Interaction in Digital News Media

Mario Pérez-Montoro
Editor

Interaction in Digital News Media

From Principles to Practice

palgrave
macmillan

Editor
Mario Pérez-Montoro
Department of Information Science
and Media Studies
University of Barcelona
Barcelona, Spain

ISBN 978-3-030-07165-3 ISBN 978-3-319-96253-5 (eBook)
https://doi.org/10.1007/978-3-319-96253-5

Softcover re-print of the Hardcover 1st edition 2018

Cover credit: stevanovicigor

This Palgrave Macmillan imprint is published by the registered company Springer Nature Switzerland AG
The registered company address is: Gewerbestrasse 11, 6330 Cham, Switzerland

To our families

Acknowledgements

This work has been made possible by funding of the Projects "Interactive content and creation in multimedia information communication: audiences, design, systems and styles" (CSO2015-64955-C4-2-R, Spanish Ministry of Economy and Competitiveness) and "Culture and Digital Contents" (2017 SGR 422, AGAUR, Government of Catalonia).

Contents

Notes on Contributors

Dr. Ernest Abadal is a Professor in the Department of Information Science and Media Studies, University of Barcelona, Spain. He has several publications on scientific communication and open access. He is principal investigator of the project "Open Access to Science in Spain" (Spanish R+D Plan) and coordinator of the research group "Culture and Digital Contents."

Dr. Alexis Apablaza-Campos is an Associate Professor at the School of Journalism and Corporate Public Relations, UNIACC University, Chile, where he teaches in the areas of corporate reputation, online journalism, and social media. He is currently researcher of the Doctoral Program of the Department of Communication, Universitat Pompeu Fabra, Spain, and collaborator of the DigiDoc Research Group.

Dr. Lluís Codina is an Associate Professor in the Department of Communication, at the School of Communication, Pompeu Fabra University, Spain. He is currently the Director of the Master in Social Communication Program at this university. He is member of the Digital Documentation and Interactive Communication Research Group (DigiDoc) and director of its Research Seminar.

Dr. Javier Díaz-Noci is a Professor in the Department of Communication, Pompeu Fabra University, Barcelona (Spain), where he teaches subjects related to digital journalism and to research methods in communication. He has been visiting scholar at the universities of Oxford (UK) and Federal of Bahia (Brazil). He has Ph.D. in both History and Law.

Dr. Pere Freixa is an Associate Professor in the Department of Communication at Pompeu Fabra University, Spain, specialized on photography, digital image, interaction design, and interactive communication. He has participated, coordinated, and conducted several courses, postgraduate courses, and investigations on digital imaging and interactivity. He is currently Editor-in-chief of academic journal *Hipertext.net.*

Dr. Javier Guallar is an Assistant Professor in the Department of Information Science and Media Studies, University of Barcelona, Spain, and he is editor of the journal *El profesional de la información*. His main research topics are content curation, digital journalism, and scientific publication.

Dr. Barbara Millet is a User Experience (UX) researcher and educator at the University of Miami. She has 20 years of research and industry experience in product design and UX. Her research interest is in design and evaluation of technology-mediated communications to improve user performance in socio-technical domains.

Dr. Rafael Pedraza-Jiménez is an Associate Professor and Serra Húnter fellow in the Department of Communication at Pompeu Fabra University, where he coordinates the DigiDoc Research Group. During his academic career, he has participated and/or led several research projects related to communicative aspects on the Web. He has also published numerous works in international journals and books. Some of its main research interests lie in Digital media, Online journalism, Web quality, Information retrieval, and e-tourism.

Dr. Mario Pérez-Montoro is a Professor in the Department of Information Science and Media Studies, University of Barcelona, Spain, where he researches and teaches in the areas of interaction design and information visualization. He is currently the Director of the Ph.D. in Information and Communication Program at this University.

Dr. Joan Soler-Adillon is an Associate Professor in the Department of Media Arts at Royal Holloway, University of London, England, where he teaches on the BA program in Film, Television and Digital Production and on the BA/BSc program in Digital Media Culture & Technology. His current research is focused on digital art, immersive technologies, and on interactive documentary and storytelling.

Dr. Carles Sora is a digital media scholar and researcher at Pompeu Fabra University, Department of Communication, and a Postdoctoral Fellow at MIT Open Doc Lab, CMS/W, School of Humanities, Arts and Social Sciences. He is the director of the digital culture incubator program UPF Starting Lab and also works as media artist and interactive designer.

Xaquín Veira-González is a visual journalist, instructor, lecturer, and independent consultant. He has worked at *The New York Times*, *National Geographic*, and *elmundo.es*, and most recently, he was the Editor of the Visuals desk at *The Guardian*, where he led a 40-person multidisciplinary team of graphics artists, photographers, picture editors, interactive editors, and multimedia producers. He has also collaborated with *The Washington Post*, United Nations, Google, and the Office for National Statistics.

List of Figures

List of Tables

CHAPTER 1

Interaction Experience in Digital News Media

Mario Pérez-Montoro

1 Introduction

Since its inception, and over the many intervening decades, classic journalistic praxis has been founded on the use of text as a narrative vehicle, supported, in certain situations, by complementary images, tables, and graphs that sustain the argumentative discourse. However, technological advances, and the search for new business models that can guarantee the economic sustainability of media companies, have revolutionized this basic narrative scheme.

The rapid development of the internet has led the media to create digital news initiatives, alongside their now classic print, radio, and television variants. These technological advances have also led to the appearance of the new media offered exclusively in digital format. Web-based technologies have facilitated the creation of new content that comprises much more than the simple static combination of text and images. The ability to incorporate video, audio, and image with the basic text has

M. Pérez-Montoro (✉)
Department of Information Science and Media Studies,
University of Barcelona, Barcelona, Spain
e-mail: perez-montoro@ub.edu

M. Pérez-Montoro (ed.), *Interaction in Digital News Media*,
https://doi.org/10.1007/978-3-319-96253-5_1

opened up a plethora of new ways to narrate stories. But, above all, it is the ability to incorporate interactivity in these new contents that has allowed the consumer of these media products to become a central actor in new narrative and communicative forms.

These new narrative forms have not only been consolidated by the advances in web technologies, but also by the evolution undergone by the devices used to consume that technology and those contents. The use of traditional computers, but more specifically the appearance on the market of mobile devices (smartphones and tablets), has meant that the full potential of these new narrative proposals can be explored easily and ubiquitously, transforming the traditional consumption of journalistic information.

But the adoption of these new technologies has had a series of further consequences for the media. The migration to the web has undermined, in part, the business model and the sustainability of media companies. The need to launch a web version that can compete in the market and reach new audiences has highlighted the weaknesses of a model of economic viability based exclusively on advertising. In the web versions, the classic advertising model does not work and media firms are yet to find viable alternatives, such as a subscription-based model, that can substitute it or complement it effectively. This economic problem is also closely linked to the legal protection of digital content.

2 Digital News Media and Interaction

The new ecosystem is built around two critical concepts that give meaning to much of current journalistic praxis: namely, the digital news media and interaction.

The development of the internet, and the continuous increases achieved in connection speeds, has not only led to the parallel launching of both digital and online versions of the leading newspapers, but it also has had much broader consequences. It has led to the appearance of what has come to be known as the digital news media.

The digital news media are represented by a new type of media company that undertake digital or online journalism. Often, these are digital native business projects, without a corresponding print version. *The HuffPost* (formerly known as *The Huffington Post*, http://www.huffingtonpost.com) is a good example of this type of journalistic initiative.

These media are characterized by the fact that they generate their content exclusively in digital format and distribute them via the internet, which contrasts with the more passive experiences provided by traditional news media that publish their content via print, radio, and television media (Friedrichsen and Kamalipour 2017). The digital medium provides them with lower distribution costs and opens up possibilities to implement new business models and to experiment with narrative creativity (Herbert 2000; Kawamoto 2003, among many others).

In this context, one of the common traits characterizing the digital news media is the intensive use of interactives in their journalistic content.

In general, interactivity can be understood as the potential relationship of bidirectional dialogue between a system and its user. Normally, this dialogue aims at achieving a specific goal, that is, the carrying out of some kind of activity in the system by the user by means of some kind of action or manipulation of that system.

The main characteristic feature of interactivity is that both the system and its user can alternate their roles as sender and receiver in that dialogue. This is a property directly attributable to the system that facilitates this switching of roles. All user actions are restricted by the system, but at the same time, the response of the system depends on the actions performed by the user.

Systems have different levels and degrees of interactivity, from the lowest, in which the user simply activates the system (pressing "play" on a video on our computer screen, for example) to the highest, in which the system changes the range of possible responses depending on the actions the user makes (playing a video game, for example).

If we translate this concept to journalism, an interactive can be understood as a special kind of digital content with which the user can interact in a reciprocal or bidirectional manner, thanks to its specific structure and design. This characteristic can then be used to obtain alternative narrative resources and resources with a high degree of communicative efficiency from this content. Here, different degrees or levels of interactivity are also available.

At the lowest level, we find those contents that allow the user to decide the pace and direction of the narrative. Contents in which the user can move forwards and backwards in the narrative using the scroll option (referred to typically as scroll telling) is an example of this level of interaction. The interactive "The Dawn Wall. El Capitan's Most

Unwelcoming Route" published by *The New York Times* in 2015 (https://www.nytimes.com/interactive/2015/01/09/sports/the-dawn-wall-el-capitan.html) provides users with this technique, as they explore the route and ascent of The Dawn Wall on El Capitan made by a couple of mountaineers.

At the highest level, we find those digital projects that allow the user to create and transform new content and to establish new narrative strategies for the consumption of that new content, by exploiting their interactive resources. The report, "Connected China", published by Reuters in 2013, provides a good example of this degree of interactivity (http://china.fathom.info). In this case, Ren Chua and his team designed a project in which the interaction design of the visualizations in the interface cannot be separated from the information structure. The resulting product is a complex, dynamic system, capable of incorporating new data and of allowing the user to set out on their own journeys and to construct their own stories. Over an 18-month period, they compiled information that they then codified in the database and which they could then base their system on. The design of the visualizations drew on journalistic criteria, and enhanced those solutions that made the complex interrelations visible (Freixa et al. 2017; Qiu and Zhang 2013).

3 A Polyhedral Scenario

The scenario created by the new media cannot, however, be examined from a single perspective; rather, its polyhedral nature means it has to be addressed from more than one point of view. This book seeks to analyze the multidimensional phenomenon of the digital news media centering the discussion around the importance of the role played in it by interactivity.

In meeting this objective, we have divided this book into eight chapters, which can, in turn, be grouped into two main blocks: an in-depth study of the intrinsic characteristics of the interactive products used in the digital news media, on the one hand; and an examination of other, more extrinsic, issues that are affected by products of this type, on the other.

In the first of these blocks, in analyzing the intrinsic characteristics of interactives, we look at aspects related to storytelling, at contents that include information visualization and those that facilitate immersive experiences, and at user experiences associated with these digital contents.

In the specific case of storytelling, Chapter 2, entitled "Content Access, Storytelling and Interactive Media", examines the use of interactives as a narrative resource in online journalism and describes the evolution undergone by the media in recent years as regards their use of these resources. We show how these new forms of storytelling are revolutionizing the basic concepts of the interactive documentary, including the role of stories and users' direct access to primary sources.

The next two chapters examine two special types of new journalistic content: those that include information visualization as a narrative resource and those that facilitate immersive experiences. Chapter 3, entitled "Information Visualization in the Digital News Media", analyzes the added value of content that incorporates information visualization and explains why the classic distinction between infographic-data visualization fails to help us understand new journalistic contents. For this reason, an alternative taxonomy is proposed that provides a more adequate characterization and which allows us to analyze the current use of visualization in the media. The chapter also identifies new trends in the type of content being offered by the new media. Chapter 4, entitled "Facing Reality Through Immersive Journalism", analyzes the new narrative possibilities provided, and the new challenges faced, by immersive technologies. Among other questions, it examines how virtual reality addresses questions related to realism, empathy, and interactivity.

This first block concludes with a chapter dedicated to the design of these interactive products. Specifically, Chapter 5, entitled, "UX Research Methods for Designing Interactive Media", examines how user experience (UX) is a critical element for the success or failure of interactive media products. The chapter explores different methods used in UX research, from interviews and observations to usability tests, eye tracking, and other physiological measures. Finally, based on these methods, various ways in which these interactive multimedia products can be improved are proposed.

The second block examines a series of more extrinsic issues involving the relationship between interactive contents and the digital news media: their role in the media's business models, the legal issues associated with this type of content and the scientific production related to the subject of interactives.

The search for economic viability is one of the main concerns of the digital news media. Chapter 6, entitled "Newsonomics and Interaction: The Present and Future of the News Media", analyzes shifting trends in the industry's economic models that can uphold the business sustainability of the news media and the role played by interactives (attracting subscribers and keeping them loyal, among others) in these models.

Closely related to these questions of economic viability is the legal treatment afforded interactive contents. Chapter 7, entitled "Authors' Rights and the Media", examines the latest steps being taken toward the reform of the laws on intellectual property and authors' rights, especially in the European Union, and how the new digital market requires these legal reforms adopt a more company-centered conception of intellectual property based on the notion of collective work. The chapter also examines how the emergence of user-generated contents is causing changes to this legal structure.

The block ends with a bibliographic review of academic studies conducted to date with a specific focus on interactive products developed in the context of the digital news media. Chapter 8, entitled "Scientific Production on Interaction", these studies are reviewed to determine, among other things, the evolution of this literature, its authorship (including joint studies undertaken by one or more authors and their institutional affiliations), the journals most frequently publishing articles in this field, and the specific subjects these articles address.

All the trends, challenges, and lessons that can be extracted from these two blocks, and which have an obvious bearing on interactive content in the digital news media, are identified in the final chapter (Chapter 9) of this book.

References

Freixa, Pere, Mario Pérez-Montoro, and Lluís Codina. 2017. Interacción y visualización de datos en el periodismo estructurado. *El profesional de la información* 26 (6), 1076–1096. ISSN 1386-6710.

Friedrichsen, M., and Y. Kamalipour (eds.). 2017. *Digital Transformation in Journalism and News Media: Media Management, Media Convergence and Globalization*. New York: Springer.

Herbert, John. 2000. *Journalism in the Digital Age: Theory and Practice for Broadcast, Print and On-line Media*. New York: Taylor & Francis.

Kawamoto, Kevin. 2003. *Digital Journalism: Emerging Media and the Changing Horizons of Journalism*. Lanham: Rowman & Littlefield.

Qiu, Yue, and Wenxiong Zhang. 2013. Connecting China, Visually. Reporters Help Tell Chinese Political Stories in an Interactive Way. *Columbia Journalism Review*, April 15.

CHAPTER 2

Content Access, Storytelling, and Interactive Media

Pere Freixa

1 Introduction

In January 2017, ProPublica and a consortium made up of 80 entities, including leading news organizations, such as *The New York Times*, *NBC News*, *Chicago Globe*, and *The Guardian* as well as the universities of Berkley, CUNY and Georgetown, and research centers such as Google News Lab, launched the project *Documenting Hate* (ProPublica 2016; *The New York Times*, 2017), an ambitious exercise in journalistic collaboration that seeks to collate reliable data on hate crimes in the United States. The project represents a complex information system, and one that would be unimaginable outside the web. As such, it is a typical product of the digital medium, combining as it does data management and coding, audience participation, and the creation of news stories. One year after its launch, the project managers were able to confirm the real need for such an initiative given the lack of institutional data on hate crimes, and to recognize the importance of user collaboration, which proved indispensable for the gathering of information.

P. Freixa (✉)
Department of Communication, Pompeu Fabra University, Barcelona, Spain
e-mail: pere.freixa@upf.edu

M. Pérez-Montoro (ed.), *Interaction in Digital News Media*,
https://doi.org/10.1007/978-3-319-96253-5_2

Rachel Glickhouse, the project manager explains, "We decided to try collecting data ourselves, using a mix of social media newsgathering and asking readers to send in their personal stories" (2017). The users' stories and testimonies are indexed and archived in an open access database, which can be consulted directly by the general public, while enabling journalists to both document and create news and journalistic information. The system can be accessed free of charge and all individual contributions can be consulted via an interface that allows content location by a range of parameters, including author, location, and subject. As Glickhouse reports, the stories provided by anonymous users are complemented by data obtained by the computer system itself, which analyzes and locates hate crimes in news stories on the web: "The Documenting Hate News Index (…) takes a raw feed of Google News articles from the past six months and uses the Google Cloud Natural Language API to create a visual tool to help reporters find news happening across the country. It's a constantly-updating snapshot of data from this year, one which is valuable as a starting point to reporting on this area of news" (Rogers 2017).

Documenting Hate is possibly the largest structured journalism project (see, for example, Chua 2010; Wojcik 2015; *BBC News Lab* 2015; Freixa et al. 2017) designed to date. Indeed, it embodies the five components that make up information systems of this kind: (1) the definition of a specific information *system* for the topic or situation addressed, which allows its characteristics to be established; (2) a proposal for *data* coding and data collection, which includes a parameterized indexing service and metadata appendix; (3) information layers to organize user *access* to the information contained; (4) the assignment of a central role to *interactivity* and procedures of interaction to ensure dialogue with the audience and the activation of data processing procedures; (5) and, finally, an *interface* via which interaction occurs and interactive dialogue can be formalized (Freixa et al. 2017). Thus the project seeks to provide journalists with access to the data stored on the platform so that they can generate news stories that make this particular issue more visible and, thus, bring public pressure to bear on this social problem. The characteristics of the dataset mean it can be exploited both locally and nationally: "The hope is that many stories, interactives, and a comprehensive national database will emerge and paint a fuller picture of the scope of hate crimes in the U.S." (Wang 2017). As well as being a leading example of structured journalism, *Documenting Hate* also falls within the tradition of the collaborative culture that has emerged in recent years on the web and which is characterized by attempts to promote the contribution of content by users, converted into co-creators (Lasica 2003; Gaudenzi 2014) or citizen journalists (Bruns 2005) of the data that feed the system and allow the generation of news stories and documentaries information. In short, using the term coined by Berger, we are witnessing the possibility of developing a participative journalism: "[which] is about the construction of a democratic community. Unlike the neoliberal ethos, journalists address audiences not as consumers of politics but as producers" (2000: 86).

This chapter examines the use of interactive resources in online journalism and in digital documentaries. Seven journalistic projects covering a wide range of applications and genres have been selected as case studies, including audiovisual reports, collaborative works, structured journalism, immersive journalism, archive studies, transmedia projects, and social journalism. Together, they allow us to identify, describe, and list different communication strategies that share a common factor, namely, the central role played by interactive discourse in their conceptualization, as well as the key role they play in the reception and meaning of the message. We highlight the dual nature that interactive communication has undergone in digital media. On the one hand, interactivity has become an essential factor for interconnecting and organizing the elements that make up the discourse and which allow the user, in the reading process, to construct meaning. The digital text assumes the discursive dimension (Nash 2012, 2014) that is derived from the incorporation of interactivity as an authorial, rhetorical resource that allows the emergence of meaning in the semiotic reception (Walsh 2011). Good examples of this are provided by the multi-awarded projects *A Short History of Highrise* (2013), by Katerina Cizek, for *The New York Times* and the National Film Board (NFB) of Canada; *Bear71* (2012), by Jeremy Méndez and Leanne Allison for the NFB and *Snow Fall* (2013), by John Branch, for the NYT, which won, among others, a Pulitzer Prize. Moreover, as can be seen in *Documenting Hate*, interaction not only organizes the discourse, but also, through the interface design, it allows the user to access and consult the data encoded and structured in its databases, that is, the foundations of digital text (Manovich 2001), thus facilitating the development of content and information.

2 Early Web Documentaries

In 1997, photojournalist Susan Meiselas began to publish online pages from her *akaKurdistan* project (Meiselas 1997a), with the support of Picture Projects, an independent production company, created in 1995 by Alison Cornyn and Sue Johnson that specializes in using "new technologies and documentary photography to examine complex social issues" (Cornyn 2010: 2). The project brings together materials that Meiselas had been collecting for five years about the Kurdish people and their lands: old postcards and photographs bought in street markets and obtained from private archives, maps, and stories told by anonymous members of the public. As she herself recognizes, the project seeks to create a virtual territory without limits or borders, a meeting place that "provides the opportunity to build a collective memory with a people who have no national archive". In 1991, during the first Gulf War, Meiselas covered the war in northern Iraq, the area of the country where the Kurds are in a majority, for Human Rights Watch. Her pictures and photojournalistic reports have been published, among others, in *The New York Times Magazine* (Miller 1993).

While the online *akaKurdistan* project includes none of her photographs documenting the atrocities committed on the streets of Arbil and Koreme, Meiselas invites visitors to her website to explore Kurdish history and culture using two semantic layers, a physical map of the region and a timeline, comprising images and information that she has digitized and indexed. In two other sections of the project, "Identify Images" and "Add a Story", users are called upon to collaborate by contributing materials. They can also upload information about images about which nothing is known, and which form the "Unknown Image Archive". "Do you know anything about this image?"—Meiselas asks on a page on which she presents a dozen photographs. The visitor clicks on the photograph to obtain an enlarged image, together with texts and comments that other users have been adding since 1997.

These are images that the author has collected, digitized, and returned to the web in order to renew a dialogue with the Kurdish community, scattered in diaspora around the world. "I have found [pictures] by visiting homes, as well as by going to archives, that without the eye of the 'other'—the traveler, the Westerner—there would be few images of the past, and it is indeed those photographs that provide people with a sense of who they have been, in order perhaps to make sense of who they are and who they will be" (Harris 1993: 24).

The *akaKurdistan* project can be considered one of the first interactive documentary archives created on the network by journalists. It was designed to complement the book and the exhibition *Kurdistan: In the Shadow of History* (Meiselas 1997b), and its value, even now, twenty years after it was published, lies in its ability to anticipate future developments in this field of journalism: it recognizes the audience's potential to generate collective stories when that audience is allowed direct access to the sources of information, to the archive. As Martin Hadis points out, "*akaKurdistan* cleverly combines pictures, time and narrative to build an image, not this time of a specific person, but of a people and a culture" (2002: 56).

Out My Window (2010) was the second, and the most ambitious, interactive web documentary to be created by Katerina Cizek during her time working at the NFB in Canada as part of its *Highrise* project. It was presented on October 16, 2010 as one of the first 360° interactive documentaries: "Over 100 people have joined us on this project: photographers, journalists, architects, residents, activists, digital developers, researchers around the world came together to bring you these incredible stories of inspiration, community and resilience" (Cizek 2010a). *Out My Window* experiments with the discursive possibilities of interactive media in its various dimensions: in its exploration of digital technologies, in its rhetoric of interaction as discursive forms, and as feedback as a key element of collaborative creation. In the words of O'Flynn, "This interactive documentary highlights the tensions of life in suburban high-rises and, in doing so, creates humanized counter stories to media and government-constructed narratives of high risk/priority communities in decline" (2014: 7).

The project explores personal stories recorded in 13 different cities around the world. The characters and experiences are presented in a simulation of an immersive virtual space in which the viewer-user-participant is invited to visit and explore the seemingly infinite spaces of the high-rise buildings. Cizek incorporates elements of the immersive exploratory mode (Ryan 2001), employed widely in videogames and in interactive projects of cultural dissemination (Ribas 2001). But perhaps the element the author defends most strongly is a commitment to participatory processes and work on the web as the foundation for documentary story telling. In the words of Gerry Flahive, the producer of *Highrise*, "We began to think that maybe we could actually do a large-scale collaborative media project about how the city is changing (...) It's great to have the freedom to not know what end-product we are developing"

(Krinsky 2010). The authors place the centrality of documentary discourse at the heart of the process of ideation and realization, as well as in the nature of the materials obtained—the stories of the participants converted into photographs, videos, and texts. The elaboration of the declarative virtual device remains open until it is decided it should be fixed in the form of an interactive web audiovisual or as a physical performance in an interactive installation in festivals and exhibition centers, as happened at the IDFA DocLab in Amsterdam: "The project extends the stories and images of our 360° web-based documentary into physical space. How do stories about space (originally created for the computer screen) translate into life-size images, within a physical space?" (Cizek 2010b).

3 Interaction Tools for Online Journalism and Webdocs

It is widely accepted that digital technology has facilitated the process of media convergence and that this has been achieved; thanks to the consolidation of the internet. Both the traditional and the new media have used and colonized the web, which in turn has become the central axis of the *digital media*, the scenario, or ecosystem from which information processes are currently articulated. Journalists have seen their work routines transformed while, at the same time, the media has undergone a radical change. The digital media has incorporated interactivity as its defining element, understood as a continuum that allows the application of different intensities or levels of interaction depending on the technologies used for communication. In Jensen's already classical definition, interactivity supposes "a measure of a media's potential ability to let the user exert an influence on the content and/or form of the mediated communication" (1998: 201).

Interactivity forms part of web-based communication in its multiple dimensions. Since the early years of online journalism, interactivity has been considered in relation to the potential of hypertext and hypermedia links (Pavlik 2001; Aston 2003; Canavilhas 2006), the inheritance of the foundational traditions of hypertext as a narrative and communication resource (Nelson 1983; Landow 1991). For other authors, interactivity has been considered as a technological and procedural resource that can be incorporated into journalistic practice. It facilitates communication between audience and writer, exploiting such resources as chats, forums, and email (Schultz 1999; Chung 2007; Stroud et al. 2016). Interactivity in the digital media has also been analyzed as a technological possibility or restriction defining and, at the same time, conditioning access and the communication model (McMillan 2002). It is considered a constituent element of journalistic formats, since it allows new genres to be defined (Palacios and Diaz-Noci 2007; Larrondo 2010) as well as new professional routines—and promises (Deuze 2003; Domingo 2008).

Interactivity can, therefore, be considered an inherent value of the media that has come to characterize the digital text. Indeed, it is the rhetorical element that differentiates the digital text from other formats. It defines exploration as the way to approach the text (Aarseth 1997) and, in the experience of its reception, it allows the user to perceive the narrative value of the content explored (Ryan 2004). It also allows us to reformulate the relationships that authors and users maintain with the content and the system with which they interact. The fragmentation of information, the hypertext link between contents and the twists of the plot are, as can be seen in the works studied, some of the resources that the interactive text offers the user to explore and build the interactive experience. As Kate Nash puts it, "Interactivity is often identified as the characteristic that distinguishes emerging forms of documentary from film and television, changing not only modes of engagement, but the form of the text itself" (2014: 50).

The possibility of cataloging and coding information, establishing hypertext links to this information, and presenting it through interfaces to users to explore, modify, or consume converts the process of the ideation and creation of interactive items into a highly specialized exercise that requires skills related to design of the interface, the usability, the structure of the information, and the codification of contents, among others. Interactive communication has emerged as a specialized skill (Soler-Adillon et al. 2016) in the digital newsrooms and laboratories that the news media has designed to explore new journalistic formats (Salaverria 2015).

To traditional multimedia units, such as texts, images, animations, and videos, we need to add the data that computer systems can process and convert into information—for example, generic data, user data, and numerical or statistical data: web presence, engagement and the searches performed, what users publish on social networks, the data provided by the devices themselves in relation to user location, and all the specific actions that can potentially be monitored—form part of the data universe that informs us of the present and that is incorporated into the informational flow (Dovey and Rose 2012).

4 Content Access and Interaction

One of the main contributions of interactivity to online journalism has been to allow the public access both to the story of the events and the documentation that supports it. Access to information often goes hand in hand with an invitation to participate in the stories told, as we have seen in *akaKurdistan*, *Highrise*, *Out My Window*, and *Documenting Hate*. In these cases, users can contribute their personal stories or give their opinions and so expand the documentary's resources which form part of the information product. By extension, users participate in the web documentaries by offering—voluntarily, consciously, or unconsciously, according to the project—their device data: including, location, web-based searches, and engagement. Data visualization, structured journalism, and interactive documentaries all require the design of interactive communication strategies that can stimulate and facilitate access to information.

Since the first web mashup created by Holovaty—*Chicagocrime*, published in 2005 (Holovaty 2006, 2008)—structured journalism (Chua 2010; Freixa et al. 2017) and data journalism (Lewis and Westlund 2015; Craig 2015) have experimented with the possibilities of transforming processed information into a story. Typically, it is numerical data that are explored using interactive visualization media—"Creating a work in new media can be understood as the construction of an interface to a database (…) the interface can also translate the underlining database into a very different user experience (…) The new media object consists of one or more interfaces to a database of multimedia material" (Manovich 2001: 226–227). In 2016, Southern California Public Radio (KPCC) launched *Officer Involved*, a magnificent exercise in investigative journalism that is presented in the form of a web documentary combining different elements of data journalism, storytelling, and access to sources of information. *Officer Involved* reports the 375 deaths produced in Los Angeles County, USA, between 2010 and 2015, as a result of police shootings. Among them, "Upwards of 120 of the individuals were either under the influence of alcohol or drugs, or there was a mention of mental illness. More than 40 of those shot were into the latter category" (Johnson 2015). The documentary combines the different dimensions of the interactive story as described by Pavlik and Pavlik: immersive environments, content distributed in multiple media, use of dynamic narratives, and non-linear narrative structures (2017).

5 Author Storytelling and User Narrative Control

Most authors who make interactive documentaries exploit the resources of interaction design. Developed originally as the specialist resources of video games, for usability, human-computer interaction, and within the cultural and entertainment industries, the most recent, award-winning works of interactive journalism employ interactive discourse as the central element for the organization of their stories. As such, most incorporate narrative disruption, discontinuity, multichannel development, and transmedia strategies in the construction of their works. These interactive stories experiment with new rhetorical devices to capture and maintain user interest. The most successful experimental works, in terms both of their conceptualization and technical or formal resolution, allow a rapid transition to standardization. They are readily clonable models given their technological reproducibility and can be incorporated into content management systems and editing programs. "New content management systems (…) permit journalists to work with text, sound, video, and photographic assets, as well as with links with drop and drag simplicity, enabling them to build graphically well-designed multimedia stories with basic interactive capacities" (MIT Open Documentary Lab 2016: 33).

The organization of information in semantic—including maps, indexes, and timelines—and morphological layers—by media, size, or format—converts the publication of interactive texts into a task of modular assembly. Specialized content management software programs quickly incorporate the procedures and resources used in successful pilot projects. The author of the interactive selects and combines those resources that she wishes to use for organizing a specific story and she organizes them in a hierarchical way in the interface. Some resources, such as parallax scrolling (Frederick 2013; Freixa et al. 2014), facilitate the introduction of new forms of long form journalism or literary journalism: "this new wave of literary journalism is characterized by executing literary techniques through multiple media and represents a gateway to linear storytelling in the hypertextual environment of the Web" (Jacobson et al. 2016). The simultaneity and combination of layers is perceived by users as alternatives offered by the work in order to travel through the content.

In 2015, the Council on Foreign Relations published an interactive entitled *InfoGuide: The Sunni-Shia Divide*. It employs numerous modular resources. For example, parallax scrolling—moving the navigator using the scrollbar—allows the user to give the story structure, to organize the presentation of the multimedia resources and its semantic layers. It facilitates a low intensity interaction, one that is almost passive, a conceptualization of interaction as a kind of reactive dialogue. The use of low intensity forms of interaction is combined with active, hypertext, and exploratory forms, in which the audience decides when to pause or to continue the flow of information. Any breakdown in the story's continuity only occurs when the user performs an action that disrupts that flow. This approach to a historical situation of sectarian conflict is justified by the user's potential interest in exploring complementary information about it, consulting the original documentation on which the project is based or exploring other parts of the site. Similarly, the principal element of interaction in *Snow Fall: The Avalanche at Tunnel Creek* and *Officer Involved* is that of parallax scrolling, allowing the user to navigate the interface.

Other interactives employ more dynamic forms of interaction, where the viewer is expected to take active control of the narrative, in a negotiation that is understood to constitute an exploratory experience. In 2015, Angela Carabalí and Thibault Durand presented *Pregoneros de Medellín* (Criers of Medellín), an interactive collage that skillfully combines multimedia resources that are explored by users as they take a virtual tour of the city of Medellín. This webdoc offers an immersive scenario constructed from photographs, obtained from the Google Street View interface. The route taken through the streets, accompanied at all times by the audio files captured in situ, allows the user to meet the story's main characters: five criers or street vendors who use their songs to sell their wares. The user walks through a city that has been visually recreated from a subjective point of view, as occurs in a large number of video games. The visitor's tour, which allows the user to stop, go forward, or retrace his steps, maintains its temporal-spatial continuity and plausibility by employing an urban soundscape: "Using a series of interactive cinematographic techniques, the cartography offered by

Pregoneros de Medellín seeks to represent the experience of listening in an urban space characterized by the plethora of its acoustic environment" (Jaramillo-Arango 2018: 189). According to its author, the perception of Medellín's soundscape is a complex exercise in the combination of geo-located sound recordings (Durand 2015). Different audio files are superimposed one on top of another and their volume is turned up or down depending on the location of the viewer in the city they are exploring.

As in traditional panoramic representations (Freixa 2005), the immersive interface is accompanied by the graphic map which allows the detailed recreation of a stroll a visitor might take, in this case, through the streets of Medellín. On encountering the street vendors, access to the audiovisual content is activated, in the form of videography capsules, which are presented on screen in conventional film format. The interactive is inspired by the exploratory tradition of video games, basically by the decision to represent the user with a symbolic avatar, the subjective point of view of the camera. The virtual space, the story's universe, simulates the unrestricted exploration typical of games, although in this case, all routes and experimentation are guided.

6 Planning: Participation and Technology

Pregoneros de Medellín, in common with *Chicagocrime* and *akaKurdistan*, was designed and produced outside the usual circuits of audiovisual production and of the coverage provided by the news media. As such, they do not present the structures, resources, and constraints of corporations and companies dedicated to the generation of information content. These are projects that bear a highly personal signature. Susan Meiselas designed her interactive to build links within the Kurdish diaspora by using images and oral narratives. It offers a space to meet and to exchange stories. After designing her archive of materials, she provided the functionalities that allowed her to set about generating a collective memory. In *Chicagocrime*, Holovaty experimented with the possibilities offered by mashups in 2005: combining disparate information, statistical data, with the Google Maps interface, discovering the potential of geolocating information, and exploring, for the first time, the relationships between different data that share metadata for informational purposes. As he explains, at that time, "just the mere fact that somebody had mixed Craigslist data with Google's maps was new and remarkable" (Holovaty 2008). This exercise in visualization, interface design, and interaction was translated into political actions carried out by Chicago's residents, who used the web to demand interventions from their political representatives in their neighborhoods. It is a project that was designed without layers of journalistic information. Neither Holovaty nor the audience adds stories or new data to the system. Holovaty simply demonstrates the communicative strength that can be achieved with data visualization, coding, and parameterization.

Fast-forward a decade, and the *Proyecto Quipu* (or The Quipu Project), published on the web in 2015, was designed to report data and impact what might be defined as a specific community. It is the outcome of a long documentary process and a considerable amount of collaboration. Work began in 2011, when Rosemarie Lerner and María Eugenia Court started to investigate the forced sterilizations carried out in Peru in the late 1990s, during President Fujimori's mandate and as part of the National Program of Reproductive Health and Family Planning (Caceres-Alvarez 2017). The aim, in common with Meiselas before them, was to create a project with and for a given group, to activate participation in a documentary that offers the possibility to establish dialogue and links with a silenced and untold story. In both cases, the authors seek to counter the loss of collective memory (Meiselas 1997a; Court and Lerner 2015a).

In *Proyecto Quipu,* interactivity takes on a systemic dimension: "From the outset, we designed the Project in collaboration with the people who were sterilized in Peru. They are our partners in a project created with them, not for them. It is this approach that has generated the project's unique structure" (Court and Lerner 2015a). The decision was taken to adopt a strategy that involved contacting the victims and recording their individual stories, which were then filed and indexed. In the interactive, the oral testimonies of the victims form an open access collection, both in terms of its continuing expansion and its consultation. The stories are presented on the interface by means of a visual and interactive representation of a *quipu*, an Andean system of talking knotted cords, which serves to articulate the collective story and as a symbolic representation of the collective memory.

The project's authors seek the empowerment of the communities among which the observation is conducted. They believe this can be achieved; thanks to the energizing capacity that the initiation of the observation process is capable of generating. The project "provides a media platform through which witness testimony can be recorded, gathered and heard in order to support an activist movement (…) the participants are the subjects of the struggles and the producers devise strategies which cede significant editorial control to them" (Aston et al. 2017: 51). Uniquely, it pursues a second level of participation with the audience via a series of concrete actions proposed by the authors: financial donations, personal testimonies, and political actions (Vázquez-Herrero and Moreno 2017). The audience is the receiver of the audiovisual story constructed and edited by the affected party and with their direct testimony, insofar as they can directly access the archive available on the interface. "In Quipu, we find an example of a new participatory media form, located within the Fogo Process tenets of both 'horizontal' and 'vertical' communication while also offering a deep and enriching listening and a framework for interactivity, connection and dialogue" (Mitchell 2015).

One of the most important aspects of *Proyecto Quipu* lies in its having assigned procedural value to the technology, displacing its usual structural significance. As with *Out My Window*, the technology allows the documentary process, once initiated, to acquire its own shape and to be developed. Specific choices are determined by the procedural needs that the project identifies and defines as it develops. Gerry Flahive, producer of *Highrise*, claims, "We're platform-agnostic; we don't have to make any specific thing. What we tried to do (…) was explode or expand or retrieve what the definition of documentary is. Now it's even easier to think about that" (Krinsky 2010).

In *Proyecto Quipu*, the information system is organized by establishing, in the first place, two scenarios for participation: that of the dialogue with the testimonies and that of the audience. The former takes place in the territory, in the locations occupied by the victims, in the small rural settlements scattered throughout the Andes. The latter is global and takes place on the web. In the case of the former, technological resources based on the mobile telephone and local radio stations are used: "The challenge facing documentary, as with any user-centered design challenge, is to tailor participation methods to users' needs. Quipu's telephone line is a good example of a sensitive method of tailoring executory participation to rural participants" (Green et al. 2017: 6325). For the design of the interactive, it was decided to use open-source resources, typical of OpenICT4D projects (Mitchell 2015). The project impacts directly on the value attached to participation, in that it offers the possibility of sharing the experiences maintained, though in most cases respecting the participants' anonymity: "Individuals who call the phone-line are also able to listen to the archived testimonies, providing an opportunity to learn about others' experiences of unconsented sterilization in the country, and to understand how their testimony contributes to an emerging collective narrative" (Brown and Tucker 2017: 1187). As the projects' authors stress, *Proyecto Quipu* corresponds to what we would define as an information system (Court and Lerner 2015b). In an initial phase, basic questions concerning technology, procedures, planning, and financing are defined. In its actual execution—which extends over several years—questions related to discourse are redefined and the interactive itself is formalized. Currently, the system remains active on the web. It has no closing or expiration date. As is the case with other information systems, its duration, a priori, is infinite since, potentially, it can continue incorporating contributions both from victims and the audience.

Proyecto Quipu can be considered a project in transmedia documentary given that it incorporates mediated participation in its conceptualization process and in the creation of content (Aston et al. 2017; Fox 2017; Ortuño and Villaplana 2017). It does not correspond strictly with Henry Jenkins' original definition, in which transmedia is understood to be "a process where integral elements of a fiction get dispersed systematically across multiple delivery channels for the purpose of creating a unified and coordinated entertainment experience" (2007). In the case of *Proyecto Quipu*, as in other works that use the term transmedia to define themselves, including, for example, *Pregoneros de Medellín*, the term is dislocated only to be relocated as a specific feature of the process of ideation and participatory creation: "The notion of participation that we wish to emphasize as being a part of transmedia activism is that which is related to the concept of production by the people" (Ortuño and Villaplana 2017: 124). These are works and projects of citizen empowerment that are part of the practices of transmedia activism that Lina Srivastava defines as "the coordinated co-creation of narrative and cultural expression by various constituencies who distribute that narrative in various forms through multiple platforms, the result of which is to build an ecosystem of content and networks that engage in community-centered social action" (Jenkins 2016).

7 Interaction as a Narrative Form

Narratology studies have highlighted the discursive difficulties encountered by interactive messages. Indeed, the interruptions in a story that occur in texts made up of fragments connected by hyperlinks and which the audience has to navigate their way through, does not facilitate the dramatic development of the story: "If interactivity requires the audience to involve itself in the direction of the plot, clearly interactivity and plot are incompatible" (Crawford 2004: 50). Crawford reemphasizes the doubts concerning the narrative possibilities of the media as formulated by Manovich (2001) and which Pope has analyzed, since their reception and on more than one occasion (Pope 2006, 2010, 2017). The loss of interest on the part of the audience often leads to their abandonment of the exploration or their reading of the text: "… the experience of highly non-linear narrative progress, combined with user-unfriendly interfaces and disruptive interactivity, could break the desirable balance of effort and reward, a balance that leads to flow, essential to reading pleasure" (Pope 2017: 3).

The creation by an author of an interactive story and a user's experimentation with that story allow us to consider interaction as a narrative form; that is, as a communicational procedure, with characteristics that facilitate the achievement of potentially very different meaning experiences for each of the users involved. This understanding of interaction as a key element in the development of the story means our having to recognize its rhetorical value—the "consideration of discourse calls for analysis of the relationship between user actions and the discourse of the documentary" (Nash 2014: 60), and the fundamental role played by the reader in the finalization and elaboration of the journalistic message in disruptive narrative sequences. Experimentation with an interactive text, whether it is a dramatic fiction or an informative piece, allows meaning to emerge. In the words of Richard Walsh, the narrative emergence offers "the prospect of reconciliation between the conflicting values of narrative satisfaction and player autonomy" (2011: 72). But the emergence of meaning cannot be associated solely with the process carried out by the user. The processing of fragments of content, as well as the coding of this processing by computer systems—Murray's story-generating systems (1998)—create mechanisms of narrative content.

The process of creating an interactive product requires that an author has the ability to organize the units of content in semantic or morphological layers, that is, at what might be considered a higher level. These layers need to be hierarchized in the interface to facilitate certain possibilities of interaction and, consequently, of potential narrative sequences. Through interaction, the system recovers, from what might be considered the lower level—that is, the database and the archive—the encoded contents, which are presented and formalized through the interface. On the other hand, the interactive text responds to a systemic structure with a specific life cycle (Freixa 2015) that may or may not allow modifications, expansions, and transformations. These can be carried out by their authors or result from the interactive dialogues held with the audience.

The debate concerning the forms of both interactive documentaries and interactive journalism allows us to identify the different approaches that converge in the field of interactive communication in the digital media. Here, emphasis is placed on those dominant aspects on which a specific interactive system focuses and of which it is made up: namely, the conversational, the hypertext, the experiential, and the participatory (Aston and Gaudenzi 2012); based on an internal/external and exploratory/ontological interactivity (Ryan 2001); the procedural, participatory, spatial, and encyclopedic (Murray 1998).

A consideration of the systemic dimension of interactive texts allows them to be categorized and enables us to organize, both in the process of creating the texts and in their analysis, the different elements that constitute them. These are: (1) the definition of the system itself and the practices it presupposes; (2) the data, the minimum content units, and their coding; (3) the procedures for accessing and processing the content, either by coding behavior or navigational structures; (4) the modes of interactivity, understood in their broadest sense, that the system incorporates; and (5) the interface or interfaces that facilitate the dialogue between the system and the different actors that interact with it. Some of the projects analyzed allow us to contemplate a sixth constituent element, the transmedia narrative strategy, which is derived from the temporal exploration of the decisions taken regarding elements 1, 4, and 5.

Each of the interactive projects presented constitutes a unique combination of the different elements making up an interactive system. Some of them, such as *Highrise*, *Out My Window*, and *Proyecto Quipu*, focus their attention on the participatory process that defines the system, or on the value of the participation of the audience in terms of contributing content, the case of *akaKurdistan*, *Documenting Hate*, *Proyecto Quipu*, and *A Short History of Highrise*. The definition of the content units, the database, the coding processes, and metadata associated with them is especially relevant in *Chicagocrime*, *Officer Involved*, and *Documenting Hate*. *Infoguide: The Sunni-Shia Divide*, *Bear71* and *Pregoneros de Medellín* distribute their contents in different layers that are organized in a hierarchical manner through the interface. These three projects use different interactive strategies: immersion and exploration, linear storytelling, and spatial exploration. Some works, such as *Snow Fall*, *A Short History of Highrise*, and *Officer Involved*, opt for several forms of simultaneous interaction of different intensity. A highly reactive resource, such as scrolling, is employed throughout *Snow Fall* and *Officer Involved*. *A Short History of Highrise* exploits the video bar as a basic element for exploration. At the same time, other resources are offered, including hypertext links, timelines, and visual indexes that allow alternative and expanded explorations of the main story.

Interactive documentaries and structured journalism offer alternative modes for understanding the role of information insofar as they allow us to rethink relations between (1) the information, which is conceived as data; (2) the different actors associated with it: professionals, reporting communities, the media, and the audience; and, finally; (3) the text itself, understood in a broad sense as multimedia, mutable, modifiable, expandable, and transmedia.

References

Aarseth, Espen J. 1997. *Cybertext: Perspectives on Ergodic Literature*. Baltimore, MD: Johns Hopkins University Press.

Aston, Judith Y. 2003. Interactive Multimedia: An Investigation Into Its Potential for Communicating Ideas and Arguments. PhD thesis, Royal College of Art, London.

Aston, Judith Y., and Sandra Gaudenzi. 2012. Interactive Documentary: Setting the Field. *Studies in Documentary Film* 6 (2): 125–139.

Aston, Judith Y., Sandra Gaudenzi, and Mandy Rose. 2017. *I-Docs: The Evolving Practices of Interactive Documentary*. New York: Columbia University Press.

BBC News Lab. 2015. A manifesto for structured journalism. *BBC News Lab*, July 7. http://bbcnewslabs.co.uk/2015/07/07/a-manifesto-forstructured-journalism.

Berger, Guy. 2000. Grave New World? Democratic Journalism Enters the Global Twenty-First Century. *Journalism Studies* 1 (1): 81–99.

Brown, Matthew, and Karen Tucker. 2017. Unconsented Sterilisation, Participatory Story-Telling, and Digital Counter-Memory in Peru. *Antipode* 49 (5): 1186–1203.

Bruns, Axel. 2005. *Gatewatching: Collaborative Online News Production*. New York: Peter Lang.

Caceres-Alvarez, Andrea. 2017. "Proyecto Quipu", el documental interactivo sobre las esterilizaciones forzadas de los 90. *El Comercio*, July 5, 2017. https://elcomercio.pe/luces/cine/proyecto-quipu-documental-interactivo-esterilizaciones-forzadas-90-439938.

Canavilhas, João. 2006. *Web Journalism: From the Inverted Pyramid to the Tumbled Pyramid*. Covilhã, Portugal: Biblioteca On-line deficiências da comunicação.

Chua, Reg. 2010. Structured Journalism. (Re)structuring Journalism: Rethinking Journalism and the Business of Journalism from the Ground Up. *Structure of News*, August 12, 2010. https://structureofnews.wordpress.com/2010/08/12/structured-journalism.

Chung, Deborah Soun. 2007. Profits and Perils: Online News Producers' Perceptions of Interactivity and Uses of Interactive Features. *Convergence* 13 (1): 43–61.

Cizek, Katerine. 2010a. Introducing: Out of My Window. Highrise Director's Blog, October 16, 2010. http://highrise.nfb.ca/blog/page/5/.

Cizek, Katerine. 2010b. Behind the Scenes of "Out My Window Story Space Installation". Highrise Director's Blog, November 12, 2010. http://highrise.nfb.ca/blog/page/5/.

Cornyn, Alison. 2010. Picture Projects Portfolio. Picture Projects http://picture-projects.com/wp-content/uploads/PPportfolio.pdf.

Court, Maria, and Lerner, Rosemarie. 2015a. The Project. Blog Proyecto Quipu. http://blog.quipu-project.com/about.

Court, Maria, and Lerner, Rosemarie. 2015b. The System. Blog Proyecto Quipu. http://blog.quipu-project.com/about/#system.

Craig, Heather. 2015. Interactive Data Narrative: Designing for Public Engagement. PhD thesis, Massachusetts Institute of Technology, Cambridge.

Crawford, Chis. 2004. *Chis Crawford on Interactive Storytelling*. Berkeley: New Riders.

Deuze, Mark. 2003. The Web and Its Journalisms: Considering the Consequences of Different Types of Newsmedia Online. *New Media & Society* 5 (2): 203–230.

Domingo, David. 2008. Interactivity in the Daily Routines of Online Newsrooms: Dealing with an Uncomfortable Myth. *Journal of Computer-Mediated Communication* 13 (3): 680–704.

Dovey, Jon, and Mandy Rose. 2012. We're Happy and We Know It: Documentary: Data: Montage. *Studies in Documentary Film* 6 (2): 159–173.

Durand, Thibault. 2015. How We Created an Immersive Street Walk Experience with a GoPro and Javascript. Medium, May 19, 2015. https://medium.com/@tibbb/how-we-created-an-immersive-street-walk-experience-with-a-goproand-javascript-f442cf8aa2dd#.frhcagsiw.

Fox, Broderick. 2017. *Documentary Media: History, Theory, Practice*. New York: Routledge.

Frederick, Dede M. 2013. The Effects of Parallax Scrolling on User Experience and Preference in Web Design. PhD thesis, Purdue University, Indiana.

Freixa, Pere. 2005. La fotografía panorámica y la representación del territorio: antecedentes para una indexación virtual del mundo. Actas del Primer Congreso de Historia de la Fotografía, 105–115. Zarautz: Photomuseum.

Freixa, Pere. 2015. Special Features in Online Journalism. Ten Years of Premios Goya and Oscar Awards in Elpais.com (2005–2014). *El profesional de la información* 24 (3): 291–300.

Freixa, Pere, Carles Sora, Joan Soler-Adillon, and J. Ignasi Ribas. 2014. Snow Fall and A Short History of the Highrise: two approaches to interactive communication design by *The New York Times*. *Textual & Visual Media*. 7: 63–84.

Freixa, Pere, Mario Pérez-Montoro, and Lluís Codina. 2017. Interaction and Data Visualization in Structured Journalism. *El profesional de la información* 26 (6): 1076–1090.

Gaudenzi, Sandra. 2014. Strategies of Participation: The Who, What and When of Collaborative Documentaries. In *New Documentary Ecologies. Emerging Platforms, Practices and Discourses*, ed. Kate Nash, Craig Hight, Catherine Summerhayes, 129–148. Houndmills: Palgrave Macmillan.

Glickhouse, Rachel. 2017. What We Discovered During a Year of Documenting Hate. Propublica, December 26, 2017. https://www.propublica.org/article/what-we-discovered-during-a-year-of-documenting-hate.

Green, David Philip, Simon Bowen, Jonathan Hook, and Peter Wright. 2017. Enabling Polyvocality in Interactive Documentaries through 'Structural Participation'. In *Proceedings of the 2017 CHI Conference on Human Factors in Computing Systems*, 6317–6329.

Hadis, Martin. 2002. From Generation to Generation: Family Stories, Computers and Genealogy. PhD thesis, Massachusetts Institute of Technology, Cambridge.

Harris, Melissa. 1993. Susan Meiselas. *Aperture* 133: 24–31.

Holovaty, Adrian. 2006. A Fundamental Way Newspaper Sites Need to Change. Adrian Holovaty blog, September 6, 2006. http://www.holovaty.com/writing/fundamental-change.

Holovaty, Adrian. 2008. In Memory of Chicagocrime.org. Adrian Holovaty blog, January 31, 2008. http://www.holovaty.com/writing/chicagocrime.org-tribute.

Jacobson, Susan, Jacqueline Marino, Gutsche Jr., and E. Robert. 2016. The Digital Animation of Literary Journalism. *Journalism* 17 (4): 527–546.

Jaramillo-Arango, Julián. 2018. Cartografías de la sorpresa: prácticas artísticas y paisajes sonoros urbanos en Colombia. *Cuadernos de Música, Artes Visuales y Artes Escénicas* 13 (1): 173–191.

Jenkins, Henry. 2007. Transmedia Storytelling 101. In *Confessions of an Aka-Fan*, Henry Jenkins. March 21, 2007. http://henryjenkins.org/blog/2007/03/transmedia_storytelling_101.html.

Jenkins, Henry. 2016. Telling Stories: Lina Srivastava Talks About Transmedia Activism (Part One). In *Confessions of an Aka-Fan*, Henry Jenkins. January 19, 2016. http://henryjenkins.org/blog/2016/01/telling-stories-lina-srivastava-talks-about-transmedia-activism-part-one.html.

Jensen, Jens. 1998. Interactivity: Tracking a New Concept in Media and Communications Studies. *Nordicom Review* 19: 185–202.

Johnson, Pamela K. 2015. New Report Analyzes L.A. County Officer-Involved Shootings. *NBC News*, December 19, 2015. https://www.nbcnews.com/news/nbcblk/call-more-transparency-after-police-involved-shootings-mentally-ill-n480301.

Krinsky, Tamara. 2010. Vertical Integration: The NFB's 'High Rise' Project Tackles Urban Living. Documentary.org. IDA, International Documentary Association, March 2, 2010. https://www.documentary.org/content/vertical-integration-nfbs-high-rise-project-tackles-urban-living.

Landow, George P. 1991. *HyperText: The Convergence of Contemporary Critical Theory and Technology*. Baltimore: Johns Hopkins University Press.

Larrondo, Ainara. 2010. The Potential of Web-Only Feature Stories. A Case Study of Spanish Media Sites. *Journalism studies* 12 (2): 188–204.

Lasica, Joseph D. 2003. What is Participatory Journalism. *Online Journalism Review* 7. http://www.ojr.org/ojr/workplace/1060217106.php.

Lewis, Seth C., and Oscar Westlund. 2015. Big Data and Journalism: Epistemology, Expertise, Economics, and Ethics. *Digital Journalism* 3 (3): 447–466.

Manovich, Lev. 2001. *The Language of New Media*. Cambridge: MIT Press.

McMillan, Sally J. 2002. A Four-Part Model of Cyber-Interactivity: Some Cyber-Places Are More Interactive Than Others. *New Media & Society* 4 (2): 271–291.

Meiselas, Susan. 1997a. akaKurdistan: A Place for Collective Memory and Cultural Exchange. On-line. http://www.akakurdistan.com.

Meiselas, Susan. 1997b. *Kurdistan: In the Shadow of History*. New York: Random House.

Miller, Judith, and Susan Meiselas. 1993. Iraq Accused: A Case of Genocide. *The New York Time Magazine*, 12–32, January 3, 1993.

Mitchell, Mary. 2015. Where Voice and Listening Meet: Participation in and Through Interactive Documentary in Peru. *Glocal Times*, 22–23.

MIT Open Documentary Lab. 2016. *Mapping the Intersection of Two Cultures: Interactive Documentary and Digital Journalism*. Cambridge: Massachusetts Institute of Technology.

Murray, Janet. 1998. *Hamlet on the Holodeck: The Future of Narrative in Cyberspace*. Cambridge: Massachusetts Institute of Technology.

Nash, Kate. 2012. Modes of Interactivity: Analysing the Webdoc. *Media, Culture and Society* 34 (2): 195–210.

Nash, Kate. 2014. Clicking on the World: Documentary Representation and Interactivity. In *New Documentary Ecologies*, ed. K. Nash, C. Hight, and C. Summerhayes, 50–66. Houndmills: Palgrave Macmillan.

Nelson, Ted. 1983. *Literary Machines*. Sausalito, CA: Mindful Press.

O'Flynn, Siobhan. 2014. Psychogeography as Social Activism in Katerina Cizek's Digital Documentaries Highrise, the 1000th Tower and Out My Window. *LISA* 12 (1).

Ortuño, Pedro, and Virginia Villaplana. 2017. Activismo Transmedia. Narrativas de participación para el cambio social. Entre la comunicación creativa y el media art. *Obra digital: revista de comunicación* 12: 123–144.

Palacios, Marcos, and Javier Díaz-Noci (eds.). 2007. *On-line Journalism: Research Methods. A Multidisciplinary Approach in Comparative Perspective*. Bilbao: Universidad del País Vasco.

Pavlik, John V. 2001. *Journalism and New Media*. New York: Columbia University Press.

Pavlik, John V., and Jackie O. Pavlik. 2017. Understanding Quality in Digital Storytelling: A Theoretically Based Analysis of the Interactive Documentary. In *Digital Transformation in Journalism and News Media*, ed. M. Friedrichsen and Y. Kamalipour, 381–396. Cham: Springer.

Pope, James. 2006. A Future for Hypertext Fiction. *Convergence* 12 (4): 447–465.

Pope, James. 2010. Where Do We Go from Here? *Convergence* 16 (1): 75–94.

Pope, James. 2017. Further on Down the Digital Road. Narrative Design and Reading Pleasure in Five New Media Writing Prize narratives. *Convergence*, online publication.

ProPublica. 2016. Documenting Hate. About. ProPublica, September 8, 2016. https://projects.propublica.org/graphics/hatecrimes.

Ribas, J. Ignasi. 2001. Cultural Dissemination and Interactive Audiovisual Communication. *Temes de Disseny* 18, 194–204.

Rogers, Simon. 2017. A New Machine Learning App for Reporting on Hate in America. The Keyword. Google. *Journalism & News*, August 18, 2017. https://www.blog.google/topics/journalism-news/new-machine-learning-app-reporting-hate-america/.

Ryan, Marie-Laure. 2001. Beyond Myth and Metaphor: The Case of Narrative in Digital Media. *Games Studies: The International Journal of Computer Games Research* 1: 1.

Ryan, Marie-Laure (ed.). 2004. *Narrative Across Media: The Languages of Storytelling*. Lincoln and London: University of Nebraska Press.

Salaverría, Ramón. 2015. Los labs como fórmula de innovación en los medios. *El profesional de la información* 24 (4): 397–404.

Schultz, Tanjev. 1999. Interactive Options in Online Journalism: A Content Analysis of 100 US Newspapers. *Journal of Computer Mediated Communication* 5: 1.

Soler-Adillon, Joan, Carles Sora, Pere Freixa, and Joan-Ignasi Ribas. 2016. A Profile of the Interactive Communication Professional: Foundations, Current Trends and Perspectives. *El profesional de la información* 25 (2): 196–208.

Stroud, Natalie-Jomini, Joshua M. Scacco, and Alexander L. Curry. 2016. The Presence and Use of Interactive Features on News Websites. *Digital Journalism* 4 (3): 339–358.

The New York Times. 2017. Why We Need a Project to Document Hate Crimes. Editorial Board: Opinion Pages. *The New York Times*, January 17, 2017. https://www.nytimes.com/2017/01/17/opinion/why-we-need-a-project-to-document-hate-crimes.html.

Vázquez-Herrero, Jorge, and Gisela Moreno. 2017. Documental interactivo iberoamericano: proximidad y transformación social. DOC On-line: Revista Digital de Cinema Documentário, Special Issue, 109–130.

Walsh, Richard. 2011. Emergent Narrative in Interactive Media. *Narrative* 19 (1): 72–85.

Wang, Shan. 2017. ProPublica is Leading a Nationwide Effort to Document Hate Crimes, with Local and National Partners. NiemanLab, January 23, 2017. http://www.niemanlab.org/2017/01/propublica-is-leading-a-nationwide-effort-to-document-hate-crimes-with-local-and-national-partners.

Wojcik, Laura. 2015. Structured Journalism, the Next Revolution in Storytelling?. Medium, October 4, 2015. https://medium.com/interactive-journalism/structuredjournalism-the-next-revolution-in-storytelling-91557c48c121.

Web Documentary Projects Cited in Text

akaKurdistan. 1997. http://www.akakurdistan.com.

A Short History of the Highrise. 2013. http://www.nytimes.com/projects/2013/high-rise/index.html.

Bear71. 2012. http://bear71.nfb.ca.

Chicagocrime. 2005. http://www.chicagocrime.org/ [closed in 2008, out of service].

Documenting Hate. 2017. https://projects.propublica.org/graphics/hatecrimes.
Highrise, Out My Window. 2010. http://interactive.nfb.ca/#/outmywindow.
InfoGuide: The Sunni-Shia Divide. 2015. https://www.cfr.org/interactives/sunni-shia-divide#!/?cid=otr-marketing_url-sunni_shia_infoguide.
Officer Involved. 2016. http://projects.scpr.org/officer-involved.
Pregoneros de Medellin. 2015. https://pregonerosdemedellin.com/#es.
Proyecto Quipu. 2015. https://interactive.quipu-project.com/#/en/quipu/intro.
Snow Fall: The Avalanche at Tunnel Creek. 2013. http://www.nytimes.com/projects/2012/snow-fall/index.html#/?part=tunnel-creek.

CHAPTER 3

Information Visualization in Digital News Media

Mario Pérez-Montoro and Xaquín Veira-González

1 Introduction

The development and global adoption of the internet has impacted every corner of our society. There are very few areas that have not been influenced, transformed even, by the emergence of this new infrastructure and its intensive use.

In the case of the media, this influence is self-evident. Television networks, newspapers, film studios, and the multimedia industry have all had to reconsider their business models, and their production and distribution processes over the last two decades.

However, it is in the newsrooms where these transformations have been most far-reaching. At risk of being forced out of the market, newspaper companies have had to combine their traditional print editions,

M. Pérez-Montoro (✉)
Department of Information Science and Media Studies,
University of Barcelona, Barcelona, Spain
e-mail: perez-montoro@ub.edu

X. Veira-González
Department of Computer Science, Applied Mathematics and Statistics,
University of Girona, Girona, Spain

M. Pérez-Montoro (ed.), *Interaction in Digital News Media*,
https://doi.org/10.1007/978-3-319-96253-5_3

distributed via their usual sales outlets, with new digital versions made available via their websites (cybermedia). A number of new (and, even, traditional) proposals in the industry have resulted in newspapers opting to distribute exclusively—free of charge or paying a fee—via their web version.

Against this backdrop, the newsrooms have had to change their production strategies. Initially, they would first design their paper edition and then, based on that, they would design a digital or web edition. However, today, some newsrooms think first about their digital edition and then about the mobile edition of their paper (leaving the print edition until last); or, even, thanks to the widespread adoption of devices of this type, they think first about the mobile edition and then the web edition.

In this new scenario, the intensive use of information visualization in journalism has become one of the main new narrative techniques for storytelling. In this chapter, we address this special type of narrative visualization. To do this, we begin by analyzing the added value of information visualization in the media. Next, we seek to address the classic distinction between the concept of infographics and that of data visualization. We show the weaknesses of such a distinction and propose an alternative (multifaceted) taxonomy that allows a more exhaustive analysis of products of this type. Based on an analysis of a selection of visual contents, the chapter concludes by identifying the main patterns and trends underpinning the current role of information visualization in the newspaper industry.

2 The Value Added of Information Visualization

The widespread introduction of the internet has not only led to a change in the production models of the press, but it has also led to profound changes in the consumption habits of its products.

Traditionally, print newspapers were bought early in the morning and consumed until mid-afternoon. By the end of the day, as the news stories could not be updated, they had lost much of their informative power.

The new media, in contrast, present a different pattern of consumption. Besides being consulted at various points during working hours, their consumption is concentrated above all in the evening, after work, back in the reader's home. This change comes hand in hand with an increase in the consumption of these digital contents in tablets—the reader, from the comfort of their own home, can explore the news stories on high quality screens, as opposed to engaging in the much less comfortable interaction sat in front of a desktop computer.

The fact that much of the consumption of cybermedia is being conducted on mobile devices, such as tablets, is impacting decisions related to interaction design and the information architecture of these websites. For example, a leading newspaper like *USA Today* (http://www.usatoday.com) has radically overhauled the design of its web version (in this instance, opting for a responsive type). Its design criteria is no longer based on the behavior of its users in the desktop version but rather based on their consumption of the news using mobile devices.

It is in this new digital context that the role of visual content, and in particular information visualization, has acquired central importance.

In contrast with the classic media where the text of a newspaper article explained the story and the graphics or images provided support or evidence for what was being narrated, in the new digital media, the visuals no longer occupy this secondary role. Thanks to their interactive dimension, these visual products now occupy a predominant position in the narrative of the news story.

But the value of visualization goes well beyond that of a simple narrative resource. Today, thanks to large screens and the gesture navigation of the new devices, visual contents can be offered in all their splendor and so play an important role in capturing readers. And it is precisely in these environments that the offer of free-access information visualizations in the cybermedia is playing a key role in marketing plans to attract users that consume other paid content. Information visualizations, with their analytical and narrative power, can help attract and retain new users. For example, newspapers such as *The New York Times* (www.nytimes.com) offer a limited number of high quality products for free so that, having exceeded that number, the user is willing to pay to continue to have access to this quality content.

But in addition to attracting new users willing to pay for content, the visualizations allow the cybermedia that include such content a direct return on their investment (ROI) (Plaisant 2004; Smiciklas 2012). Basically, and among other consequences, content that includes visualizations or infographics results in a significant increase in user interactivity on social platforms with respect to that content.

3 Infographics and Data Visualization: A Classic Distinction

The classic debate centered on the differences between information graphics and data visualizations has been shown to be something of an artificial distinction. The industry has outgrown any differences and visually-driven formats—just like static, print infographics—are a mixed bag of devices, borrowing methods, and techniques from many disciplines to tell news stories that combine text, visual and multimedia elements, and interaction.

The distinction used to be justified as follows: infographics were graphic representations combining text and images to present information that exploited visual structures and from which readers could gain certain additional insights. Infographics might contain data visualizations, but the visuals were primarily pictorial, i.e., they depicted real-life objects, visible phenomena, using different levels of iconicity ranging from the realistic to the most abstract and schematic.

Data visualizations, on the other hand, were abstract graphic representations of data and data relationships. They were considered to serve primarily analytical goals and, while infographics were heavily authored, data visualizations were explorable and unguided. They presented no iconic relationships with real-life objects; they were abstractions that were designed to encode visually the values in the data and to highlight data relationships. However, these conceptions provided a somewhat narrow view of the possibilities—and the actual uses—of information visualization.

The roots of this debate lay in the different educational backgrounds of the professionals producing infographics in newsrooms and the academic analyses of the output of their work. The earlier emphasis on graphic design backgrounds—with a nose for journalism—gave way in the past decade and a half to computer scientists—with a nose for journalism and an eye for visual design.

The professionals, practices, and techniques of information visualization (InfoVis), the computer science that studies visual representations of data for communication, began to seep into newsrooms. Journalism happily adopted some of these techniques and applied them to messages addressing a larger audience with its different needs, priorities, and reading habits.

Data visualization (DataViz) became the new buzzword in and around newsrooms—constituting a veritable buzzfeed—as the output from graphics desks shifted from diagrammatic explanations to abstract data representations (Cairo 2017). The sector started to talk more about DataViz than infographics, as distinctions began to be drawn between them. Critics conflated data visualization with data art and visual analytics, especially with devices that facilitated exploratory data mining. However, these are important considerations since the role of information is not to entertain or dump data, but rather to reveal and provide context.

Yet, as we have been at pains to stress, the two sides to the debate have been talking at cross-purposes. Information graphics is all-encompassing—at times too much so. It includes diagrammatic renderings of processes and events, the inner-workings of machines, schematics, flowcharts, cartographic representations of social behaviors, and, yes, abstract representations of large sets of data. It is what Tufte (1983) described as "visual explanations;" what Costa and Moles referred to as "educational (didactic) images" (Costa and Moles 1991). Data visualization is a subset of information graphics.

And that is not the end of the story. The current trend is toward the use of narrative devices that can weave video, photo, text, and interactives, to tell a visual story. Publishers that are aware of their audience's hunger for more visual stories are investing in teams that are capable of conceiving and producing this integrated visual storytelling, and a few leading newsrooms in the world have expanded beyond the traditional boundaries of information graphics to become visual desks.

In the field of information visualization, from which we take our cue as regards, the taxonomy we outline later in this chapter, the systematic study and categorization of these digital, visual stories, or narrative visualizations (Segel and Heer 2010) is still less than a decade old. Until that date, computer science studies had focused primarily on visualizations as separate entities, paying very little attention to the relationship between them and the larger narratives in which they were embedded. Current research has shifted its attention toward how to tell complete story arcs anchored in visualizations, and it raises questions about the roles of the author, narrative style, and rhetorical devices when examining the sequencing of text and visualization. The reason for this shift is that because visualizations are turning into the default techniques to present what reporters and analysts extract from their data sources, it has become necessary to understand the inner workings of these narratives, how visuals work in conjunction with text, or audio, or interaction, or other visuals, and what the building blocks of that skeleton—i.e., the visual structure that combines them to deliver the journalistic message—are.

Much of the research coming out of InfoVis continues to focus—quite logically—on how these narrative techniques work in data visualizations: how sequencing and accumulation turn a data visualization, for example, on climate change into an instant classic, myth-busting essay as in Bloomberg's "What's Really Warming the World?" (https://www.bloomberg.com/graphics/2015-whats-warming-the-world/), how framing through personalization turns, for example, a map of house prices into an anger-inducing revelation for the audience as in *The Guardian*'s "Unaffordable Country" (https://www.theguardian.com/society/ng-interactive/2015/sep/02/unaffordable-country-where-can-you-afford-to-buy-a-house), or how template-based language generation can rewrite a story into thousands of localized stories as in *The New York Times*'s "The Best and Worst Places to Grow Up" (https://www.nytimes.com/interactive/2015/05/03/upshot/the-best-and-worst-places-to-grow-up-how-your-area-compares.html).

Newsrooms have pushed forward the boundaries of how to structure these stories as they pile on the use of multimedia devices. Text can dissolve into images that take over the screen to display visually what the reader was possibly already imagining, as in *The New York Times*'s influential "Snowfall" (http://www.nytimes.com/projects/2012/snow-fall/index.html); visuals and voices can drive the narrative and fade into the text that provides the context, as in *The Washington Post*'s "Fenced Out" (https://www.washingtonpost.com/graphics/world/border-barriers/europe-refugee-crisis-border-control/); users can swipe screens up and onwards—on the story—or left and inwards—deeper on that stage—with each screen using the multimedia element best suited for that story block, as on the small screen version of *The Guardian*'s "Mekong: a river rising". In these narrative visualizations, each story unit can be realized as an appropriate multimedia element, connected to the adjacent units in the same way that a sentence is connected to the next sentence in a paragraph, the way comic-book panels build up, or the way a shot in a movie makes sense when seen in context with the shots that come before and after it. These new types of storytelling devices bring new editing needs—they call for holistic editing—and a new set of categories.

And although the future seems to lie in digital stories, the end goal, when all is said and done, is not that dissimilar from that of the static, print, all-encompassing visual explanations which we seem to have forgotten about.

4 A New Taxonomy

"If you ask something of the reader, something spectacular has to happen in return." This powerful soundbite from Archie Tse, deputy Graphics Director at *The New York Times*, from his influential talk at Malofiej (Tse 2016), sought to explain how his paper has transitioned from reporting and developing interactive visualizations to conceive, report, and write stories, like those described above, which integrate text, static visualizations, and other multimedia elements. It is a way to simplify production, in part, due to the multidimensional characteristics of digital platforms, as content now needs to live in devices with different resolutions, capabilities, affordances, in different contexts, and with different user habits.

As usual, the problem was how this idea was translated to the wider audience, the mangled understanding of what "spectacular" actually meant, and the narrow view afforded interaction in this context. For one thing, the need for something "spectacular" to happen in response to a user action was understood as something that was carried out using multimedia elements, not so much as the result of an establishing shot followed by the reveal, to put it in more narrative terms. The idea also turned into an argument for removing interaction all together when this meant very specific types of superficial interactions, which according to the NYT's metrics their readers were not using, such as hovers, or interactions that could be realized without really requiring the user to act, such as location-based needs or multimedia autoplays. What it was not though was a call to remove the interaction from narratives that emphasize personalization and frame stories in terms of the user, or game-like narratives.

Developing this idea, it becomes apparent that the classic distinction between infographics and data visualization is not at all illuminative. It fails to help us understand the phenomenon of information visualization in the media, and sheds no light on what Tse might have been trying to convey in relation to quality. Very few journalistic creations match exactly with one or other of these two types of communicative proposals.

These creations simultaneously employ aspects drawn both from the domain of infographics and from that of data visualization. What we need, therefore, is a classification that provides a more adequate characterization and that allows us to analyze the current panorama of visualization in the media.

Logically, the first step in designing such a classification is to review the various proposals made to date in the specialist literature on visualization research.

Leaving to one side, the various reformulations and variants of the classic infographic-data visualization distinction (Cairo 2017; Tufte 1983; among others), there would appear to be a certain degree of consensus that allows current visual proposals to be divided in two main groups that depend on the navigation system being implemented (McKenna et al. 2017). In the first group of this standard classification, we find stories that readers navigate using a click/tap input (stepper mode). These stories are visualized at the discretion of the user, in a step-by-step fashion, clicking through the narrative as though it were a slideshow. In the second group, we find stories that readers navigate using a scroll input (scroller mode). In this case, the user can pan up and down through the story using the scroller on their device, maintaining narrative continuity without the disruptions characteristic of the first case.

The products associated with the first group have the advantage of overcoming the problems associated with those based on scrolling, including, among others, the excessive weight of the pages that support this type of navigation or the frequently unintuitive exploration that occurs when the visual story contains elements of a focalized or hierarchical narrative type. The products associated with the second group, unlike those in the first, ensure stories are fully consumed.

This classification, although interesting, is similarly not, especially, illuminative when it comes to analyzing the current panorama of visualization in the media. Once again, it suffers from being a hierarchical classification generated from a single criterion. As in the earlier case, current information visualization proposals offer such a rich variety that extends well beyond a single excluding criterion, as in this classification based on the type of navigation.

What is required is an alternative classification that can shed more light on the analysis of visualizations, a faceted (non-hierarchical) classification that allows us to examine these productions in a polyhedral fashion. Here, the differences between a simple hierarchical classification and a faceted classification are substantial, insofar as the former comprises a single hierarchical taxonomy and each domain object to which it applies falls in just one of the classification's extremes. A faceted classification, in contrast, is a method for simultaneously classifying the same set of objects (belonging to the domain) from multiple points of view or based on multiple criteria. Technically, a faceted classification is a controlled documentary language formed, in turn, from the aggregation of various classifications or facets. Each classification or facet is parallel to all the others and they are all at the same semantic level and each object in the domain must be classed in each and every one of those classifications or facets of which it is made up.

A number of faceted classifications have been attempted for the analysis of narrative visualization with data (Segel and Heer 2010; among others). But they suffer various limitations inasmuch as they fail to address in an inclusive and simultaneous fashion all, and not just one part, of the characteristics of these visual productions.

The basic structure of our proposal draws its inspiration from the facets described by Segel and Heer (2010), but we adapt and extend this by including other facets that we and other authors have identified. The resulting classification or taxonomy (Table 1) comprises the following five facets or sub-classifications: narrative genre, visual narrative, narrative structure, driver of the interaction, and the visualization-story ratio. Below we explore each facet in the taxonomy, which enables us to provide a good description of the current panorama of visual narrative in the media and to draw interesting conclusions.

4.1 Narrative Genre

The narrative genre is the first of the facets or subcategories proposed for conducting the analysis. Depending on the narrative style of the visualization, we can identify seven distinct genres: magazine style, annotated chart, partitioned poster, flow chart, comic strip, slide show, and video (Segel and Heer 2010). However, they are not, it should be stressed, pure, and exclusive genres, rather the same narrative visualization, or a part of it, might be classified within one or more of these subgenres.

To illustrate these genres, examples can be readily extracted from the media. Although there seems to be a convergence toward a very definite

Table 1 Narrative visualization taxonomy

Narrative genre						
Magazine style	Annotated chart	Partitioned poster	Flow chart	Comic strip	Slide show	Video

Visual narrative		
Visual structuring	*Highlighting*	*Transition guidance*
Establishing shot/splash screen	Close-Ups	Familiar objects (but still cuts)
Consistent visual platform	Feature distinction	Viewing angle
Progress bar/timebar	Character direction	Viewer(Camera)motion
"Checklist" progresss tracker	Motion	Continuity editing
Navigation input	Audio	Object continuity
	Zooming	Animated transitions

Narrative structure		
Ordering	*Interactivity*	*Messaging*
Random access	Hover highlighting/details	Captions/headlines
User directed path	Filtering/selection/search	Annotaions
Linear	Navigation buttons	Accompanying article
Story progression	Navigation progress	Multi-messaging
Story layout	Navigation feedback	Comment repetition
	Very limited interactivity	Introductory text
	Explicit instruction	Summary/synthesis
	Tacit tutorial	
	Stimulating default views	

Interaction driver	
Author driven	*Reader driven*
Linear ordering of scenes	No prescriberd ordering
Heavy messaging	No messaging
No interactivity	Free interactivity

Ratio visualization-story			
Q1	Q2	Q3	Q4

type of story format—which we explain below—most newsrooms still demonstrate some variety in their narrative genres. *The New York Times*, for example, employs a wide range of visualization formats, although most of its visual stories are magazine style, static charts embedded in the flow of the story—such as, 'What Would It Take to Fix New York's Subway?' (https://www.nytimes.com/interactive/2017/12/22/nyregion/what-would-it-take-to-fix-new-yorks-subway.html), the paper also relies heavily on annotated charts and maps—as in 'The Islamic State: From Insurgency to Rogue State and Back' (https://www.nytimes.com/interactive/2017/10/22/world/middleeast/isis-the-islamic-state-from-insurgency-to-rogue-state-and-back.html)—and videos—as in the forensic '10 Minutes. 12 Gunfire Bursts. 30 Videos. Mapping the Las Vegas Massacre' (https://www.nytimes.com/video/us/100000005473328/las-vegas-shooting-timeline-12-bursts.html). On occasions, video is not used as the delivery method for the entire narrative, but rather as a small fragment of the piece—the case for example of the vintage videogame-style simulations of the Times' piece 'How Uber Uses Psychological Tricks to Push Its Drivers' Buttons' (https://www.nytimes.com/interactive/2017/04/02/technology/uber-drivers-psychological-tricks.html). Their piece 'LeBron James Scores 5,995th Playoff Point, Taking the Record From Michael Jordan' (https://www.nytimes.com/interactive/2017/05/25/sports/basketball/lebron-career-playoff-points-record.html) is both an annotated chart and a partitioned poster. Likewise, their multimedia formats for what we would call correspondent's dispatches, such as 'Tour a City Torn in Half by ISIS' (https://www.nytimes.com/interactive/2017/02/22/world/middleeast/solomon-isis-front-line-iraq-diary.html), are slideshows that help fragment the narrative in steps that cover the entire canvas, without allowing the user to drill deep on each step.

4.2 *Visual Narratives*

The second of the facets concerns the visual narratives implemented in the work. Here, we specifically analyze their visual structuring, visual highlighting techniques, and transition guidance (Segel and Heer 2010).

In the case of visual structuring, this means examining the use made of the following mechanisms: establishing shot/splash screen, consistent visual platform, progress bar/timebar, "checklist" progress tracker, and the navigation input of button, scroll, and slider (McKenna et al. 2017). For instance, the main, scrollable visualization from the Post's "Why MLB hitters are suddenly obsessed with launch angles" (https://www.washingtonpost.com/graphics/sports/mlb-launch-angles-story/) uses a consistent visual platform, and changes and annotates the chart as the user scrolls, indicating with navigation dots on the right where the user is in the stepper. And stories about places, such as the NYT's "A Crack in an Antarctic Ice Shelf Grew 17 Miles in the Last Two Months" (https://www.nytimes.com/interactive/2017/02/07/science/earth/antarctic-crack.html), *The Guardian*'s "Missing flight MH370—a visual guide to the parts and debris found so far" (https://www.theguardian.com/world/ng-interactive/2017/jan/17/missing-flight-mh370-a-visual-guide-to-the-parts-and-debris-found-so-far), and the Post's "What is North Korea trying to hit?" (https://www.washingtonpost.com/graphics/world/north-korea-targets/?utm_term=.0105d76dc7dc), usually start with an establishing shot—an overview of the location and the specific areas of interests—that serves to set the scene.

In the case of highlighting strategies, this means analyzing the use of such mechanisms as close-ups, feature distinction, character direction, motion, audio, and zooming implemented in the piece. The Times's "Harriet Tubman's Path to Freedom" (https://www.nytimes.com/interactive/2017/02/24/travel/underground-railroad-slavery-harriet-tubman-byway-maryland.html), for example, uses animation of the background map to anchor the transitions between locations. The Post's "How water damages a flooded house—and how parts can be saved" (https://www.washingtonpost.com/graphics/2017/national/flooded-homes/) uses feature highlighting to establish the visual focus of the annotation at each step.

Finally, there are the techniques of transition guidance: familiar objects (but still cuts), viewing angle, viewer (camera) motion, continuity editing, object continuity, and animated transitions. Reuters' "A deadly crossing" (http://fingfx.thomsonreuters.com/gfx/rngs/MYANMAR-ROHINGYA/010051JR3GY/index.html) uses different size camera shots of the same characters at different points in the narrative for continuity—all static; while the Times's "Hurricane Irma Is One of the Strongest Storms In History" (https://www.nytimes.com/interactive/2017/09/09/us/hurricane-irma-records.html) keeps animating and transforming the objects, in this case the hurricanes' path, throughout the views—transitioning from map to chart views seamlessly. In the Times's "Escaping the Inferno" (https://www.nytimes.com/interactive/2017/09/09/us/hurricane-irma-records.html), the camera motion on each visualization continues from the last shot of the previous one, so it picks back the visual frame of reference even though the viewer has left it behind a few scrolls or swipes ago.

4.3 Narrative Structure

The third of the facets concerns the narrative structure of the journalistic production analyzing its ordering, interactivity, and messaging (Segel and Heer 2010).

In the case of the first tactic, ordering, the analysis examines random access, user-directed and linear paths, and story progression, that is, the possible story paths that might occur—linear, linear skip, and tree/graph style (McKenna et al. 2017) and the possible story layout—document, slideshow, and hybrid (McKenna et al. 2017). Non-linear ordering has almost completely disappeared from narrative visualizations and, in the few examples where there is no prescribed ordering, the visualization is an isolated device within an article, as in Axios' "The flow of goods between states" (https://www.axios.com/the-flow-of-goods-between-states-1513304375-5d9d9ddc-b0fe-4d0d-a556-dab4279acbe0.html). Even the Pudding's "How Robert Glasper sampled Miles Davis on 'Ghetto Walkin'" (https://pudding.cool/2017/03/sampling/) is a slideshow with a strict linear ordering of the content, with each step triggered by non-traditional user inputs like "Click along the dotted line to crop the sample"—although it also allows the user to layer the components of the audio track at any point.

Interactivity includes such methods as hover highlighting/details, filtering/selection/ search, navigation buttons, navigation progress—which describes how the reader perceives their placement within the entire story using text, dots and infovis (McKenna et al. 2017), navigation feedback—which combines animated transitions with additional animations of story text or other components, such as fading or movement (McKenna et al. 2017), very limited interactivity, explicit instruction, tacit tutorial, and stimulating default views. The Pudding's "An Interactive Visualization of Every Line in Hamilton" (https://pudding.cool/2017/03/hamilton/), which can be read as a tacit tutorial that leads to the freely explorable visualization in the last step, also has stimulating default views that allow for further exploration within some of the steps.

Messaging addresses such techniques as captions/headlines, annotations, accompanying article, multi-messaging, comment repetition, introductory text, and summary/synthesis. Most visualizations in our collection are integrated and interconnected with the text in the article, so much so that some articles are nothing but the annotation of the chart, taken out of the chart space, and turned into caption or headlines within the text body, as in the *Los Angeles Times*' "This isn't the best Dodgers team ever—but it's still pretty great" (http://www.latimes.com/projects/la-sp-dodgers-best-season-ever/).

4.4 Interaction Driver

The fourth facet analyzes what is responsible for driving the narrative, although in many cases a balance is struck between author-driven and reader-driven stories (Segel and Heer 2010).

The first option examines author-driven narratives with respect to the existence or otherwise of such properties as the linear ordering of scenes, heavy messaging, and no interactivity. Most stories fall within the author-driven setup, especially those from traditional media outlets. For instance, *The Guardian*'s "How to finish a novel: tracking a book's progress from idea to completion" (https://www.theguardian.com/books/ng-interactive/2017/mar/20/how-to-finish-a-novel-tracking-book-progress-wyl-menmuir) has heavy messaging, no interactivity at all, and linear ordering. The focus is on the semantic integration of visuals and text, so the story reads in and out of the visuals, which are heavily captioned and annotated.

The second option examines the freedom enjoyed by the reader in driving the story, identifying whether the properties of no prescribed ordering, no messaging, or free interactivity occur. The few examples that allow for total control over the order in which the user accesses the information are searchable databases like the Post's "A database of the president's false and misleading claims since Jan. 20" (https://www.washingtonpost.com/graphics/politics/trump-claims-database/) or "The Fact Checker: Trump's promises" (https://www.washingtonpost.com/graphics/politics/trump-promise-tracker/).

4.5 Visualization-Story Ratio

As we have noted, traditionally, a newspaper story was narrated using a large body of text, embedded in which were graphics or images providing evidence or related details. Today, this narrative scheme has been turned upside down and these graphics and images have acquired their own specific weight within the story that extends beyond that of mere support.

In this last facet, we analyze the visualization-story ratio, that is, the weight of the information visualization with respect to the whole story. To evaluate this, we create a scale of quartiles: Q1, Q2, Q3, and Q4. The productions in the first quartile (Q1) have a visualization-story ratio higher than 75%; those in Q2 have a ratio between 50 and 75%; those in Q3 have a ratio between 25 and 49%; and, those in Q4 have a ratio below 25%. At the high end of the scale, we find pieces like *Los Angeles Times*' "Don't waste your time at Disneyland. Here's how to avoid the lines" (http://www.latimes.com/projects/la-fi-disneyland-ride-wait-time/). This has a ratio of over 80%: it comprises a 500-word article with seven blocks of charts, the last of which, showing the wait times for individual rides, accounts for about half the entire story. At the low end of the scale, many of Quartz's single-chart-surrounded-by-article have a ratio under 25%, including, for example, "England says Oliver is the most popular boys' name, but it's actually Muhammad" (https://qz.com/1082778/popular-baby-names-muhammad-is-actually-the-most-boys-name-in-england-and-wales-not-oliver/): a 300-word article with a single static chart.

5 Patterns and Trends

The faceted taxonomy outlined above allows us to analyze the current panorama of visualizations in the news media and to draw a number of interesting conclusions.

In carrying out our analysis, we adopted the following methodological strategy. First, we selected a series of digital media which we consider, along obviously with others, to be leaders in the development of innovative strategies for incorporating information visualizations in their journalistic work: Axios (www.axios.com), *Los Angeles Times* (www.latimes.com), National Public Radio (www.npr.org), Quartz (qz.com),

Reuters (www.reuters.com), *The Guardian* (www.theguardian.com), *The New York Times* (www.nytimes.com), The Pudding (pudding.cool), *The Washington Post* (www.washingtonpost.com), and Tableau Public (public.tableau.com). We should perhaps point out that Tableau Public is not strictly speaking a digital medium, but rather a platform for visualizations created by users with access to the open, free version of the program for the generation of Tableau visualizations. We opted to analyze its visualizations because it is a scenario where professionals hang their productions and, therefore, it is an ideal environment in which to identify innovations and trends in the visualization field.

Having selected the media organizations, we examined the contents that they had published during 2017. We evaluated over 400 items and ended up with a final sample of 61 for further analysis, which thanks to their information visualizations can be considered as good, innovative narrative proposals. We then generated a system in a private webpage in which we were able to navigate freely through these contents and access them. When visiting a specific content, the systems offer a dropdown menu on the right containing the faceted classification that allows us to click on the specific characteristics of each facet that the content satisfies. The system also allows us to conduct a descriptive statistical exploitation of the results of the analysis.

The analysis of these contents using the system and the faceted classification enabled us to extract important ideas as regards the patterns and trends presented by these media visualizations.

Indeed, a number of trends are immediately apparent. Thus, most of the visual stories analyzed have a linear order; they are semantically interconnected with the accompanying article—to the point that text which would previously have been used as an annotation now forms part of the body of the article—and they have very limited interactivity—in fact, most remove superficial interaction, such as details-on-demand, altogether. Steppers—with very few exceptions but including Reuters' "Europe Elections: Europe's shift right - EU and national parliamentary election votes by ideology" (http://fingfx.thomsonreuters.com/gfx/rngs/FRANCE-ELECTION-FARRIGHT/010040TK1SP/index.html)—now use "scrollytelling," a design pattern in which the visual sticks to the viewport while the text annotation responds to the user's scroll: every time a new annotation is revealed, it triggers a new state, an animation, a transition, or a highlight on the visual.

These trends seem to represent a fairly pragmatic way of responding to the needs created by the many screen sizes they have to serve, from the range of mobile and desktop sizes, but employing the now widely accepted "mobile-first" strategy. A linear story with visual elements interwoven, at times like a set of stacked narrative blocks, allows authors to focus either on the information, on the reporting, or on the design of each visualization or interactive, instead of on the overall narrative interface. This continuous scrolling adapts well to the natural gesture for reading on both mobile and desktop devices, and while the practicality of it is understandable, and while it has become predominant, we would not prescribe it as the only solution, because it is linked to the text as the narrative driver. Visually-driven narratives, as is the case of slideshows, use an equally simple interface to jump from block to block—swipe or tap on the mobile; arrow or click on the desktop—but the reading is not the same as with continuous scrolling. As slideshows take over the entire screen, they allow for a pause, and in that pause, the block could be anything from a video, to an interactive, to a copy block, or even a stepper using two directional swiping—down to move forward in the story, left to go deeper on the step, or vice versa.

Anyway, continuous scrolling is the norm, and as part of that norm, we have identified a few patterns that are perhaps worth highlighting. In a subjective, least to more complex order, they are "intro and chart," "multiple views," "guided dashboards," "quick overview, story is in the details," "quick overview, annotated chart," "complex overview, quick details," and the "martini glass structure."

The first pattern, "intro and chart" is common in the visualizations of Quartz, *Los Angeles Times*, but especially those of Axios. The website's "Atlantic hurricanes" (https://www.axios.com/1-atlantic-hurricanes-1515110846-8b55a5d4-193d-45c2-8e94-7d49d331f5a9.html) serves here as the simplest version of this archetype. The short introduction explains what the graphic is about, how to decode the visualization and what the hover contributes. Category 5 hurricanes are highlighted in red and annotated in the visualization. It is, above all, a quick read: a visual interface for the data, with no scenes, very limited interactivity and messaging, and although the user is free to explore each hurricane, the details are simple. It follows Axios' "smart brevity" premise and it unpretentiously delivers on what is promised: here you have every Atlantic storm tracked.

The second pattern is that of "multiple views," as typified by the Times' "Six Charts That Help Explain the Republican Tax Plan" (https://www.nytimes.com/interactive/2017/09/27/us/politics/six-charts-to-explain-the-republican-tax-plan.html). This pattern does not require consistency in the narrative blocks nor does it carry the objects through the story. It has a strong linear narrative driven by the text, and the visualizations are static. It uses the visuals to provide proof of the story told in the text. And the use of color is adapted to whatever is on screen. When the plot is broken down in narrative blocks, its flexibility makes it well suited for breaking news, developing stories: it keeps the editing focus on the overall narrative, while the narrative blocks of copy and visuals can be moved around.

The third pattern is commonly used for stories in which the structure of the data is set but its values cannot be controlled, as is the case of election results or polls, and issue trackers. These "guided dashboards," like the Post's "A database of the president's false and misleading claims since Jan. 20" (https://www.washingtonpost.com/graphics/politics/trump-claims-database/) offer a set of filtered views that give the user an idea of the scope of the data together with some significant annotations. They are linear in the sense that they are stacked, so the user sees one before scrolling to the next, but their only narrative thread in our case study would be that they go from overview, to superlatives, to searchable database, and indeed most could be better understood as a partitioned poster. In the Post's database, the interaction is limited to filtering the database, with the most sophisticated being in the third block.

The fourth pattern is the "quick overview, story is in the details," which is a common feature in *The Washington Post*, *The New York Times*, and *The Guardian*, whose "The three-degree world: the cities that will be drowned by global warming" (https://www.theguardian.com/cities/ng-interactive/2017/nov/03/three-degree-world-cities-drowned-global-warming), we use here to define the model. It starts with an overview—in this case doubled—first global, then focused on Asia. In this model, the overviews are quick reads, single charts that are a visual answer to the statement in the caption, headline, or whatever prominent text accompanies them, clearly highlighted, and with no or very limited interaction. The first part of the overview in this piece uses an autoplay sequence to present the global warming projections. The color blue used to highlight the projections is then used to highlight the most affected cities, using color to focus rather than giving it any specific meaning.

The "details" are large scale maps of the most interesting cities—an editorially driven author selection—that autoplays to show the extent of the sea-level rise overlaid on top of the population density. Because the visual pattern is repeated in all the detailed blocks, there is no need to explain the color-coding of the visualization anywhere else than in the first map.

The fifth pattern, "complex overview, quick details," shifts the focus of the story to the beginning as in the Times' "The Islamic State: From Insurgency to Rogue State and Back" (https://www.nytimes.com/interactive/2017/10/22/world/middleeast/isis-the-islamic-state-from-insurgency-to-rogue-state-and-back.html). This pattern engages the user at the top with a sophisticated overview, in this case an annotated chart that follows the scrollytelling pattern, then it offers the rest of the story as a text-driven narrative with embedded visuals. At each step, the main visualization fades the cities in or out—which are sized based in relation to their actual area. We understand that the choice of the scroll to trigger the views—as opposed to a stepper or an autoplay animation—is a way of ensuring the user continues to read the rest of the story in a natural way. The narrative almost follows an inverted pyramid style with the most important details being at the top, while the rest follows a pattern similar to that of "multiple views," with a few visuals that offer a different summary view of the data interspersed in the text.

These two models, which to some degree mirror each other, are two different solutions to attempts to ensure reader engagement on longer visual stories. While the first quickly gets the reader scrolling and goes from general details to detailed stories, the second hooks the user at the top then slowly releases their attention. It would be interesting to test, using analytics, if the time spent per narrative block does or does not align with our theory. In the "story is in the details" pattern, the "details" are the main focus of the story and a repetitive pattern is used that can take many shapes: an autoplay video, a set of small multiples, an interactive map—such as those on the similarly themed and structured "What 500-year flooding could look like around five cities" (https://www.washingtonpost.com/graphics/2017/national/harvey-flood-compare/) from the Post, or even an annotated chart—like that in the Times' "Every Tax Cut and Tax Increase in the House G.O.P. Bill and What It Would Cost" (https://www.nytimes.com/interactive/2017/11/15/us/politics/every-tax-cut-in-the-house-tax-bill.html).

The last pattern, the well-known martini glass structure is the one used on The Pudding's "An Interactive Visualization of Every Line in

Hamilton" (https://pudding.cool/2017/03/hamilton), an ambitious piece that makes use of almost every trick available to the visualization designer. It visualizes each data point—a line from Lin-Manuel Miranda's musical—and carries it from the splash screen, where they make up the play's Broadway promotional poster, to the arrangement of 46 circles for the 46 songs, to the filtered views of Angelica's and Eliza's stories, to the final view where the user can explore, filter, and interact with them. Regardless of the arrangement, the user can hover over each data point to investigate the details of the line. It uses the scrollytelling pattern so each copy block triggers an animated transition that ends on a new arrangement of the visualization; within each step, the user can further interact or filter the view from the text on the left side—the first step on Angelica's and Eliza's stories are actually default views that invite further filtering. The story acts as a tacit tutorial for the final tool, which allows the user to freely explore the entire dataset based on character and theme filters. Annotation, captions, headlines, and other prominent copy connect the text and the visualization by literal reference and by the consistent use of color. The story has an experimental nature: it's a complex balance between linear narrative and free exploration that was more common before the "mobile-first" strategy took hold in newsrooms—it confesses in the intro that it is best viewed in a high resolution modern browser.

Finally, while generally we can conclude that these are models of excellence in linear narrative visualizations, we must also recognize that their formats are, as we have pointed out, restricted by production routines. We are certain that as the industry's priorities crystalize and the study of audience behavior takes center stage in strategic decisions, we will see more formats that target narrower consumer habits rather than trying to service them all, and as a result, new standards for visual storytelling will emerge that are platform-specific.

We can foresee the impact that such technologies as augmented or virtual reality, which for the time being news outlets have had to limit to well-placed experiments, will have once they become commonplace, offering narrative visualizations a wealth of untapped possibilities. We have also observed the influence that experimental spaces such as The Pudding can have in positively advancing the medium. In sandboxes like this, the restrictions and the needs to serve a wider audience can to some extent be disregarded as developers make advances in terms of angles, formats, styles, and structures.

As narrative visualizations become increasingly popular devices to deliver the news and outlets use them as a way to engage and retain readers, we will have access to an even larger collection of pieces for research. And as perspectives from communications and from InfoVis converge, interact, and influence one another, we should gain more insights into design patterns, narrative techniques, and the journalistic strategies that shape them. Yet, the overriding aim should always be to understand, to prescribe methods, and to define standards so as to convert these communication devices into effective mechanisms that can help audiences understand and interpret the world around them, making sense of the noise, and making decisions as informed citizens.

References

Cairo, A. 2017. *Nerd Journalism*. Barcelona: Universitat Oberta de Catalunya.

Costa, J., and A.A. Moles. 1991. *Imagen didáctica*. Barcelona: CEAC.

McKenna, S., N. Henry Riche, B. Lee, J. Boy, and M. Meyer. 2017. Visual Narrative Flow: Exploring Factors Shaping Data Visualization Story Reading Experiences. *Eurographics Conference on Visualization (EuroVis)* 36 (3): 377–387.

Plaisant, C. 2004. The Challenge of Information Visualization Evaluation. In *AVI '04 Proceedings of the Working Conference on Advanced Visual Interfaces*. New York: ACM.

Segel, E., and J. Heer. 2010. Narrative Visualization: Telling Stories with Data. *IEEE Transactions on Visualization and Computer Graphics* 16 (6): 1139–1148.

Smiciklas, M. 2012. *The Power of Infographics*. Indianapolis: Pearson Education.

Tse, A. 2016. *Why We Are Doing Fewer Interactives*. Available https://github.com/archietse/malofiej-2016/blob/master/tse-malofiej-2016-slides.pdf.

Tufte, E. 1983. *The Visual Display of Quantitative Information*. Cheshire: Graphic Press.

CHAPTER 4

Immersive Journalism and Virtual Reality

Joan Soler-Adillon and Carles Sora

1 Introduction: Immersive Journalism

The digital technologies used in journalism today are fundamentally different from the media ecosystems that dominated this profession at the end of last century. In recent years, digital journalism has been presented with new digital story forms using interactive and mobile platforms that expand the boundaries of storytelling and create new relations with consumers, as they are able to reach larger audiences in a wide variety of ways. These new platforms have fostered a series of innovations that impact the entire profession, from the moment that news are reported, to the process of distribution, and audience reach at the receiving end. The 2015 Pew Report claims that almost two-thirds of Americans now use their phones to follow

J. Soler-Adillon (✉)
Department of Media Arts, Royal Holloway, University of London,
Egham, Surrey, UK
e-mail: joan.soler-adillon@rhul.ac.uk

C. Sora
Department of Communication, Pompeu Fabra University, Barcelona, Spain
e-mail: carles.sora@upf.edu

C. Sora
School of Humanities, Arts and Social Sciences,
MIT Open Doc Lab, CMS/W, Cambridge, MA, USA

M. Pérez-Montoro (ed.), *Interaction in Digital News Media*,
https://doi.org/10.1007/978-3-319-96253-5_4

breaking news, and this new scenario is growing around the globe, in a process that will change how we consume and produce news forever. In the words of the Executive Editor of *The Guardian*: "If you are not building for mobile, you are building for the past" (Matias 2012).

In this new mobile journalism scenario, several platforms have proliferated: from mobile-first webs, tablet, and phone apps to Augmented Reality and Virtual Reality (VR) experiences. And from these platforms, new formats and genres have emerged, such as short factual pieces with immersive 360-degree video, VR non-fiction productions, and interactive documentaries. Initially developed in research laboratories—such as the pioneering studio run by Nonny de la Peña (2010)—over the last decade, immersive journalism has now left academic laboratories to take up a key role in the coverage of many news companies. In November 2015, *The New York Times* was one of the first early adopters of this technology when it distributed Google Cardboard viewers among its Sunday edition subscribers while publishing the first journalistic VR piece, "The Displaced," a story about the lives of three refugee children forced to leave their homes in war-ravaged countries. Since then, several US and European newspapers have delivered their own immersive stories.

VR and 360 films are being used to allow audience to experience incidents and situations at firsthand, placing the viewer at the center of the experience and, thus, generating the sense of being in another place and time, living other people's lives and stories. However, newsrooms recognize that there is still not enough "good content" (Watson 2017). In what are still the early stages of creation, every production has had to face their own challenges in terms of technical and language conventions that remain very much work-in-progress and which need to be consolidated (Sirkkunen et al. 2016; Sora 2017; Watson 2017). Based on recent state-of-the-art reports from research institutions (Watson 2017; Uricchio et al. 2015) and a number of publications in the literature, we seek to contribute to this field by discussing some of the ideas that are central to these discourses, both from the theoretical and the creative point of view.

With this in mind, we undertake an analysis of several projects in immersive journalism from the perspective of content analysis and also from that of audience reception, without considering pipeline and production features, which although very relevant, do not inform us about the user experience. Our analysis of reception involves a study of the technological characteristics of the immersive experience and the psychological perceptions that the product generates. To do so, we have chosen a number of recent immersive productions, some of which made by *The Guardian* and *The New York Times*, two newspapers that are leading digital innovation media with award winning VR projects. These productions will help us devise and build our theoretical framework and, subsequently, extract and identify relevant considerations and tendencies.

The main objective underpinning our research is the development of a theoretical framework for the analysis of new immersive journalism. This is to be based on four broad and highly pertinent topics that are already in discussion on the research literature, namely: "storytelling," "empathy," "immersion," and "interactivity." It is our contention that these four concepts encapsulate the main challenges faced by these new digital journalism experiences, and that to ensure the successful implementation of VR, it is critical that we understand how users perceive and are affected by VR stories. Drawing on previous research in the design and analysis of VR productions for journalism (e.g., Shin and Biocca 2017; Sirkkunen et al. 2016; de la Peña et al. 2010), we undertake an analysis of immersive journalism experiences, focusing on the study of the design, narrative, and user experience features of these productions.

Although the concept of immersion using VR technology has been widely covered in fields such as computer science or media studies, much work has to be done in order to understand the terms on which the technology is addressed in VR stories and how people experience and react to immersive journalism pieces. This is a topic of some relevance in that it covers both cognitive and experience design parameters, as well as components related to the generation of emotions and feelings such as empathy. Here, one of the main goals is determining whether the VR stories of other citizens produce different, stronger, or long-term emotional responses than those reported in previous newspaper and digital formats, and so increase audience's understanding of particular issues.

Storytelling and interactivity are significantly tied to each other. In the ecosystem formed by digital journalism, users typically interact with content. Thus, it is critical to understand the implications of VR stories for narrative conventions and the extent to which they are influenced by interactivity. We discuss some of the challenges of the new immersive storytelling practices, derived from the technical specificities of creating and presenting stories in 360 degree environments. With an eye on the conventions of cinema, we identify uses and patterns that typify the new audiovisual techniques, before shifting our attention to address how interactivity is being reshaped to become an important aspect of these new immersive features proposed for the contemporary journalistic audiences.

We hope that this text will help tackle future research questions and offer a solid basis for the narrative analysis of products of this type. In short, that it will help analyse and study immersive journalism at this critical juncture in the development of the discipline.

2 Immersive Storytelling

Immersive storytelling refers to the use of VR technologies and 360 degree video in order to deliver both fiction and non fiction stories. In recent years, technological advances have facilitated the appearance of a very relevant number of new projects and initiatives that take advantage of the potentialities of the medium. While there is an undeniable connection with the VR practices that originated in the late 1980s, the new context affords a much bigger range of options, both from the creators and the receivers end. In particular, 360 degree video has allowed journalism and documentary to expand and find news way of engaging with audiences. While we are arguably still in an initial phase, and in the process of remediating form earlier practices, the ubiquity of smartphones capable of displaying immersive video has been a key element for its inclusion in journalistic practices. As new VR devices become mainstream, we can expect immersive storytelling to consolidate as a narrative form, and it is thus relevant to review some of the central aspects of how this process is unfolding.

2.1 *Making Sense of It All*

Immersive technologies afford a myriad of new possibilities for journalism, but also present new challenges. As we are slowly witnessing the commodification of VR devices, and while still in the infancy of mainstream narrative in 360 degrees, this is an interesting moment to analyse what this move from the flat to the immersive screen means in terms of storytelling and, particularly, for journalism.

Immersive journalism refers to the use of VR technology in order to create first person experiences of events, locations, and stories (de la Peña et al. 2010). In recent years, and especially since 2015, the popularization of the cardboard has opened the door for VR to become mainstream. While arguably this process is still ongoing and still presents important challenges (see the following sections), it has fuelled the creation of content to be distributed to the wider public, as exemplified by platforms such as NYTVR, *The Guardian* VR or BBC Taster.

This new coming of VR is not alien to the same discourses that framed the medium in the late 80s and 90s, but precisely because of its much wider spread, and particularly with the appearance of 360 video, some other concepts have become common place to explain and design successful experiences in it. Presence, realism, empathy, or interactivity are amongst these, and are discussed in the following sections of this chapter.

The overall picture, thus, does not significantly differ from the early discourses, but a renovated interest has facilitated the appearance of new models that aim at understanding the specificities of this form of storytelling. The MAIN model (Sundar et al. 2008, 2017) studies how modality (the means by which information is conveyed) and interactivity (as user ability to control and act on it) relate to how strong the sense of presence and realism or credibility is experienced in this type of experiences. In a recent study, its authors acknowledge that, while VR and 360 video offer a more natural and intuitive interaction than that of multimedia projects, it is in fact the emotional intensity of the stories what most affects the experience that can be broken down into three basic ideas: being-there, interaction, and realism. Additionally, it warns that while VR and 360 video do enhance the cognitive retention (memory) and sharing intention of the journalistic stories, what they call the "bells and whistles" heuristic (the technological novelty effect) can in fact affect negatively the trust in the stories presented. Another recent model presents an analytical tool to study how the viewer is presented and how she can participate in 360 video journalistic pieces. While warning of a possible loss of interest if the content is not good enough once the novelty wears off, it advocates for an understanding through the ideas of immersive narrative, perception, and the representation of plausible spaces (Benítez-de-Gracia and Herrera-Damas 2018).

These efforts, and their connection to earlier VR literature, demonstrate that, on one hand, the theorization of the new wave of VR and 360 video is strongly linked to the original VR era. Many of the fundamental ideas are still under discussion. What has radically changed are the uses, content, and audience reach, which goes hand in hand with a more general implementation of digital media that has not only facilitated this reappearance of and old technology, but also blurred the distinction between the real and the virtual that was so strong in the first VR discourses. And as these new technologies become more and more available, and conquer new domains, it is relevant to discuss how much of the current discourses are already medium specific and how much are, still, remediations of pre-existing ones.

2.2 *Still Remediating?*

In short, remediation is the representation of one medium in another; the borrowing of what is known and common in an existing medium by the newer one (Bolter and Grusin 2000: 45). VR, and 360 video in particular, are not alien to this practice, and in fact we'll argue here that there is still a great deal of remediation practices in immersive storytelling. Three areas that are easily identifiable here as sources to remediate from are interactive documentary (or multimedia, if we want to use an almost deprecated term), film, and theatre.

Interactive documentary is a broad descriptor of non-linear factual storytelling. Projects that aim at documenting the "real" using digital technology (Aston and Gaudenzy 2012) fall into this category, which has been well covered in the literature and, particularly, in a recent monograph (Aston et al. 2017) and on the National Film Board and Docubase web pages. It is in fact a practice that, like VR, connects to a previous technological instantiation, although in this case this is seldom recognized. In the 1990s, before the popularization of the web, a great deal of work was done using CD-ROM as a support, many of which anticipated practices and methods later reintroduced in the interactive documentary domain (see, e.g., Ribas 2010).

Now, VR and 360 video documentaries are remediating interactive documentary, along with documentary in general. In part, because of a straight-forward fact that many of those working in immersive storytelling have previously worked on interactive online projects. However, as discussed below, the implementation of interactivity in these projects is still problematic, especially on the lower end of the technology, which is that through which the projects are currently able to reach a wider audience. Yet, it is precisely interactivity, quite obviously, what defines interactive documentary. The non-linear stories are presented in a way that affords the action of a non-passive audience. According to Domínguez-Martín

(2015), there are three main ways in which the viewer can affect the story: by changing the order in which the narration unfolds, the scenes that one will be able to watch, or by changing or selecting the narrative point of view. As discussed below, the interactivity in the mentioned low technological end of 360 video is still, generally, limited to being able to look in any direction within a scene. But this user control of the point of view does not afford the same degree of agency that one finds in controlling the narrative perspective in interactive documentary, as described in the classification just mentioned (e.g., in the project Inside the Haiti Earthquake, you could choose either of three character points of view to experience the documentary). It does obviously create a different experience, because of the specificities of both media, but this is another discussion.

The second medium from which 360 video is still in a process of remediating is film. And this is well exemplified in two technical characteristics that, in turn, affect the narrative. First, the fact that a 360 camera, by definition, sees everything around it. This has a first obvious but very important implication: filming with in 360 is not thinking about the frame anymore, but about the whole environment (which also connects to the remediation of theatre discussed below). All the conventions of the frame are gone, as authors of 360 films claim (Sora 2017), and the whole creative process becomes a hybrid between theatre and cinema, where things have to be staged all around the camera and not just in front of it. This means that scripting, storyboarding, and even the shooting practices themselves have to be redesigned.

Additionally, technically this presents the challenge that the camera will even see its own support (typically a tripod). In cinema, we don't see the supporting artefact. The camera and all what goes with it are hidden by the nature of its mechanics. The art and science of the boom mike is to keep it close but always out of the frame, and the convention is that we will never see the lightning system in a movie or anything close to giving away how the scene has been constructed. But in 360 video, all these elements have to be hidden from the camera if we want to keep the illusion that the artefact is not there. And this is one of the reasons why most pieces will have mostly or exclusively static shots, as removing the tripod in post-production is then much cheaper than when the camera is moving.

It becomes relevant, here, to ask whether the need to remove the tripod is a case of remediation of cinematic practices, and how much effort and creative compromise should be put into it. In Gabo Arora's "The Last Goodbye," there is a final scene in which the camera is moving along with the main character as he speaks. If you look down, you can see the shadow of the moving camera along the path and even the wire that supports it. Regardless of whether this is there because of production costs or as a creative decision, the answer to the question of whether or not this has an impact on the viewer's experience of the film is relevant in regard to the remediation issue.

Another good example of this new set of challenges is movement. Camera dollies, hand-held, and grip equipment are means of obtaining the desired effect when shooting conventional film. But moving the camera in 360 film is much more problematic. Interestingly enough, it is precisely the same effect that makes the 360 point of view such a powerful experience what provokes that most movements will feel rather unnatural to the viewer. It is a very well-known fact that camera movement in VR or 360 video often provokes motion sickness to viewers. To put it simply, the same agency we are given to look around is taken away from us as soon as our disembodied self starts moving without us being the originators of this movement.

Take as an example "Home: Aamir" directed by Saadati, Coffey, and Norris. This 360 documentary, winner of the Journalistic Achievement Jury Prize at SIMA 2017, presents the live of Aamir in the refugee camp of Calais, as he explains his experiences while we are placed inside the spaces he used to live in. After some static shots inside burned out tents and alike, there is a moment when the camera starts moving to follow a path within the camp. As soon as the camera starts moving, we lose much of our sense of agency, as it is no longer us controlling our movements, how much ever limited these were. Of course, this is not a problem specific to that film, but to all 360 films with moving shots. One way to deal with the unnaturalness of this is to integrate the movement not only in the narrative but in the first person experience. Shelmerdine's "Catatonic" (2015) is a short VR horror film that cleverly situates the viewer in a wheelchair that is pushed around a 1950s mental asylum. By doing this, the piece creates movement that doesn't feel like an awkward flying around, but which is integrated in the story. At the same time, it solves the proprioception problem by giving the user arms and legs within the shot—and because it's on a wheelchair, it makes sense, at least from the narrative point of view that they are not under your control.

Finally, a third medium that VR and 360 video in particular draw from is theatre. Because of the nature of how 360 video is shot, the creative experience becomes a sort of in-between of film and theatre. As said above, scripting and storyboarding changes and are not about what is in front of the camera anymore, but what is around it. Therefore, shots have to be conceptualized and staged very differently than when only pointing to one direction. This has all kinds of narrative implications, from visual cues, to sound design, or composition, in order to direct the gaze of the user toward the desired point, and yet offer her something interesting should she choose to look elsewhere on the scene.

But the similarities with theatre are not just there. As noted by Victoria Mapplebeck, VR offers a story-being experience, and as such the traditional techniques of cinema storytelling are not always useful. For example, it is best suited for stories that unfold in real time, rather than told in the past tense; which is likely to be the reason why so many theatre directors have taken to the new medium (Mapplebeck 2017). Indeed, some of the most innovative VR pieces have integrated directly theatre techniques into the experiences. "Alice: The Virtual Reality Play" is a 2017 piece directed by Mathias Chelebourg that blends theatre and animation using live actors whose voices sync perfectly with those of the animated characters that the audience sees through the headset, creating a very compelling first-person theatrical experience.

In a similar, yet more intimate, approach to storytelling, another reactive theatre piece that has recently demonstrated the potential of using actors in sync with VR experiences is "Draw me Close," a 12 minute piece directed by Jordan Tannahill in 2017, in collaboration between the National Film Board of Canada and London's National Theatre. It tells the past and present story of the author's relationship with his mother as they deal with her terminal cancer diagnosis. The person experiencing the piece will put on the headset and then enter a virtual (and real) room to meet the virtual mother. As they engage in conversation, the movements of the animated mother on the headset will be sync and in place on the virtual space according to those of an actress in the real space, and so will the mouth movements as the actress speaks. This creates a very powerful experience for the viewer, who becomes completely immersed, and not just technologically, in the experience. Common problems with VR experiences such as lack of proprioception and of haptic feedback are solved, so to speak, by bypassing the technology with the use of real spaces, objects, and actors mapped onto the virtual space. This comes to two stellar moments in the piece, when mother and son hug, and when the mother tucks the viewer to bed. As narrated by those who have experienced it, this is an incredibly moving moment, especially if viewers find in it a strong connection to their own personal story (Mapplebeck 2017).

One could argue that these last two pieces are more a case of hybridation than one of remediation. However, in any case the links between theatre and VR go far beyond this type of experiences. And be it theatre, film, or interactive documentary, it is clear that these older practices are informing VR and 360 video storytelling. The question is whether these connections will stay strong as the new medium leaves the current stage and moves to one of stronger consolidation, in which it becomes a suitable alternative to tell stories that aim at reaching the wider audiences.

3 The "Empathy Machine" Slippery Zone of Virtual Reality Documentaries

Over recent years, we have seen how news organizations and NGOs have been innovating in the field of digital narratives to reach new audiences (Sora 2015). These practices have ranged from the use of new digital formats, such as interactive online documentaries (Aston and Gaudenzi 2012) and transmedia projects to the use of new virtual reality (VR) formats and 360-degree immersive videos. All of these projects have had a significant impact on both the media and social media and have been won acclaim and awards at documentary film festivals.

VR films and documentaries have emerged in an attempt to offer real immersive experiences and also to help citizens to connect and create bonds by becoming more empathetic toward each other. Evangelists of this new immersive medium maintain that the technology offers a revealing new experience that allows us to live the lives of others, literally to put ourselves into another person's shoes—for example, their struggles or the risks to which they are exposed—in their impact-film mental frameworks. They argue that this new medium, through its technical capabilities, offers a new way to produce impact by others' lives, bringing us a little closer to what cinema, theater, literature, and other artistic media have done before.

In the majority of these films, spectators are situated in the eyes of another person who is placed in their home location—or in transit—and surrounded by their relatives. Some of the experiences involve a 360 film, during which participants can move their gaze and turn their head without affecting the film, and in others, those that involve real-time generated images (virtual reality), the audience is able to explore the space by moving around or pointing in a particular direction. The majority of these films show tough personal experiences. Most of these social experiences attempt to foster an empathetic relationship with the audience, trying to bring about action and, therefore, positive change in the world. And most of them are part of wider communication campaigns.

From the beginning of this new hype of creating digital content to cover social issues, a particular concept has been at the center of discussions and has generated as many followers as detractors: the empathy produced by social issues content. Empathy has been used as part of public discourse in promoting action and social change by world news organizations such as *The New York Times*, *The Guardian* and PBS—to mention just a few and NGOs and social institutions including the United Nations and Doctors Without Borders, which disseminate worldwide humanitarian crises, for example those of refugees and climate change, through VR experiences. The United Nations has already released four VR films and has a program based on VR impact. "Clouds over Sidra" was the first documentary in this UN VR series. The film was made in collaboration with the company Here Be Dragons and was directed by Gabo Arora and Chris Milk—both pioneers in this new wave of VR. It tells the story of the daily lived experience of a twelve-year-old Syrian refugee living in the Za'atari camp in Jordan—home to 84,000 refugees. These projects have been widely reported on in the press and have been acclaimed at several festivals around the globe; their impact has been significant, due to their potential for creating empathetic responses in viewers.

What is really important to see here is that this new phenomenon has been driven mainly by the major tech companies that are investing billions in its logistics, and also in its content, which will, in the end, be their real value that will convince audiences to adopt the medium. It is also easy to observe how tech innovators have been connecting VR and empathy getting vast impact in media. Mark Zuckerberg, Facebook's CEO, recently virtually transported himself to Puerto Rico for an—ill-considered—demo of the future VR platform Facebook Spaces, in an attempt to emphasize the potential of watching other people's catastrophes. It was a bizarre scene. The experience of watching the avatar of a billionaire tech man in a scenario of the aftermath of Hurricane Maria, which devastated the lives of so many people, was a complete failure. The day after, in reaction to the backlash, Zuckerberg apologized, saying,

"When you're in VR yourself, the surroundings feel quite real. But that sense of empathy doesn't extend well to people watching you as a virtual character on a 2D screen. That's something we'll need to work on over time." (Matyszczyk 2017).

Although, as a creator, his role and "responsibility" was slightly different, another important force in the emergence of this VR empathy hype was Chris Milk, a renowned artist and the CEO of a VR company called Within. Milk used—coined—the term "the ultimate empathy machine" in a very successful TED talk in 2015. Milk said of VR: "It's a machine, but through this machine we become more compassionate, we become more empathetic, and we become more connected. And ultimately, we become more human" (Milk 2015).

And it looks like the strategy of using "empathy" as a hook is starting to have an impact, at least in terms of fundraising. It was said during a VR conference entitled "Versions: The Creative Landscape of Virtual Reality," held in New York in 2017, that after a number of VR screenings in economic forums, including Davos, funding for a UN campaign doubled. And this seems to have happened because of the impact that the film "Clouds Over Sidra" had on the participants, although there is no evidence that this was not due to the novelty of the technology. But then, we should ask ourselves whether those who attend this type of forum are the real "final recipients" of this empathy concept; if they are, we should review its objectives.

3.1 Empathy and Immersion

While the possibilities of VR as an empathy tool in storytelling are creating great expectations, the concept of empathy has produced significant differences of opinion and a lack of consensus regarding its nature across different disciplines, including psychology, ethnology, and neuroscience (Sánchez 2017). There are almost as many definitions of empathy as scientists who have been studying the phenomenon for decades. In fact, there is disagreement in the literature about its exact nature. Emotional, cognitive, and conditioning views are involved, to varying degrees (Preston and Waal 2002).

Even though the immersive feature of these projects is mentioned as the main reason empathy is produced, scientific research shows us that to this day not enough evidence of this exists (Shin 2018). It remains unclear what the key factors of a good immersive experience are, and also, whether immersion fosters empathy (Shin 2018). Moreover, the literature maintains (Reinhard and Dervin 2012) that user traits and personal contexts are one of the main factors in the creation of the meaning of immersion. And we believe that this lack of evidence of the implication of immersion in VR is exactly what is happening with the overused concept of empathy. Moreover, the particular social empathetic process that activates emotional states between individuals is still not truly understood in neuroscience (Singer et al. 2006).

In this imprecise scenario—in terms of user experience and empathy impact—supporters of VR still refer to it as the "global empathy machine" or the "ultimate empathy machine," as a machine that will drive action because it connects the public so profoundly with its content. But how can we validate or confirm that all this is really happening? Even those scholars who have contributed to the discussion of immersion in VR not being taken for granted (e.g. Shin and Biocca 2017), depict Empathy as something that "happens" in VR, without taking into account the context and personal bias or traits.

What we really know from psychology studies (Riess 2017) is that humans have a general empathetic response to the pain of others. Neurophysiological studies indicate that when people see or even imagine the pain of others, the brain activity that is activated is the same as if they were experiencing the observed pain themselves (Singer et al. 2006). But these studies have not yet been translated into VR films. Although it is true that a few VR lab experiments reveal that some aspects of empathy are triggered in particular situations (Peck et al. 2013; Hofer et al. 2017), so far there are no qualitative or quantitative indicators that might help investors, researchers, or educators to agree that this medium creates empathy, or at least, no more so than older mediums such as cinema or photography did before.

3.2 Media Coverage of Empathy

Different media have very often used the concept of empathy in a slippery, superficial way, without defining its edges without distinguishing between empathy, sympathy, and compassion, without explaining its internal bias, and taking for granted a supposed general public idea of what empathy means for the audience. And this brings up an important issue: is empathy a common-sense concept? Do we really know, and share an idea of, what empathy is? And what kind of interpretations are set aside for the purpose of connecting people's lives through immersive technologies?

This lack of a solid understanding of what empathy is and of what kind of implications it has may be part of its very complexity. But precisely because of that, some researchers are opposed to the use of virtual reality to evoke empathy with humanitarian crises. They say that empathy is strongly influenced and biased by factors such as race and similarity, an influence which in some cases could backfire (Bloom 2017), creating a certain repulsion regarding groups of race, gender, or thinking that are different from our own. Thus, this phenomenon cannot be understood as an instrumental tool for general purposes.

Therefore, not knowing about or avoiding the complexity of the phenomenon supports the use of its more superficial and irrelevant meaning. The digital media industry might be applying—and even taking profits from—this mental framework when referring to empathy and its vast potential in social development. And its long-term goals for this social engagement are not sufficiently clear.

Given that this media format has the potential to reach millions of people, it is imperative not to take any aspect of it for granted and to explore all its facets, in case empathy turns out not to be the fair fellow we believe it to be in all its aspects for this kind of purpose. We will then be able to avoid the inherent bias that it may have or avoid unintentionally generating negative stereotypes or backfire behaviors.

4 Reality and Immersion in VR Experiences

With the onset of the first techniques and theoretical frameworks of the first virtual reality wave—during the eighties and nineties—the "real" and the "virtual" were the two opposing concepts used in binary models of representation. The virtual represented all the characteristics that the real did not have. One of the most frequently cited definitions was this one by Ted Nelson: "I use the term virtual in its traditional sense, an opposite of real" (Nelson 1980; cited in Rheingold 1991: 171). Despite Pierre Lévy (1998) and other scholars and philosophers emphasizing that from a philosophical point of view the "virtual" "has little relationship to that which is false, illusory, or imaginary", this was the predominant metaphor. This distinction had important implications for the way in which the "virtual" was conceived, always as a contraposition of reality, a journey through the senses and the imaginary. From that period onwards, overused metaphors such as "immersion" and sense of "presence" were the totems upon which technologists, academics, and writers stood the concept of the "virtual" as something that replaced the real.

In contrast to this previous conception of what virtual reality was, which is still present in our digital mindset, the new wave of virtual reality documentaries—in the broad sense of immersive media experiences—presents new challenges for revisiting the understandings of and the relations between the "real" and the "virtual." As already mentioned, in recent years, there has been great enthusiasm among producers, researchers, filmmakers, artists, and journalists to explore and create VR factual films. And a few of these authors have been working conceptually with different ways, or accents, to represent "reality." Moreover, in some cases, they also use augmented and mixed reality technologies that mix, blend, and augment that which we call "real" with images that belong to the "virtual." But not matter how much all these layers and forms of digital information are based on the "real" world and its data, we might not call it "virtual" anymore. This "not that virtual" representation of the virtual is generating new approximations to the sense of presence very much discussed previously in the experimental literature of virtual reality.

If in virtual documentaries the "virtual" is no longer an opposite place to be or a replacement of the real, what is it? What types of marginal vision of "realities" are we representing in VR? What kinds of relationship can be built with our "reality?" And finally, what is the embodiment presence that the public has with this "no-longer-virtual?"

Nonny de la Peña is one of the pioneers of a new wave of experimentation with virtual reality that she calls "immersive journalism" for "the production of news in a form which people can gain first-person experiences of the events or situation described in news stories" (de la Peña et al. 2010). She has presented her work at major festivals as Sundance, Tribeca, SXSW, and the Davos Economic Forum. In a 2015 TED talk, she asked, "What if you could experience a story with your entire body, not just with your mind?" Most of the works of de la Peña are factual representations that put the user inside an emotive story, where they relive the shocking experiences of others.

"Hunger in Los Angeles," an immersive film made by de la Peña, simulates the experience of watching a man going into a diabetic coma attack at the door of a food bank in Los Angeles, with other people waiting in line to enter a church. It is a mixed virtual reality film that uses real audio documents from the scene and a 3D re-creation of the space and the people present at that moment. For the virtual re-creation of her films, de la Peña tries to create 3D models of people and buildings that look very similar to those in the real scenario. In this work, the user can move freely in the space without agency, acting as a mere spectator of the scene. This and the subsequent works by de la Peña's company, Emblematic Group are groundbreaking experiences that have achieved international interest from the film, media, and journalistic industries, and have been followed by the establishment of VR departments in several news organizations.

Without getting into a discussion now about whether this particular project represents an excessively voyeuristic exercise or about what the role of the audience is in a subjective experience of witnessing someone else's difficult real-live experience, it is appropriate to consider how virtual representations are becoming part of a new journalistic wave. In these kinds of VR projects, virtual representations are no longer fantasies or fictional representations—as described in the nineties—but real facts. And the projection of virtual worlds that will augment and complete our senses is trying to knock down our empathy barrier. These kinds of experiences are far from the narrative "holodeck" that Murray (1998) predicted because these new VR experiences are inserting into reality virtual worlds. And one of the main disadvantages that we can depict here is their lack of agency in terms of interaction. In this type of immersive experience, participants are not allowed to interact with, or even change, the unfolding of the story because if they do so they will be altering the narrative, and presumably the objectivity of the journalistic approach, blurring the boundaries between fact and fiction.

The new factual reinterpretations and the fictional VR worlds share the principle of trying to accomplish an immersive experience and, along with this, the consequent suspension of disbelief, in the same way as was understood during the first wave of virtual research: "Immersion is a metaphorical term derived from the physical experience of been submerged in water" (Murray 1998). However, this earlier definition of the virtual environment as based on the idea of the sensory-motor experience, where "the more the system blocks out stimuli from the physical world, the more the system is considered to be immersive" (Biocca and Delaney 1995), is now being called into question.

The conditions in which users, thanks to their mobile phones, today access the new factual VR experiences in remote or personal places are far from those of the scale-room lab experiments in which the first VR worlds were designed. In these experiences, as in some of the documentaries, we can see through app platforms such as Within, using the Google Cardboard, or other headsets, the interface is extremely present and creates tremendous limitations of embodiment. The paradigm of the transparency of the interface has lost its meaning in the current configurations, although the immersion is felt as a genuine phenomenon of these experiences. It seems reasonable to acknowledge at this point that the immersive experience is tied not only to the digital interface but also to other qualities such as the embodiment of the participant and the mental and personal constructors of the "virtuality."

By way of analogy, film does not depend on the projection room, the darkness, and the surrounding audio, even though all of that certainly contributes a great deal to the experience. Film is the production and editing strategies and techniques that we unconsciously absorb while we watch, and which make the experience absorbing and smooth. And reaching this point of absorption, which allows us to talk about the suspension of disbelief, has taken decades of exploration of the language of cinema. In this regard, the VR language is still taking its first steps, but the failures and pitfalls that the community of makers and academics has discussed has produced insights into future directions. One of the recursive commentaries around this is the conception of the immersive audiovisual as more an act of performance than film (Sora 2017).

Exploring other languages, such as dramaturgy and mise-en-scène, may be helpful, or videogames that strike a balance between plot, action, subjective point of view, and so on, because the fact is that in VR and immersive video mises-en-scène the role of the viewer changes radically. Professor Janet H. Murray agrees when she says that "the focus of VR design is not the camera frame, but the embodied visitor" (Murray 2016). A good example of this can be seen in the recent documentary "6×9: a virtual experience of solitary confinement" produced by *The Guardian* editors Francesca Panetta and Lindsay Poulton. This film is a 360 video experience of solitary confinement in US prisons that places viewers in a virtual segregation cell in an attempt to generate a suffocating sensation, highlighting the psychological effects of long-term solitary confinement. Storytelling with immersive video is less about telling viewers a story and more about placing them inside it.

The role of the viewer's body is another key issue. There may be more similarities than you would expect between immersive video and escape room experiences, in which participants go into a themed room that has been decorated to represent a fictional space and have to proceed according to a narrative that is not predefined but takes shape through their actions. Immersive video also falls within a genealogy of representation that can be traced back to Robert Barker's eighteenth century panoramic paintings, which placed spectators within a scene and made them feel part of it. And as professor William Uriccio recently reminded us in the first Virtual Reality and Documentary conference, the registered patents of Barker's panoramas did not only place the spectator within the scene by means of the images that filled the whole room, but also used objects and materials displayed in the middle ground between the spectator and the perspective paintings on the wall. This is something that is starting to happen at VR film and documentary festivals that features digital VR productions, such as Sundance and IDFA, at which scale-room VR films are increasingly present.

It seems that the sensation of been present inside a story suffers from the cognitive dissonance between the interface and your real surroundings, which prevents you from being totally transported to this virtual place. One could argue that some projects that make use of 360 video to show images of refugees, including "The Displaced," a *New York Times* project in partnership with Here Be Dragons, do not add anything to what television already does. And this is the tension that we have to explore: the relationship between the feelings or sensations we want to provoke in viewers and the content we show them. Film and literature create that connection with audiences, making them feel connected, and fully immersed in what they are reading or seeing. Now, we have to figure out how to re-situate this in the new medium.

Finally, also worthy of mention are those practices in which the interface becomes invisible. In the near future, documentary and journalistic projects will be designed for augmented reality displays such as the HoloLens or the future Google Lens, so that the content can be provided as an augmented layer at any time in any location. As an example of that we could mention the VR project "The Enemy," by the Berlin-based photojournalist Karim Ben Khelifa, is a scale-room virtual reality installation made in collaboration with the M.I.T. Open Documentary Lab. In this installation, participants can see a face-to-face encounter between two combatants in each of three conflict zones: the "maras" in El Salvador, the Democratic Republic of the Congo, and Israel and Palestine. The public can move physically and freely with a headset into three different spaces, where the two combatants in each conflict express their feelings and their concerns about the conflict. Subjects transit from still pictures to animated avatars of themselves that speak to the audience. In an extended version, users can download a mobile augmented reality app that enables them to take the subjects into their homes. Reliving the experience in your own real, intimate, personal space converts this kind of virtual reality documentary into something new, because your own place triggers emotional conditioners that neutral, public spaces do not, potentially making the emotional impact of the experience last longer.

The virtual and the real are two areas of thought and experience that are no longer configured as binary concepts but as juxtapositions of senses and thoughts, mixed with your presence in the construction of the so-called virtual experience. The new interfaces of virtual, augmented, and mixed, reality, as well as the new journalistic genres that are being established in these practices, are bringing the construction of the virtual experience closer to one of the most genuine and well-known immersive experiences, that of reading. This analogy with the tiniest expression of the most common "technology" for the imagination of worlds, the book, does not mean that the potential of VR is being underestimated—quite the opposite. Thinking in VR as a book could signify a considerable achievement meaning that the imaginary virtual world is no longer dependent on the technology, as it gets closer to our physical world and our imagination at the same time. VR will probably be just the first of many future storytelling technologies that will merge, and blur the limits between, the real and the virtual.

5 Interactivity Within Immersion

Immersion is just a part of the appeal of VR. The simulated digital environments that this medium offers are engaging because of how powerful the experience is. Isolating the user from the environment and giving her the ability to look around is the fundamental characteristic of both VR and 360 degree video. But the ability to interact with the content—just like with most digital environments—can also be a key part of the experience. However, while many discourses around VR and 360 videos take interactivity for granted, the type of interactivity they refer to is arguably very limited, especially when discussing storytelling-based projects and not videogames. From this perspective, it is relevant to question how should we frame interactivity in these discourses, both from the narrative and from the design points of view, and to analyse how it relates to immersion. A sound understanding of interactivity and immersion, along with the idea of participation, is useful to articulate our knowledge of the types of storytelling that can unfold in these environments.

Currently, in part because of the coexistence of a low and high technological ends of VR and immersive experiences, interactivity is strongly linked to the gaze: that is, the agency of the viewer is that of looking in any direction. But often, creators or journalistic experiences want to offer more than this, and afford that the users make choices or select different paths just as they are used to do in the web. And while in cardboard-based systems this is technologically quite limited, although not impossible, it is quite obviously in the more sophisticated systems where the possibilities of implementation grow significantly.

5.1 Interactivity, Participation, and Immersion

Immersion is, arguably, one in three key concepts that help framing the discourses on digital media. Along with interactivity and participation, it forms a triad of ideas that are at the heart of many of the culturally relevant practices afforded by the digitalization of technology. Quite usually, at least two of these concepts will be relevant in any digital media experience if not all three, with one taking the leading role in the experience of the audience in the receiving end. Immersive Journalism is a good example of this.

Interactivity refers to ability of a system to partake in the process of interaction. In the context of communication, a key aspect is the fact that the passive viewer or reader of traditional media is replaced by an active user; an entity with agency. The way this agency affects the reception of the work or the work itself is widely varied. And while interactivity is intrinsic to digital media, one can argue that not all our experiences with it are really interactive from the user experience point of view, or may at least have a very low degree of interactivity. In this context, working with interactive media not only means telling stories, but also creating and designing experiences for an active audience.

Although some authors conflate it with interactivity, it is very useful to differentiate interactivity and participation. While interaction always implies some sort of participation, this is a pertinent distinction in order to frame the different types of activities that can take place with technological systems that afford that the users take action in relation to them.

The proposal here is to understand participation as contribution: that is, the creating content by the user of the system as a different act than that of interacting with this content. Uploading picture to a social network is an act of participation, and it does involve interactivity when the actual uploading is happening, but it is a trivial and mechanistic type of interactivity.

Finally, immersion is an idea that, similarly to interaction, can appear in digital media experiences in various degrees. In the literature, definitions of interactivity usually look at the idea from the point of view of how media is presented, of user perception, and/or of how the process of interaction unfolds (Downes and McMillan 2000; Kiousis 2002; Soler-Adillon 2015; Tham 2018). In the case of immersion, we can also differentiate between a technological and a psychological component of it or, in other words, between spatial and emotional immersion (Zang et al. 2017). The first is the immersion created with systems that are designed to isolate the user from her physical environment, and give control of the point of view on a usually 360 degree scene. This type of technologies, which as mentioned above find its technological ancestors at least on Baker's panoramas of the late eighteenth century, have resurfaced in recent years with the revival of Virtual Reality. They are well-known for providing very strong experience in terms of 'sense of place', and have been linked to the creation of empathy, as they are very powerful in having the user experience a specific point of view.

There is, however, another type of immersion that relates strongly to interactivity. In this case, it is not so much the technology but the engagement that generates immersion. Playing a game in a very small screen, or a monitor a few meters away can be as immersive as using a Virtual Reality headset, if we understand immersion as this psychological loss of awareness of our immediate surroundings. It is from this point of view that some authors refer to immersive media when theorizing about wearables or the Internet of Things (Tham 2018).

It is in this context that the discussion of interactivity within immersion becomes a very interesting one. Obviously, immersion is the driving force of VR and of immersive journalism. The first-person experience (de la Peña 2010), based on the illusion of being in there (Slater 2009), is built upon the effect of technological immersion afforded by VR systems. And this preeminence of immersion leaves less room for interactivity than in other digital media experiences, especially in low-tech-based VR.

The new wave of VR came along with the promise of overcoming the problems that stopped the development of the first one by becoming a mainstream medium. The 90s equipment was too expensive and too awkward, and never got close to fulfil its initial promises. Twenty years later, VR has reemerged to reconnect with many of the early discourses. But the big difference is now on the technology. High tech VR is comparatively much cheaper than it was in the first wave, but it is still far from being mainstream yet. However, it is on its low-tech end that the revolution has happened. The Google Cardboard, in a moment when smartphones are ubiquitous in first world countries, allowed a very low entry fee to the world of VR.

5.2 *Agency as Gaze*

However, in this low-tech VR context, what Sirkkunen et al. (2016) labeled as the cardboard phase, where 360 degree video is a key player, the question of user agency remains unsolved. It does offer one very simple yet very powerful degree of interaction: the fact that the user will choose where to look at from a predefined point of view. This is in fact the whole basis of the experience and what makes it interesting. The sense of place, the being in the story rather than being told a story, is all based on the fundamental trick of VR: the immersive technology isolates you from the environment, so you become a disembodied self in an alternate word, yet with some agency in it, which allows you to look wherever you desire at any given moment.

But even within the lower end spectrum of immersive technology, with the cardboard and smartphone, the need for at least some basic interaction beyond that soon becomes apparent. However, the technological nature of the devices and how they are used presents an important challenge: if we use the phone as a screen inside the cardboard, we loose our ability to use the tactile screen, which is precisely the main means of interacting with it.

The solution, for those apps that have implemented one, is in fact usually quite simple and elegant. If the only thing you can do is look, where you look becomes the means of interacting with the interface. That is, the gaze becomes the pointer and clicker. This was the implemented solution both in the content curation app 'Within' and in the interactive VR animation "Cardboard Crash." In the first, it is just the means of selecting videos and controlling the playback without having to take the phone off the cardboard. In the second case, the interaction affords a branching experience where the user selects what will happen at a certain point.

"Carboard Crash" was produced at the National Film Board of Canada and directed by Vincent McCurley in 2015. It was a very timely piece that used the emerging VR technologies—as the name suggests, it was meant to be watched with the cardboard—to talk about yet another emerging technical issue: the ethics of autonomous cars. In a simple but very elegant VR animation, the user is put in a car driving down the road with a movement that feels quite natural to the viewer. After a few seconds, the user is warned that a collision is unavoidable and, suddenly playing the role of the algorithm deciding the movements of the car, is asked to decide how the car should react: turn left and run over a family; keep going and crash with a truck filled with explosive material; or turn right and fall off a cliff.

While interesting from several points of view, including the use of animation instead of a realistic approach, the focus is here on how the interaction is implemented. And as said, the solution is simple but effective. When the menu appears showing the three options, the user can see a point just in front of her, and this point will be controlled by the head movements. Therefore, she can use it to point to one of the three buttons representing the choices, which will show a "charging" animation as a feedback mechanism to indicate that the choice is about to be selected. If the user keeps pointing until the charging animation goes full circle, the selection has been made, and the narrative will resume on the selected branch.

A different approach to interactivity is presented in Arnaud Colinart and Amaury La Burthe's "Notes on Blindness VR," produced by Ex Nihilo, Arte France, and Archer's Mar in 2016. This is an accompanying piece to the feature documentary with the same name, which narrates the story of John Hull, a professor from Birmingham University who went blind on 1983, and who recorded his experiences on cassette as an audio diary. This VR piece uses the original audio to illustrate what Hull is narrating about how he perceives the world after loosing sight. With subtle animations, the sound perceptions are illustrated as the user turns her head around to look for what Hull is talking about. In this case, the creators implemented a very subtle but well integrated level of interactivity. While in three out of the six chapters in the piece, the only thing that changes is the point of view of the user—the gaze—in three of the others, the Oculus rift version offers a bit more to the user, thus affording a bigger sense of agency in the piece. In the second chapter, the user can use the Oculus Rift controllers to create wind. This will not only enhance the visual experience, but it also does so in terms of sound. The wind will generate noises as it triggers animations on some of the surrounding objects, which in turn makes these objects visible, as the wind "particles" will temporarily reveal their silhouettes. In the following two chapters, the interaction is somewhat similar to that of Cardboard Crash, although very differently implemented in terms of visual design. Here, there are no buttons, but objects or footsteps to activate. Upon looking at them, a series of the characteristic particles in the piece will indicate the start of the activation process. If the gaze does not move away for a few seconds, the system will trigger the result, in the form of user movement for the footsteps or a piece of animation for the objects, thus giving the user a stronger agency than that of simply looking around the scene.

Not surprisingly, the more sophisticated VR systems offer more complexity in terms of interaction. And as we move from the cardboard phase onwards, we can expect interactivity to be more present in mainstream VR experiences. From the remote controls and pointing devices of the Samsung Gear or Google Pixel, which studies have shown to be quite effective (Pakkanen et al. 2017), to the video game-like controls of the HTC Vice and the Oculus Rift, the affordances escalate in terms of how the user can interact. However, these systems are currently far from being mainstream, and if the aim of an immersive piece is audience reach, designing for some of this particular systems—like, e.g., some of the newer pieces of *The Guardian* VR for Google Pixel do—is already a big compromise that will severely limit the number of people being able to experience the work.

VR and 360 video are still heavily platform dependant once interaction beyond the gaze is an important part of the experiences. There is no such thing as platform agnostic interactive VR, yet. And with very few exceptions, the choice is still very much between audience reach and interactive complexity.

6 Conclusions

The new wave of VR, in which immersive journalism is inscribed, presents a series of challenges that need to be addressed in order to frame the discussion on the new storytelling practices afforded by its technological possibilities. From immersive video to room-scale experiences, the expected commodification of these experiences, and the resulting widening of audience reach, situates the need to articulate this theorization in a prominent position.

From a technological point of view, some of the experiences that are now being brought into the wider domain are linked to what was already experimented within the first instantiation of VR, although in a less sophisticated and extensive form. However, many of the projects discussed show significant advances both in furthering the specificities of the medium as storytelling platform, and introducing new modes of interaction and engagement with the audience. Additionally, there is one particular field, key to understand immersive journalism, which is presenting a rather new approach: 360 degree video. While technologically possible in the past, the affordances of the new cameras and visualization systems offer a radical new way of creating immersive reality-based imagery and experiences on both ends: production and reception. What is particularly interesting here is to look at how the practices are currently experimenting with the possibilities and specificities of the new medium. As we have argued, 360 video is still in a process of remediation, drawing particularly from film and television but also from theatre. The paradigm shift that represents loosing the frame and working with cameras and visualizing systems that see all around is a very significant one, and the implications pervade all aspects of creation, from the script to the final reception.

When we look at how we theorize immersive experiences, it is relevant to acknowledge that, along with the newer contributions discussed in this chapter, many of the key issues in discussing the current wave of VR find its roots in the discourses that originated over two decades ago when VR has its first appearance. Presence, embodiment, or simulation have already a long history in the literature, and the new interest on VR needs to reconnect and recognize this, and is indeed generally doing so, in order to create a coherent discourse. One of the biggest changes is, arguably, on audience reach. While we are not yet at the point where VR is a mainstream medium, the path seems to have been finally set out for good. However, some concepts have gained a new perspective precisely because of this wider reach facilitated by the ubiquitous presence of smartphones and its combination with the simplest technological form of VR: the cardboard.

Empathy is a good example of this, although still a slippery concept. It has been used rather extensively over the last few years in an attempt to present VR as a uniquely qualified medium to create this type of emotional effect, and thus being particularly adequate in order to pursue the goals of those aiming at provoking a reaction of solidarity on the viewers. Arguably, this is the main reason why NGO and humanitarian organizations became the commissioners of many of the first documentaries that used 360 video. However, there is not enough evidence that immersive technologies are in fact better than any other medium in creating empathic reactions on the audience. Furthermore, the very concept of empathy and its definition are still under discussion. So it is relevant to ask whether how the idea as it has been used is a really fundamental, ground-breaking one, or if we are looking at a rather superficial and irrelevant use, aimed at sparking the hype on the new technologies that go hand-by-hand with its promise.

In the new VR, the "virtual" and the "real" are no longer two opposite concepts. In fact, we have discussed that it is not only that the distinctions are now blurred in the context of the ubiquity of digital media, but also that the new factual VR immersive pieces go one step further in placing the real within the virtual. It is not only that the distinction is gone, but also that there is a subversion of what the virtual was in opening the door to presenting is as real, as facts to be experienced "as if" the viewer was actually not in a virtual simulation but in the real place. As discussed, this has implications in terms of interactivity, but also in terms of how immersion is being experienced. While more available than ever, it is not necessary to access to these experiences with high-end VR headsets in order to account for it as immersion. Just as we don't need (or we are no longer necessary used) to experience film in a theatre for us to engage in the story, we don't need complete physical immersion to experience VR as such.

Additionally, and as VR moves from remediation to more medium specific experiences, the VR "text" should be able to detach not only from previous media experiences but also from specific technologies. In combination with artificial and mixed reality, room-scale and larger experiences are likely to become more and more relevant. The proposed metaphor of VR as a book points at how these should evolve into affording the appearance of a type of storytelling that is truly specific to that medium.

This relates to the last part of the discussion, which looked at the concept of interactivity within immersive experiences. Of course, as it has been argued, there is a degree of interaction that is possible in any VR experience: that of controlling the point of view within the experience. However, as we move to these more complex experiences just mentioned, interactivity will need to become, and will be, better integrated. Games are currently at the forefront of this, but as said above, immersive journalism is still very much rooted in linear storytelling, and it has yet to embrace interactivity, or at least have a branch that does so in the way i-docs do it in respect to traditional documentary. To end with the above mentioned metaphor, if VR is to become a book that is truly specific and true to its full potential, it will have to be an interactive one.

References

Aston, Judith, and Gaudenzi, Sandra. 2012. Interactive Documentary: Setting the Field. *Studies in Documentary Film* 6 (2): 125–139.

Aston, Judith, Sandra Gaudenzi, and Mandy Rose. 2017. *The Evolving Practices of Interactive Documentary*. New York: Columbia University Press.

Benítez-de-gracia, Maria-José, and Susana Herrera-Damas. 2018. El reportaje inmersivo en vídeo 360°: diseño de un modelo de análisis. *El Profesional de La Información* 27 (1): 149–161.

Biocca, F., and B. Delaney. 1995. Immersive Virtual Reality Technology. In *Communication in the Age of Virtual Reality*, ed. F. Biocca, M.R. Levy, 57–124. Hillsdale, New Jersey: Lawrence Erlbaum Associates.

Bloom, Paul. 2017. It's Ridiculous to Use Virtual Reality to Empathize with Refugees, *The Atlantic*.

Bolter, Jay, and Richard Grusin. 2000. *Remediation: Understanding New Media*. Cambridge: MIT Press.

de la Peña, Nonny, Peggy Weil, Joan Llobera, Elias Giannopoulos, Ausiàs Pomés, Bernhard Spanlang, Doron Friedman, Maria V. Sanchez-Vives, and Mel Slater. 2010. Immersive Journalism: Immersive Virtual Reality for the First-Person Experience of News. *Presence: Teleoperators and Virtual Environments* 19 (4): 291–301.

Domínguez-Martín, Eva. 2015. Periodismo inmersivo o cómo la realidad virtual y el videojuego influyen en la interfaz e interactividad del relato de actualidad. *El Profesional de La Información* 24 (4): 413–423.

Downes, Edward J., and Sallly J. McMillan. 2000. Defining Interactivity: A Qualitative Identification of Key Dimensions. *New Media & Society* 2 (2): 157–179.

Hofer, Matthias, Andrew Hüsser, and Sujay Prabhu. 2017. The Effect of an Avatar's Emotional Expressions on Players' Fear Reactions: The Mediating Role of Embodiment. *Computers in Human Behavior* 75: 883–890.

Kiousis, Spiro. 2002. Interactivity: A Concept Explication. *New Media & Society* 3 (4): 355–383.

Levy, Pierre. 1998. *Becoming Virtual: Reality in the Digital Age*. New York: Plenum Trade.

Mapplebeck, Victoria. 2017. 'A Virtual Mum Put Me to Bed': A View from the VR Future of Film, The Conversation.

Matias, J. Nathan. 2012. Behind *The New York Times* Interactive Team with Aron Pilhofer, MIT Center for Civic Media.

Matyszczyk, C. 2017. Mark Zuckerberg's Virtual Puerto Rico Jaunt Misses the Mark. Retrieved from https://www.cnet.com/news/mark-zuckerberg-puerto-rico-hurricane-virtual-reality-oculus-connect-vr/. Accessed 5 May 2018.

Milk, Chris. 2015. How Virtual Reality Can Create the Ultimate Empathy Machine. TED Talks.

Murray, Janet H. 1998. *Hamlet on the Holodeck: The Future of Narrative in Cyberspace*. Cambridge, MA: MIT Press.

Murray, Janet H. 2016. Not a Film and Not an Empathy Machine. How necessary Failures Will Help VR Designers Invent New Storyforms. *Immerse*.

Pakkanen, Toni, Jaakko Hakulinen, Tero Jokela, Ismo Rakkolainen, Jari Kangas, Petri Piippo, Roope Raisamo, and Marja Salmimaa. 2017. Interaction with WebVR 360° Video Player: Comparing Three Interaction Paradigms. In *Proceedings—IEEE Virtual Reality*, 279–280.

Peck, Tabitha C., Sofia Seinfeld, Salvatori Maria Aglioti, and Mel later. 2013. Putting Yourself in the Skin of a Black Avatar Reduces Implicit Racial Bias. *Consciousness and Cognition* 22 (3): 779–787.

Preston, Stephanie D., and Franz B. M. De Waal. 2002. Empathy: Its Ultimate and Proximate Bases. *Behavioral and Brain Sciences* 25 (1): 1–20.

Reinhard, CarrieLynn D., and Brenda Dervin. 2012. Comparing Situated Sense-Making Processes in Virtual Worlds. *Convergence* 18 (1): 27–48.

Rheingold, H. 1991. *Virtual Reality*. New York: Simon & Schuster.

Ribas, Joan Ignasi. 2010. Interactive Discourse in Cultural Dissemination: Innovation and Electronic Readers. *Hipertext.net* 8.

Riess, Helen. 2017. The Science of Empathy. *Journal of Patient Experience* 4 (2): 74–77.

Sánchez Laws, Ana Luisa. 2017. Can Immersive Journalism Enhance Empathy? *Digital Journalism*. https://doi.org/10.1080/21670811.2017.1389286.

Shin, Donghee. 2018. Empathy and Embodied Experience in Virtual Environment: To What Extent Can Virtual Reality Stimulate Empathy and Embodied Experience? *Computers in Human Behavior* 78: 64–73.

Shin, D., and Frank Biocca. 2017. Exploring Immersive Experience in Journalism. *New Media & Society*.

Singer, Tania, Ben Seymour, John P. O'Doherty, Klaas E. Stephan, Raymond J. Dolan, and Chris D. Frith. 2006. Empathic Neural Responses Are Modulated by the Perceived Fairness of Others. *Nature* 439 (7075): 466–469.

Sirkkunen, Esa, Heli Väätäjä, Turo Uskali, and Parisa Pour Rezaei. 2016. Journalism in Virtual Reality: Opportunities and Future Research Challenges. In *Academic Mindtrek '16 Proceedings of the 20th International Academic Mindtrek Conference*, 297–303, October 17–18, Tampere, Finland.

Slater, Mel. 2009. Place Illusion and Plausibility Can Lead to Realistic Behaviour in Immersive Virtual Environments. *Philosophical Transactions of the Royal Society of London* 364 (1535): 3549–3557.

Soler-adillon, Joan. 2015. The Intangible Material of Interactive Art: Agency, Behavior and Emergence. *Artnodes* 16: 43–52.

Sora, Carles. 2015. Etapas, factores de transformación y modelo de análisis del nuevo audiovisual interactivo online. *El Profesional de La Información* 24 (4): 424–431.

Sora, Carles. 2017. Una inmersión en el audiovisual VR y 360. Serie DigiDoc-EPI, n. 1. Barcelona: Ediciones Profesionales de la Información S.L.

Sundar, S. Shyam, Haiyan Jia, T. Franklyn Waddell, and Yan Huang. 2008. Toward a Theory of Interactive Media Effects (TIME). Four Models for Explaining How Interface Features Affect User Psychology. In *The Handbook of the Psychology of Communication Technology*, ed. S. Shyam Sundar. Chichester: Wiley Blackwell.

Sundar, S. Shyam, Jin Kang, and Danielle Oprean. 2017. Being There in the Midst of the Story: How Immersive Journalism Affects Our Perceptions and Cognitions. *Cyberpsychology, Behavior, and Social Networking* 20 (11): 672–682.

Tham, Jason Chew Kit. 2018. Interactivity in an Age of Immersive Media: Seven Dimensions for Wearable Technology, Internet of Things, and Technical Communication. *Technical Communication* 65 (1): 46–66.

Uricchio, W., Sarah Wolozin, Lily Bui, Sean Flynn, and Deniz Tortum. 2015. Mapping the Intersection of Two Cultures: Interactive Documentary and Digital Journalism. MacArthur Foundation.

Watson, Z. 2017. VR For News: The New Reality? Reuters Institute for the Study of Journalism.

Zhang, Chenyan, Andrew Perkis, and Sebastian Arndt. 2017. Spatial Immersion Versus Emotional Immersion, Which Is More Immersive? In *9th International Conference on Quality of Multimedia Experience*, May 31–June 2, Erfurt, Germany.

CHAPTER 5

UX Research Methods for Designing Interactive Media

Barbara Millet

1 Introduction

Interactive media has greater impact when the design process is informed. Developing great products requires wide-ranging information from people who use, or might use, the product, and an understanding of the contexts of use. Only by understanding the user and the context of use do we ensure that characteristics of the product match the needs of the user. User Experience (UX) research provides this understanding and informs the design process from the perspective of the user.

1.1 What Is UX?

There are many definitions for UX, but no standard definition. The usability.gov website offers a useful definition, describing it as the "quality of the user's interaction with and perceptions of" the product and related services ("User Experience Basics," n.d.). Fundamentally, UX refers to

B. Millet (✉)
Department of Cinema and Interactive Media, School of Communication,
University of Miami, Coral Gables, FL, USA
e-mail: bmillet@miami.edu

M. Pérez-Montoro (ed.), *Interaction in Digital News Media*,
https://doi.org/10.1007/978-3-319-96253-5_5

user attitudes and behaviors influenced by product visual design, information architecture, content, navigation, and interactions when using the product (Kula et al. 2017). Ultimately, a meaningful user experience provides desired features and offers an interface design that is usable and engaging.

1.2 HCD and the Product Development Cycle

Human-centered design (HCD) is an approach for product development that focuses on end users. The term "human-centered design" originated from seminal work by leading cognitive scientist Donald Norman and human-computer interaction expert Stephen Draper (Norman and Draper 1986). HCD is also known as user-centered design and customer-centric design. Regardless of its title, the approach relies on user involvement during the design and development processes and includes the total user experience, incorporating any user interaction with the product, the brand, and the organization.

The HCD philosophy is that product design must align with user needs. The HCD process describes development efforts in which end users influence the product design. It ensures that design and development efforts result in usable products by focusing on usability goals, product functions, and user and environmental characteristics. HCD follows an "iterative cycle of investigation- usually characterized by observations, an ideation phase, and rapid prototype and testing" (Norman and Verganti 2014: 78), with each iteration building on the lessons learned from the previous cycle. This is accomplished by employing techniques and methods throughout the development cycle that focus on understanding the user and tasks, and on iterative design and evaluation. Many organizations use HCD to create products that better meet, and often exceed, user expectations.

1.3 UX Research Methods

Before product implementation, it is critical to have a clear understanding of the target users and the product domain. UX research is about understanding users, the context, and technology (Courage and Baxter 2015). It explores how users experience product interfaces and services. To do so, UX research encompasses a variety of investigative methods to provide insight into the design. These methods can be divided into two main categories: generative research and evaluative research. At the start of the project, generative research is focused on learning about product requirements from stakeholders, as well as the needs and goals of the users. UX Researchers conduct interviews, collect surveys, observe current or likely users, and review existing data. Then, iteratively throughout the development process, the researchers shift focus to product evaluation. Researchers interview users and conduct evaluations to identify opportunities for improving the product.

Many different methods have proven useful in each stage of the HCD process. UX research methods are commonly used iteratively, are not mutually exclusive, and can be adapted to accommodate specific research goals. This chapter explores the many different types of methods employed in UX research—from interviews and observations, to usability testing, to eye tracking and use of physiological measures—in defining and evaluating the user experience of interactive media.

2 Generative Research

Generative research is primarily a front-end analysis leading to concept exploration and ideation. A primary goal of generative research is that before designing a product, it is critical to have a clear understanding of the target users. Conducting generative research leads to a better understanding of those who will be using a product and the context in which it will be used, and reveals user needs and preferences through interviews, user observations, and creative activities that encourage users to express their motivations, feelings, and underlying concepts and beliefs. The information gained with these methods then serves as input to the design. It is only with this understanding that products can be designed to support user behaviors in a way that will improve the user experience. The next few sections introduce commonly used generative methods (e.g., interviews, contextual inquiry, and card sorts), describe when to use them, and provide real-world interactive media examples to illustrate their efficacy in informing design.

2.1 Inquiry

Inquiry methods focus on what people say and think (Sanders 2002), captured through techniques such as interviews, focus groups, and questionnaires. These methods provide insight into the "true user profile, user needs, and user preferences" (Wilson 2009: 31). Below we introduce three inquiry methods: interviews, focus groups, and questionnaires.

One-on-one user interviews pose questions to an individual to find out what they think, feel, and expect. Interviews may be structured (tightly guided), semi-structured, or unstructured (loosely outlined). Sessions typically range from 15 minutes to more than an hour. Interviews are ideal for understanding what an individual, without being influenced by others, thinks about a topic.

Similar to a group interview, focus groups are small groups of informed people who are gathered to address product research questions. Traditional focus groups are organized into sessions of up to 12 current or likely users in a structured discussion moderated by a trained practitioner. These sessions typically last for one to two hours. Focus groups are helpful for gathering multiple points of view in a short period of time (Courage and Baxter 2015).

Questionnaires are instruments for collecting data by asking representative users a set of questions in a specific order. The respondent usually answers the questions on their own, either online or by filling out a paper form. Questionnaires can provide useful self-reported data, demographics, and information about opinions and preferences. Questionnaires are useful in collecting large amounts of data from a large population sample in a relatively short period of time.

2.2 Observation

Observation research has its origins in anthropology, but is now used extensively in product design initiatives. Observational research is the systematic study of behavior, focusing on what people do (Sanders 2002) and how they behave in their natural environments such as at home or at work. This type of research, when used for product design is exploratory, typically conducted to gain a better understanding of the users, tasks, and environment. It is used to define requirements and inspire design ideas. Observation research is valuable in situations where researchers cannot interact directly with end users, for example, understanding the information needs of emergency-room doctors. In using this technique, the researcher directly or indirectly observes users in their environment, but does not necessarily interact with them. While observing the users, researchers make careful, objective notes about what they see, recording all accounts and observations. Researchers continue to conduct observations until they have a good understanding of the focus areas.

There are many variations of observational research. Three applied approaches are outlined here.

1. *Field Ethnography.* A person or group of people are observed by a researcher while they go about their normal lives. The duration can range from one hour to several days or even weeks. Direct observation is ideal for use in the early exploratory stages when researchers and designers need to learn more about the people for whom they are designing.
2. *Video ethnography* is the video recording of human behavior. The video records can be used to supplement field notes or to record events without a researcher present.
3. *Self-reporting* techniques are used when direct observation is not practical because of cost, time, or domain constraints. Many self-reporting techniques exist, such as written dairies, visual storybooks, and blogs (Blomberg and Burrell 2009). In these approaches, the participant engages in self-guided reporting.

For product development, it may be helpful to interact with users rather than just observing them. Researchers often mix observation activities with inquiry to get a better understanding of user needs. One commonly used method that relies on both observation and inquiry to arrive at a more comprehensive understanding is contextual inquiry. It is a technique that reveals real context and uncovers what people really do and value. A good resource for learning more about this technique is Karen Holtzblatt and Hugh Beyer's *Contextual Design: Design for Life* (2016).

2.3 Immersion

With immersion techniques, the researcher becomes the user by adopting their activities for a period time in order to understand the domain. Immersion techniques focus on what researchers do and offer tremendous context and emotional empathy. Such research experiences provide data that can be translated literally to design. Unfortunately, this approach is time consuming, heavily reliant on reflection, and limited to individual experience.

2.4 Participatory Design

Participatory design involves engaging end users in the design process to ensure the product designed meets their needs and is usable. Designers and researchers using this technique value the involvement of users, viewing them as co-creators in the design process. In contrast to techniques that focus on what people say or do, participatory design focuses primarily on what people make (Sanders 2002). This section introduces the three commonly used participatory design tools: card sorting, collaging, and interactive modeling. Card Sorting is described in greater detail given its prevalence in informing the information architecture of interactive media projects.

Card sorting (see Fig. 1) is a valuable tool to understand how people organize information. This technique is conducted by presenting participants with written or pictorial cards conveying product characteristics and then asking them to sort the cards in a meaningful way. Card sorting allows researchers to understand how users think about products, providing information about how users perceive product elements and thus enabling designers to create better navigation and operation. Given the useful information it offers, this technique is widely used to inform decisions about the information architecture of a website, mobile application, and other software programs (Pérez-Montoro and Codina 2017).

There are three types of traditional card sort exercises: (1) open card sort, (2) closed card sort, and (3) hybrid card sort. In an open card sort,

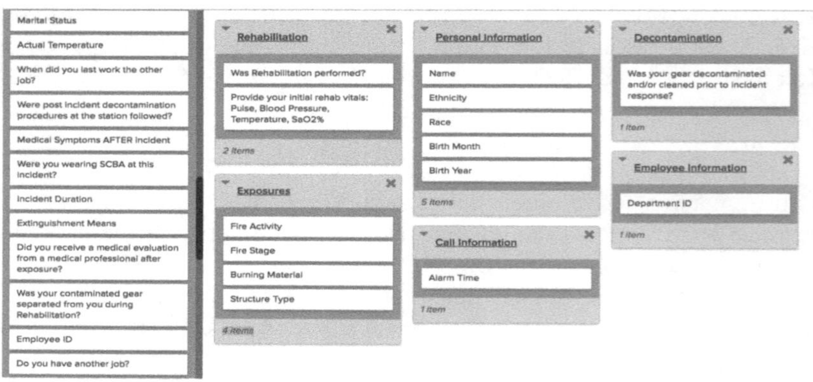

Fig. 1 Cards partially sorted into pre-determined categories

participants are given cards showing content with no pre-established groupings. They then sort these cards into groups that they think are appropriate and label each group. An open card sort is generative, is used early in the design process, and offers useful input for designing information structures of new or existing interactive media. Participation in an open card sort results in individual models that are then analyzed as a whole when the study is concluded. As an alternative to the open card, in the Modified Delphi Card Sort participants work with a proposed model that they modify throughout the study (Paul 2008). In a closed card sort, participants are given cards showing content which they subsequently organize into pre-established groups. This exercise helps validate participant agreement with pre-existing categories. Closed card sorting is both generative and evaluative: it is generative when used to add new content to an existing structure; it is evaluative when used after an open card sort to collect feedback in assessing if the information architecture implemented effectively organizes the content. The third type of card sort, the hybrid sort, is used when there is uncertainty surrounding the categories created in a closed card sort or if partial information architecture exists and new content needs to be added. In a hybrid sort, participants are given cards to sort within predetermined groups or in groups they create. Regardless of the type of sort conducted, the technique offers an understanding of how people think about information relatedness and organization, and allows for the design of linking structures to facilitate information seeking needs (Soranzo and Cooksey 2015).

Card sorts are conducted using paper cards, or software tools employing virtual cards. Many digital tools are available for conducting card sort studies. These tools allow for un-moderated, remote sessions and facilitate data visualization and analysis. For a list of digital card sort tools, see Tullis and Albert's book titled *Measuring the User Experience* (2013).

Typical card sort studies are conducted in 3 stages: planning and creation, sorting, and analysis. The planning and creation stage includes deciding what to test, determining how many participants to include the exercise, preparing the cards, and recruiting participants. To ensure reliable results from the analysis, Tullis and Wood (2004) prescribe a minimum 15 participants to be included in the exercise. As for the cards, it is not recommended that participants sort hundreds of cards, which will be too time consuming and tiring (Spencer 2009). In *Card Sorting: Designing Usable Categories* (2009), Donna Spencer recommends between 30 and 100 cards. However, researchers must be aware that the selection of items may affect the results. To avoid bias, it is best to choose items that proportionately represent product offerings. Next, in the sorting stage participants' sort the cards into groups as prescribed by the type of sort employed. Finally, the last stage requires analysis of the results.

Card sort analysis is centered on recognizing meaningful patterns in the data. The analysis phase should begin with data examination or, in the other words, cleaning up the data. For or some tips on data examination and analysis, see "Card Sort Analysis Best Practices" (Righi et al. 2013). The analysis technique, however, can vary in approach and across projects. For some studies, it may be sufficient to use the insights gathered through speaking with the participant about the results during the session that are reinforced by calculating the frequency with which items are placed in particular categories. A distance matrix facilitates exploring the item-to-item connections. The matrix provides the strength of the relationship between each pair of individual content items, and how strong a group the items form. Figure 2 represents a segment of a similarity matrix, showing the number of times, as a percentage, participants grouped each individual card with each other card in the set. The higher numbers represent stronger item-to-item relationships. For most studies, a statistical approach follows.

Statistical methods of analysis researchers most frequently use for open card sorts are cluster analysis and multidimensional scaling. Cluster analysis allows data quantification by calculating the strength of the perceived relationships between pairs of cards, based on frequency with

93										Was your contaminated gear separated from you during Post Incident Analysis?
80	80									Did you have post incident decontamination procedures at the station?
76	76	90								Were post incident decontamination procedures at the station followed?
76	76	83	90							Decontamination at Station: Washed, Rinsed, Replaced
76	76	80	83	86						Were post incident decontamination procedures at the scene followed?
66	66	80	86	83	83					Decontamination on Scene: Washed, Rinsed, Replaced
66	66	80	73	76	80	83				Did you have on scene decontamination procedures?
80	73	70	73	70	63	60	63			Was your contaminated gear separated from you during Rehabilitation?
63	63	46	53	60	56	50	50	50		Was your gear decontaminated and/or cleaned prior to incident response?
43	46	36	40	43	33	40	33	36	60	Where is your gear stored between shifts?

Fig. 2 Partial similarity matrix showing relationship strength between cards

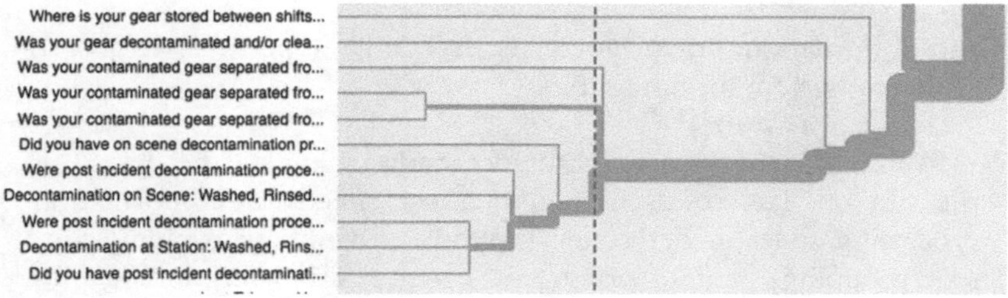

Fig. 3 Segment of an open card sort dendrogram showing cards and their hierarchical cluster groupings

which members of each possible pair appear together. Figure 3 shows a segment of the result of a hierarchical cluster analysis represented as a tree diagram or dendrogram, which help to generate ideas for grouping and labeling content. The items that joined together sooner are more similar than those that joined together later. Another way to analyze the results from an open card sort is to use multidimensional scaling (MDS). MDS converts the distance matrix into a spatial map with data points located relative to how they were perceived, such that similar items will be grouped together while dissimilar items are spread farther apart (Kruskal and Wish 1978; Borg and Groenen 1997). Fortunately, many online card-sorting applications will provide the distance matrix and will cluster results automatically.

For closed card sorting, data can be analyzed using hierarchical cluster analysis or MDS. However, useful insights are obtained by just examining the data. For example, researchers can calculate the number of times a card was sorted into predefined categories and/or display the percentage of participants who sorted cards into the categories and rank them from most popular to least popular.

Case Study 1: Card Sorting for an Exposure Reporting System for Firefighters

Product and Research Goals

A web-based application that allows firefighters to document occupational exposures to hazardous agents and facilitates access to exposure data on any internet-enabled device. The primary research objective for this study was to explore design attributes and information organization in designing a personal exposure reporting system for firefighters.

Why Card Sorting?

We conducted an open card sort study to inform the design of the system. The research examined user needs and information processing styles to determine the most appropriate content, content grouping, content order, and categorization terminology for the exposure reporting system to be developed. Figure 1 depicts a partially completed sort for the study.

How Card Sort Contributed to the Research?

Thirty firefighters sorted 68 cards into an average of 7 groups. On average, participants took 35 minutes to complete the study. A similarity matrix was created to identify key relationships between individual items (see Fig. 2). The similarity matrix depicts the cards the participants paired together in the same group most often. The darker shading represents where two cards intersect more often, as they were paired together by the participants. Figure 3 shows a segment of the result of the hierarchical cluster analysis represented as dendrogram. Study results showed how firefighters organize event-based information when describing occupational exposure incidents.

Card Sorting Explained How Firefighters Think About Incident-Based Information

For this type of information, firefighters followed a chronological pattern of organization by arranging information according to representations of a particular period of time. Based on this information, the organizational strategy for the reports was to divide topics into before-during-after segments.

Card Sorting Informed the Variables and Structure of the Exposure Reporting System

To align with established mental models for this user group, reporting instruments for each incident type were organized by phases of work: from the incident call, to activities on the scene, to decontamination procedures on scene and at the station. The research outcomes provided an understanding of mental models and user acceptance of the variables for exposure reporting. Furthermore, the card sort exercise offered a better understanding of those who will be using the system, the context in which it will be used, and the appropriate design attributes to support ease of use.

Other participatory techniques include collaging and interactive modeling. Collaging is a tool that allows users to communicate experiences through sets of pictures and words. The researcher gives users the collaging materials and a surface on which to arrange them. Collaging is ideal for giving rise to feelings and memories. Interactive modeling, on the other hand, allows users to express their ideas through low-fidelity, 2-D constructions. Such modeling enables a user to create actual interfaces with simple modeling materials. This encourages creative expression without leading to preconceived solutions.

3 Merging and Translating Insights

Generative research methods reveal user needs and preferences through interviews, user observations, and creative activities. Such creative activities encourage users to express their motivations, feelings, and underlying concepts. The information these methods provide inform the design, so that products can be developed to support user behaviors in a way that will improve the user experience. While not all generative research methods are used in every generative research initiative, merging insights from multiple research methods provide deeper understanding and interpretation of user needs. Ultimately, the selection and variety of generative research methods used depend on the specific research questions and product objectives. Regardless of the method used, translating user data is a critical step that leads to design exploration.

While research on its own can be valuable, to effectively use the insights to inform design, it must be analyzed and translated. The data collected through generative research methods are mostly qualitative. However, all share several common characteristics and phases of data analysis, such as data reduction, data display, and verification of findings. Regardless of the data type, the value of the research effort depends on appropriate analysis and translation. Analysis of qualitative data often entails examining, comparing, and interpreting patterns or themes. This data can be analyzed and synthesized from multiple angles depending on the particular research objectives.

Translation tools promote the conversion of user data into insights and design criteria by examining, comparing, and interpreting patterns or themes in the data. This allows user insights and interaction principles to be merged into practical design requirements. Translation leads to the identification of current, and more importantly, ideal behaviors.

Ultimately, identification of ideal behaviors and the exploration of design alternatives foster ideation. Approaches to ideation, although pivotal to the user experience, are beyond the scope of this chapter.

4 Evaluating Interactive Media

Once design concepts materialize, the research focus shifts to evaluating the user experience. Traditionally, UX evaluations assess the degree to which users can operate a product, the efficiency of the product, and user satisfaction with the product. Evaluative research methods are the means for such assessments, making an important contribution in developing a great user experience. Various evaluative research methods are available for assessing the user experience. Some methods make use of data gathered from users, while others rely on the judgments of UX experts, but all offer techniques to measure the user experience. Different methods are applied, in an iterative fashion, throughout the product development process, ranging from the first low-fidelity design concepts to high-fidelity design prototypes. This section presents various types of evaluative research methods including questionnaires, inspections, and user testing. It also introduces use of physiological measures that when accompanied by user testing provides a more complete assessment of the user experience.

4.1 Standardized Questionnaires

UX researchers gather information about user likes, dislikes, needs and understanding of the product by either talking to them, observing them using the product, or having them answer questions in written form or verbally. Inquiry and observation methods include focus groups, interviews, questionnaires, and field observations. As we have introduced most of these methods in the preceding sections, here we focus on three representative standardized questionnaires often used in product development to gain subjective feedback from users and measure perceived usability.

1. System Usability Scale (SUS), developed by Brooke (1996), measures perceived usability and is most often administered at the end of a user study. The SUS consists of 10 items, with mixed tone (positive and negative), and has a 5-point response scale. The SUS is the most well-known questionnaire used in UX research.

2. Post-Study System Usability Questionnaire (PSSUQ), developed by Lewis (1995), is a 16-item standardized usability instrument, comprised of three subscales (System Usefulness, Information Quality and Interface Quality), used as a product evaluation tool. The PSSUQ is typically used in combination with user testing and is administered at the end of the study.
3. NASA Task Load Index, developed by Hart and Staveland (1988), is a subjective workload assessment tool using six dimensions to measure mental workload: mental demand, physical demand, temporal demand, performance, effort, and frustration. The questionnaire uses twenty bipolar scales to obtain ratings for each dimension and is used mostly in mission critical domains.

4.2 Inspection

Inspections are diagnostic techniques whereby UX practitioners decide whether product design elements follow established UX standards and guidelines. In contrast to other evaluation methods, inspection methods rely only on expert judgment and are most often used early in the product development cycle. The objective of inspections is to find usability problems that need to be eliminated through redesign. There are three key inspection methods: guidelines review, heuristic evaluation, and expert review.

1. Guideline or standards reviews are expert evaluations of products to assess conformance against a comprehensive list of usability guidelines. Many detailed usability guidelines exist in the literature (e.g., Department of Health and Human Sciences 2006).
2. Heuristic evaluation is used both to identify elements of a design that should be kept and, most importantly, to find usability problems in a product so they can be addressed as part of an iterative design process. Heuristic evaluation involves having a small set of evaluators examine the user interface and judge its compliance with recognized usability principles (i.e., the heuristics). For example, leading web usability consultant Jakob Nielsen's (1994) main heuristics include:
   - Using simple and natural presentation
   - Speaking the user's language (rather than computer jargon)
   - Minimizing memory load on a user

- Maintaining consistency within the design and with other similar applications
- Providing feedback to users' actions
- Offering clearly marked exits
- Affording shortcuts for experienced users
- Preventing errors
- Offering good error messages
- Providing adequate help and documentation.

3. Expert review is similar to a heuristic evaluation, except that experienced usability specialists conduct the review. These usability experts typically have domain knowledge, may rely on explicit rules, and could be provided with usage scenarios. In this technique, the experts usually work alone, although aggregating the problems identified across the evaluators usually leads to a higher proportion of usability problems detected (Dumas and Salzman 2006).

4.3 User Testing

User testing encompass observing and learning from users as they work with a product before, during, and after the design and development process. The insights from this type of research are used to inform design modifications prior to product release. This section presents two user testing methods.

4.3.1 Usability Test

Usability testing is possibly the most important method for evaluating products and is considered by many as the 'gold standard' to which all other evaluation methods are compared (Lewis 2012). Usability testing originated from well-established experimental methods, where the main objective was to discover whether the product elicits the necessary human performance to meet the requirements established for it. When defects or problems are discovered, opportunities arise to refine the design.

There are two main types of usability tests: formative and summative. In formative usability tests, the goal is to reveal any potential usability problems (or defects) with the product before it gets released. These tests are conducted iteratively throughout the product development cycle to guide design. Summative tests focus on measuring and validating the usability of the implemented product and are conducted at or near the end of product development. Summative tests can be used for hypothesis testing of a single product or competitive testing between similar products (Lewis 2012; Tullis and Albert 2013).

Both formative and summative usability tests require recruiting a representative set of users, using a realistic set of tasks scenarios, and collecting data about what users say and do. What users say is captured in usability testing through the think-aloud protocol (i.e., participants talk about what they are doing during or after completing tasks), after-task and post-study interviews, and questionnaires, while what users do is captured with direct observation of the participants performing tasks. Most usability tests are conducted to identify usability issues and collect performance data such as task completion rates, time on task, and errors. User satisfaction is also captured by having participants' answers questions after each task and at the end of the test (Tullis and Albert 2013).

Usability testing can be conducted in a laboratory or done remotely. In a typical laboratory-based usability test (see Fig. 4), an evaluator observes representative users performing a series of tasks using an application or prototype. The evaluator and one or more observers in the same or adjacent room record the time it takes the users to complete each task, whether the users were successful, and any important comments or problems. To extend usability testing beyond the laboratory, remote usability testing is available. This approach uses the same basic techniques as laboratory-based tests, but the test users and evaluators may be in geographically different locations.

Fig. 4 Usability testing in the University of Miami UX Laboratory

Case Study 2: Usability Testing of a Cancer Clinical Trials Website

Product and Research Goals

The website offers individuals access to information about participating in clinical trials, a decision aid, and a search tool to find clinical trials. The primary research objective for this study was to evaluate the immediate usability of the website.

Why Usability Testing? How Was It Done?

We conducted a formative usability test to identify website strengths and weaknesses. Ten adults, with moderate-to-high health literacy and Internet experience, performed information seeking and information understanding tasks using the website. Four categories of usability metrics were collected: effectiveness, efficiency, satisfaction, and usability improvement opportunities.

How Usability Testing Contributed to the Research?

For each task, the mean time on task was less than 11 minutes and the upper limits of the confidence intervals ($\alpha = 0.10$) were all under 13 minutes. Most participants expressed that using the website to complete tasks took much longer than expected. Task success rates were low across task type, with most participants unable to complete tasks successfully when using the website. After task satisfaction scores ranged from 3.4 to 6.3 (7 is the best rating), with clinical trial search tasks ratings slightly poorer than other task types. After finishing all tasks, participants completed a System Usability Scale. The SUS is at 10 item survey in which participants rate (on 5 point Likert scale) their level agreement. For analysis, the 10 ratings were combined into an overall score. The overall score was 61, which is in the direction of unfavorable perceived usability. Fifty-three usability problems were detected, most of high to moderate severity. Figure 5 shows the important aspects of the data (efficiency, effectiveness, and user satisfaction) collected and an overall usability score. From this information it is evident that there are vast opportunities for improvement.

Usability Testing Identified Significant UX Problems with the Website

Participants experienced issues with website navigation, information organization, and design saliency across platforms. Participants also experienced difficulty in understanding clinical trial study descriptions and using search to find trials.

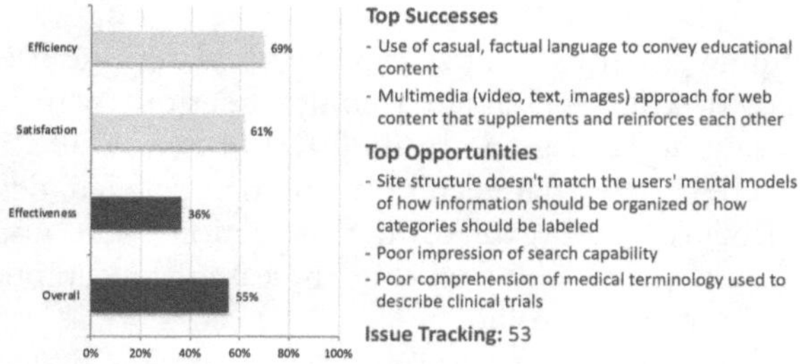

Fig. 5 UX scorecard. Note: Colors not apparent in grayscale print

First click information is very telling about whether the information is organized in a matter that aligns with a user's mental model. For the task that required finding general information about clinical trials, the participants expected this type of information to be directly on the home page, accessible in the "Learn more" button overlaid on the home page, top-placed image, or searchable across the website content. Unfortunately, these first clicks lead to task failures as the information was only available via the "What is a Clinical Trial" link on the main navigation. Beyond the first click data, we found many examples of issues with the information architecture, navigation, and design affordances (i.e. lacking adequate affordances for interaction).

In trying to find clinical trial tasks, participants' information seeking strategy was search dominant, with all participants using search over browse by category. Participants also relied on multi-keyword and conversational queries (sentences), with minimal changes to their search strategy after many failed attempts. The problem was that the site search function was limited in capability for processing user queries. It didn't work as well as Google or other major search engines with many reasonable search queries resulting in error (no search results). Search needs to support queries with multiple terms or natural language. Furthermore, few participants used advanced search (filter and sort) and those that did used it incorrectly.

Another critical issue was the use of medical jargon in clinical trial information. Although the educational content on the website was easily understood by the participants, the language used in the clinical trials description hindered comprehension (with this content measuring at 12th grade reading level). Specifically, information provided in the trial inclusion criteria, detailed description of trial procedures, and technical details sections were not easy to understand. Excessive white spacing increased consumption time and required excessive scrolling.

Usability Testing Assessed User Satisfaction with the Website

Self-reported data provides important information about user's perceptions of the website and their interactions with it. At an emotional level, it tells you how users feel about the website. For this we used the most widely used tool for assessing perceived usability of a product- the SUS. The overall mean SUS score for the website was 61 in the direction of unfavorable perceived usability. However, unprompted verbal expressions also provide valuable insights into a participant's emotional response for the website. Overall, participants expressed satisfaction with the purpose and aesthetics of the website. Participants were also interested in using the website after the study as many participants asked for the website address before leaving the session.

4.3.2 A/B and Multivariate Testing

The A/B test is a type of live-site study with two variants, A and B, which are the control and treatment in an experiment. The two versions (A and B) compared are identical except for a design variation that may affect a user's behavior. Version A could be the currently used version (control), while Version B is modified in some respect (treatment). In online settings, the goal is to identify changes to web pages that increase or maximize an outcome of interest (e.g., click-through rate for news articles). For instance, an A/B test can be used to explore if click rates improve with photo placement alternating between left and right (version A) or always to the right of the article (version B) content for an online newspaper (as cited in Tullis and Albert 2013). Research has found that improvements can sometimes be seen through testing elements like layouts, images, copy text, headlines, fonts, and colors.

The standard approach to A/B testing is to randomly split traffic to version A and version B. Traffic redirection can be equally split or not, with a smaller percentage of visitors redirected to the experimental version. As an extension to A/B testing, multivariate testing is used when multiple variables (e.g., headline, text, and layout) are manipulated and the interaction between the variables needs to be explored to determine the optimal combination. In this case, all variations must be tested in parallel. Both A/B testing and Multivariate testing require carefully designed experiments and large sample sizes to statistically analyze the findings and uncover what works best.

4.4 Behavioral and Physiological Measurements

Understanding how users feel and what attracts attention when using interactive media can facilitate the optimization of the experience to promote certain responses (e.g., happiness) and avoid others (e.g., frustration). Traditional research relies on self-reports and observations to capture emotional and cognitive aspects in the user experience. With self-reports, participants are asked to describe what they think about the product being evaluated. These methods are subjective and are usually measured with various types of rating scales (e.g., Likert or semantic differential scales). While verbal or written responses can produce quantifiable data, they are most often and best used to provide insights rather than metrics. Similarly, observations reveal interface effectiveness and efficiency, but emotional response remains hidden (Kula et al. 2017). To capture objective, observable responses to interface interaction, researchers are exploring use of behavioral and physiological measurements as supplements to traditional methods.

Physiological measures have previously been used in human factors studies to capture indicators of mental effort and stress (Vicente et al. 1987; Wilson and Sasse 2000). Physiological techniques have been shown to provide valuable measures of visual attention, cognitive workload, and emotions. Now, in UX research, physiological data is also being used to measure engagement with user interfaces. The use of physiological measures, in combination with traditional UX methods, help practitioners to better measure the user experience as they provide complementary information on how users feel about the interface. Another advantage in using physiological measures is that, unlike traditional methods, they offer continuous information throughout the interaction (Mandryk et al. 2006).

Recent technology developments have made psychophysiological measurement systems more affordable and less cumbersome. Many UX practitioners are now employing these systems in product research and assessment. The future will be about using technology to learn more about the user experience, getting beyond performance and self-reported satisfaction to exploring physiological response and behavioral change. The next sections introduce some behavioral and physiological measures used, describe how these measures are collected, and explain their inferred meaning. Eye tracking is described in greater detail given its wide use in UX Research.

4.4.1 Exploring Eye Movements: Eye Tracking

Eye Tracking offers unique insights into visual behavior that cannot be discovered through participant observation, questionnaires, or interviews. At the most basic level, eye tracking measures visual activity. Specifically, this technology identifies where someone is looking and measures the characteristic of the eye and eye movement. Where do participants look? For how long? What do participants ignore? What are participants' eye movements and focus across the interface? Although, the concept for eye tracking is easy to understand, both the process and interpretation of results are complex.

Eye tracking captures foveal vision, which is vision in the center of the field of vision, where visual acuity is greatest. This information is useful as gaze is typically associated with where attention is directed (Bjoko 2013). To capture visual activity, researchers use special eye tracking equipment (see Fig. 6). The eye tracker, either remote or head-mounted, consists of hardware and software components which record eye movements when looking at computing displays, physical objects, and spaces. Generally, eye tracking systems include cameras, projectors, and sophisticated algorithms to capture eye movements. Projectors shine near-infrared light on the eyes and the cameras capture visible ocular features (e.g., pupil) and record the reflection of the light from the retina (to locate the center of the pupil) and from the cornea (i.e., corneal reflection). Algorithms use details about the location of the corneal reflection relative to the center of the pupil to determine where the person is looking. Other information such as changes in pupil diameter and blink frequency is also captured by the eye tracking system. The combined data is saved for processing with eye tracking analysis software.

Fig. 6 An eye tracking system from Tobii

Researchers typically analyze eye movements in terms of fixations and saccades. A fixation is pause of eye movement on a specific area of the visual field, while saccades are rapid eye movements between fixations tracing the eye's movement among areas of focus. Common metrics using this data include number of fixations, fixation duration, time to first fixation, and fixation sequence. Beyond the analysis of eye movement, eye characteristics can be examined to measure the participant's cognitive state. For example, the pupil contracts and dilates in response cognitive processing, arousal, and engagement. Typically, the larger the pupil diameter the greater the level of engagement.

There are many different methods of visualizing eye data. The most common approaches explore where participants focus their gaze (e.g., heat map) and investigate the visual path (gaze plot) of one or more participants across the interface. Typically, these visualizations are used to aggregate the eye activity across several participants for a specified time interval. This enables researchers to get an overview of the viewing behavior across multiple participants. In aggregation, the visualizations smooth over differences in individual viewing behavior. For good practice, visualizations should also be generated for each individual as participants approach interfaces differently, and it is important to consider viewing behaviors and usability problems experienced one participant at a time.

The heat map (Fig. 7) indicates which aspects of the interface are attracting visual attention. Heat maps represent where participants focus their gaze based on the number of fixations or the duration of gaze on an area of the interface. Generally, a color scale relating to temperature is used to represent the value measured. For example, the longer participants' look at a fixed position, the hotter the area indicated by warm to

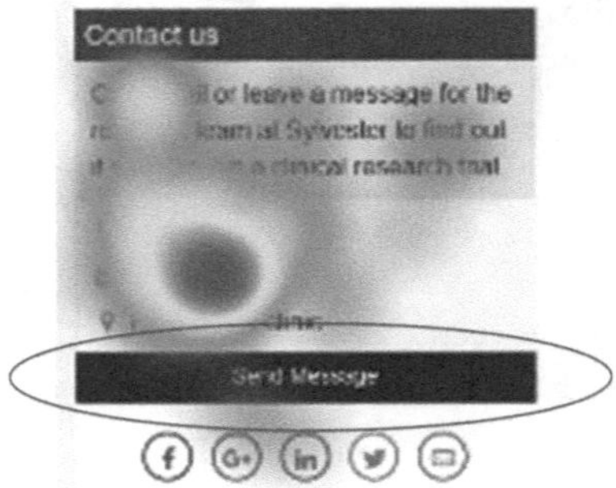

Fig. 7 Example of a heat map of a cancer clinical trials website showing distribution of eye movements of several participants in the study. Note: Colors not apparent in grayscale print

hot colors (e.g., red). Hence, a red spot over an area of the interface may indicate that several participants focused on that part of interface for a longer period of time. When participants look at an area for less time, the colder the area indicated by cold colors (e.g., blue, green).

Gaze plots (see Fig. 8), also known as scan paths, depict a series of dots indicating fixations and fine lines indicating saccades. The size of the dots represent the duration of fixations, with longer fixations indicated by larger dots and shorter durations represented by smaller dots. The dots are numbered to show the order in which the fixations occurred. Typically when gaze plots illustrate gaze activity of one or more participants, different color coding is used in order to distinguish between participants.

Eye tracking in UX research is used most commonly to determine where participants look and for how long, as well as what was ignored. Understanding where people look or don't look for information or features reveals whether or not participants discovered an aspect or element of the interface. Such analysis provides interesting insights into the overall gaze behavior. This information is used to inform interface design changes that are needed to increase saliency of information or features.

UX researchers use eye tracking to evaluate interfaces for the optimal user experience. Eye tracking allows exploration of interface design impact on the user experience. It is flexible technique that works with a variety of research methods, including interviews, observation, user testing, and a/b testing. Eye tracking complements traditional methods by offering insights into what participants say and do. Eye tracking also facilitates diagnosing usability issues as it uniquely provides information about the interaction that isn't articulated by participants or observed

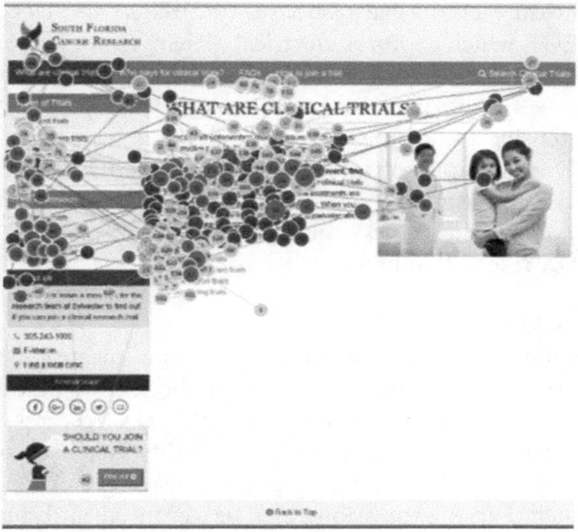

Fig. 8 Example of several participants' scan path of eye movement on a cancer clinical trials website. Note: Colors not apparent in grayscale print

by the researcher. Eye tracking provides objective data that reveals the behavior behind usability issues, allowing effective recommendations to be made.

4.4.2 Understanding Emotions

Emotions are a momentary physiological response characterized by two dimensions: arousal and valence. Arousal is the experience of change in the bodies' physiological activity, providing information about emotional intensity. Valence is a quality for positive and negative emotions. Individual elements of interactive media design can trigger positive or negative emotions, influencing the overall user experience. Hence, measuring user's emotional response to interactive media is important. The next sections describe several techniques for measuring emotions.

Brain Activity

Brain activity is associated with cognitive and emotional states. Research has shown that specific patterns of brain activity are associated with emotional states such as frustration and engagement (Tullis and Albert

2013). To measure emotional response, researchers use electroencephalography (EEG), which captures electrical activity of the brain using electrodes positioned at various points on the scalp. EEG accurately reveals emotional state of the user but does not provide precise data about emotional intensity. Other physiological measures have been used more widely in UX evaluations of interactive media than EEG. This is likely due to the cost and difficulty in implementation, as well as the expertise required to collect and process the data. It may be that EEG is not yet suitable for UX research in practice.

Facial Expression

Facial expressions are a form of nonverbal communication characterized by movements of one or more muscles of the face. These movements communicate an individual's emotional state. UX researchers monitor participant's facial expressions to provide insights into user engagement, which is the degree of emotional response a user feels when interacting with a product. Facial expressions can be captured and analyzed with three different approaches: facial electromyographic activity (EMG), manual coding of facial activity, and automatic facial expression analysis using computer-vision algorithms.

Facial EMG measures facial muscle activity by detecting surface voltage during muscle contraction (Potter and Bolls 2011). This involves putting electrodes on the skin of the face to measure electrical activity of the muscles underneath. EMG has been used extensively to measure emotional valence (see Cacioppo et al. 1986; Hassenzahl and Sandweg 2004; Mandryk et al. 2006) because it is precise and able to detect miniscule responses with temporal precision. However, data collection is intrusive as electrodes attached to cables are placed on the participants face and the data capture tends to contains electrical noise.

An alternative to facial EMG is facial expression coding. Based on the formative work by a Swedish anatomist Hjortsjö (1969), Ekman and Friesen developed the Facial Action Coding System (FACS 1978). The FACS is a classification system mapping emotions to a distinct set of facial expressions, muscle movements, and head positioning that can be reliably identified. These analyses were historically conducted by trained researchers reviewing videos of faces. However, recent advances in technology have automated this process. Software using a webcam automatically detects the face, codes facial expressions, and identifies emotional states. Facial expression analysis is a useful method for measuring the valence and types of emotion experienced by participants. However, this approach is less accurate than EMG and may not capture subtle interactions.

Electrodermal Activity

Sweat glands in the skin cause conductivity to change, resulting in electrodermal activity (EDA). Sweating is controlled by the sympathetic nervous system. Increases in moisture on the skin caused by sweating are associated with increased sympathetic nervous system activity indicating anxiety or stress.

To measure skin conductance, EDA equipment is used. This equipment directly measures skin conductivity between electrodes. EDA is used to measure arousal, but also reflects cognitive load as increases in arousal are associated with cognitive demands. In UX, EDA is used to provide insights into emotional states. EDA is helpful in detecting engagement intensity and difficulty of use when users interact with a product, but is not an effective measure of valence or identification of the types of emotions experienced.

4.4.3 Cardiac Activity

A common approach for measuring arousal or stress is to capture cardiac activity. Cardiac activity is assessed by the increase and decrease in heart rate, which is the number of heart beats per minute (Potter and Bolls 2011). As heart rate is coupled to the autonomic nervous system activity (Anttonen and Surakka 2005), it offers a suitable measure for exploring how people feel. Capturing and processing cardiac activity relies on two technologies: electrocardiography (ECG) and photoplethysmography (PPG). ECG measures bio-potential produced by electrical signals that control contraction and expansion of the heart. PPG relies on light-based technology to sense blood volume changes in microvascular tissue.

In UX research, an important metric for heart rate is how much it varies. Heart rate variability (HRV), a derived measure, captures variation in time intervals between heart beats and is an indicator for arousal. Overall, HRV is an indicator of physiological arousal, with decreased arousal associated with high HRV and increased arousal associated with a low HRV. HRV is also used to measure cognitive processing. For example, cardiac activity was used to assess cognitive processing of news media in several published studies (as in Wise et al. 2009; Potter and Keene 2012).

On its own, HRV has had limited use in user experience research as it is not always possible to pinpoint what is the true source of stress (Tullis and Albert 2013). However, several UX research efforts have explored the use of both HRV and EDA as indicators of stress in user test settings. For example, Ward and Mardsen (2003) found that both EDA and heart rate reflected greater stress when interacting with poorly designed websites. While cardiac activity provides a practical and objective measure of emotional response and cognitive processing, it is most effective when combined with other physiological measures.

4.4.4 Multiple Physiological Measures

UX researchers can now objectively explore users' emotional response to interactive media, and evaluate how interface design influences human performance and engagement. Use of physiological recordings provides reliable measurement of cognitive effort, arousal, and emotional response when users interact with product features. However, each physiological measure only reveals a portion the user experience. For more comprehensive assessment, it is important to implement multiple physiological measures in parallel to allow comparison of findings. Furthermore, the use of physiological measures, in combination with traditional methods, provides a better evaluation of the overall user experience.

5 Conclusion

User-experience research methods are invaluable for producing data and insights to inform product design. At every stage in the HCD process, different UX research methods can keep product development efforts on the right path and aligned with real user needs. Although UX research should be performed across the stages, the earlier the research is conducted the more impact the findings will have on the product. Each UX research method has its strengths and weaknesses. Supplementing each method with a range of other approaches allows triangulation of findings to safeguard against misleading outcomes.

Companies in various industries have already made user experience a key part of their product development processes. A poor user experience can result in great cost to business, not only in lost sales, but also in customer satisfaction, productivity, and additional support needs required for an inadequately designed product. Poor interface design, if found early in development, can be improved to reduce or eliminate serious problems, rather than having to make costly changes after the fact. Addressing UX early in the design process is an advantage for all.

References

Anttonen, J., and V. Surakka. 2005. Emotions and Heart Rate While Sitting on a Chair. In *Proceedings of CHI 2005 Conference*, April 2–7, ACM, Portland, OR.

Blomberg, J., and M. Burrell. 2009. An Ethnographic Approach to Design. In *Human-Computer Interaction: Development Process*, ed. A. Sears and J. Jacko, 71–94. Boca Raton, FL: CRC Press.

Bojko, A. 2013. *Eye Tracking the User Experience: A Practical Guide to Research*. New York: Rosenfeld Media.

Borg, I., and P. Groenen. 1997. Multi-Trait-Multimethod by Multidimensional Scaling. *SoftStat* 97: 59–65.

Brooke, J. 1996. SUS: A "Quick and Dirty" Usability Scale. In *Usability Evaluation in Industry*, ed. P. Jordan, B. Thomas, and B. Weerdmeester, 189–194. London, UK: Taylor & Francis.

Cacioppo, J.T., R.E. Petty, M.E. Losch, and H.S. Kim. 1986. Electromyographic Activity Over Facial Muscle Regions Can Differentiate the Valence and Intensity of Affective Reactions. *Journal of Personality and Social Psychology* 50 (2): 260.

Courage, C., and K. Baxter. 2015. *Understanding Your Users: A Practical Guide to User Requirements Methods, Tools, and Techniques*. San Francisco, CA: Morgan Kaufmann.

Department of Health and Human Sciences. 2006. *Research-Based Web Design & Usability Guidelines*. http://www.usability.gov/guidelines/. Accessed March 14, 2018.

Dumas, J.S., and M.C. Salzman. 2006. Usability Assessment Methods. *Reviews of Human Factors and Ergonomics* 2 (1): 109–140.

Ekman, P., and W. Friesen. 1978. *The Facial Action Coding System (FACS): A Technique for the Measurement of Facial Action*. Palo Alto, CA: Consulting Psychologists Press.

Hart, S.G., and L.E. Staveland. 1988. Development of NASA-TLX (Task Load Index): Results of Empirical and Theoretical Research. In *Human Mental Workload*, ed. P.A. Hancock and N. Meshkati, 139–183. Amsterdam: Elsevier.

Hassenzahl, M., and N. Sandweg. 2004. From Mental Effort to Perceived Usability: Transforming Experiences Into Summary Assessments. In *CHI'04 Extended Abstracts on Human Factors in Computing Systems*, 1283–1286, April, ACM, New York.

Hjortsjö, C.H. 1969. *Man's Face and Mimic Language*. Lund, Sweden: Studentlitteratur.

Holtzblatt, K., and H. Beyer. 2016. *Contextual Design: Design for Life*, 2nd ed. Cambridge, MA: Morgan Kaufmann.

Kruskal, J.B., and M. Wish. 1978. *Multidimensional Scaling*, vol. 11. Beverly Hills and London: Sage.

Kula, I., R. Atkinson, R. Branaghan, and R.D. Roscoe. 2017. Assessing User Experience via Biometric Sensor Affect Detection. In *End-User Considerations in Educational Technology Design*, ed. R.D. Roscoe, S.D. Craig, and I. Douglas, 123–139. Hershey, PA: IGI Global.

Lewis, J.R. 1995. IBM Computer Usability Satisfaction Questionnaires: Psychometric Evaluation and Instructions for Use. *International Journal of Human-Computer Interaction* 7 (1): 57–78.

Lewis, J.R. 2012. Usability Testing. In *Handbook of Human Factors and Ergonomics*, 4th ed., 1267–1312. New York: Wiley.

Mandryk, R.L., K.M. Inkpen, and T.W. Calvert. 2006. Using Psychophysiological Techniques to Measure User Experience with Entertainment Technologies. *Behaviour & Information Technology* 25 (2): 141–158.

Nielsen, J. 1994. Heuristic Evaluation. In *Usability Inspection Methods*, ed. J. Nielsen and R.L. Mack, 25–62. New York: Wiley.

Norman, D., and S.W. Draper (eds.). 1986. *User Centered System Design: New Perspectives on Human-Computer Interaction*. Mahwah, NJ: Lawrence Erlbaum Associates.

Norman, D.A., and R. Verganti. 2014. Incremental and Radical Innovation: Design Research vs. Technology and Meaning Change. *Design Issues* 30 (1): 78–96.

Paul, C.L. 2008. A Modified Delphi Approach to a New Card Sorting Methodology. *Journal of Usability Studies* 4 (1): 7–30.

Pérez-Montoro, M., and Ll Codina. 2017. *Navigation Design and SEO for Content-Intensive Websites: A Guide for an Efficient Digital Communication*. Oxford: Elsevier (Chandos).

Potter, R.F., and P. Bolls. 2011. *Psychophysiological Measurement and Meaning: Cognitive and Emotional Processing of Media*. New York and London: Routledge.

Potter, R.F., and J.R. Keene. 2012. The Effect of Sports Fan Identification on the Cognitive Processing of Sports News. *International Journal of Sport Communication* 5 (3): 348–367.

Righi, C., J. James, M. Beasley, D.L. Day, J.E. Fox, J. Gieber, C. Howe, and L. Ruby. 2013. Card Sort Analysis Best Practices. *Journal of Usability Studies* 8 (3): 69–89.

Sanders, E.B.-N. 2002. From User-Centered to Participatory Design Approaches. In *Design and the Social Sciences: Making Connections*, ed. J. Frascara, 1–8. London: Taylor and Francis.

Soranzo, A., and D. Cooksey. 2015. Testing Taxonomies: Beyond Card Sorting. *Bulletin of the Association for Information Science and Technology* 41 (5): 34–39.

Spencer, D. 2009. *Card Sorting: Designing Usable Categories*. Brooklyn, NY: Rosenfeld Media.

Tullis, T., and B. Albert. 2013. *Measuring the User Experience: Collecting, Analyzing, and Presenting Usability Metrics*. Waltham, MA: Morgan Kaufmann.

Tullis, T., and L.E. Wood. 2004. How Many Users Are Enough for a Card-Sorting Study? In *Proceedings of the Usability Professionals Association Conference,* June 7–11, Minneapolis, MN.

User Experience Basics. n.d. Retrieved from https://www.usability.gov/what-and-why/user-experience.html. Accessed April 3, 2018.

Vicente, K.J., D.C. Thornton, and N. Moray. 1987. Spectral Analysis of Sinus Arrhythmia: A Measure of Mental Effort. *Human Factors* 29 (2): 171–182.

Ward, R.D., and P.H. Marsden. 2003. Physiological Responses to Different WEB Page Designs. *International Journal of Human-Computer Studies* 59 (1–2): 199–212.

Wilson, C. (ed.). 2009. *User Experience Re-Mastered: Your Guide to Getting the Right Design*. Burlington, MA: Morgan Kaufmann.

Wilson, G.M., and M.A. Sasse. 2000. Do Users Always Know What's Good for Them? Utilising Physiological Responses to Assess Media Quality. In *People and Computers XIV—Usability or Else!*, 327–339. London: Springer.

Wise, K., P. Bolls, J. Myers, and M. Sternadori. 2009. When Words Collide Online: How Writing Style and Video Intensity Affect Cognitive Processing of Online News. *Journal of Broadcasting & Electronic Media* 53 (4): 532–546.

CHAPTER 6

Newsonomics in the Interactive Era: Dimensions of Sustainability in the News Media

Alexis Apablaza-Campos, Lluís Codina and Rafael Pedraza-Jiménez

1 Introduction: Interactive Communication and Sustainability

The different digital formats that quality newspapers are currently experimenting with are related, albeit indirectly, with the overall profitability and sustainability of the news media and their business models, although

A. Apablaza-Campos (✉)
School of Journalism and Corporate Public Relations, UNIACC University, Santiago, Chile
e-mail: a_apablaza@boleteador.com

L. Codina · R. Pedraza-Jiménez
Department of Communication, Pompeu Fabra University, Barcelona, Spain
e-mail: lluis.codina@upf.edu

R. Pedraza-Jiménez
e-mail: rafael.pedraza@upf.edu

M. Pérez-Montoro (ed.), *Interaction in Digital News Media*,
https://doi.org/10.1007/978-3-319-96253-5_6

at first glance they may well give the appearance of occupying different dimensions.

The main reason why this is so—and this is an argument that is very well captured by a number of recent studies (Hansen and Goligoski 2018; Nafría 2017a; Kleis Nielsen 2016; Newman 2018)—is that these new digital formats, especially those that are interactive, directly increase the number of ways in which readers can interact with the news media, generating a form of engagement that, in turn, cultivates reader loyalty.

In fact, what the most proactive media firms in this field are doing is to envisage digital formats as a way to attract new audiences—in some cases to increase their website traffic and influence, which in turn boosts their advertising revenue; and, in others, as an instrument of added value that encourages potential readers to subscribe to their sites.

This chapter undertakes an analysis of different initiatives taken in the field of interactive communication in the US (most notably by *The New York Times*), Latin American and European media.

The key feature of the cases we consider is undoubtedly their exploratory nature. With the exception of very few firms, and here again *The New York Times* stands out, most are currently experimenting with new sections in an attempt to expand their user bases and to reach new social sectors. Increasingly, what we are witnessing is the creation of new innovative sections, such as those dedicated to leisure and cooking, as well as new formats, especially those using immersive journalism, combining different forms of virtual and augmented reality, to support investigative and community journalism.

Some newspapers of course aim to exploit the exclusive content provided by their new sections of visual and immersive journalism, based on high levels of interactivity, as they explore the viability of paywalls.

2 News Media Outlets and New Business Formats

The origin of most of these new paths of exploration can be traced back to the belief that for decades, the news media and, as such, the whole journalism industry have been deep in the throes of crisis. Arguably, this idea has gained greater credence of late as a result of the social repercussions surrounding the problems of truthfulness with which the content of certain news sources has been tainted. The impact at the international level has been such that in 2016 the editors of the Oxford English Dictionary chose as their word of the year "post truth", followed, in 2017, by "fake news" (*BBC News*, 2017).

However, the content of the news media is not the only problem. For more than a decade now, traditional media formats have been trying to reinvent themselves as they seek to live side by side with the internet. Their audience and readership figures, along with their advertising revenue, have been subject to continuous fluctuations, albeit in a general downward direction. As a result, while some have managed to adapt to new formats, for others the digital challenge has become a question of simple survival.

Since the creation of the World Wide Web, more than 25 years ago now, and, more particularly, since the emergence of news media in what are exclusively digital formats (over more than a decade ago), the very survival of newspapers (and, more generally, the world of printed publications) has been called into serious question.

Although most of the world's leading newspapers survive, there has been a progressive fall in the sale of print editions and in their spending on advertising, two trends that have been accompanied by insufficient advertising in digital formats. These trends have been identified in many studies, including a report published by the Brookings Institution in the United States:

> As circulation has plummeted, so has the number of newspapers. There were 1,749 American newspapers in 1945 and by the end of 2014, the number had shrunk to 1,331. Once again, when these numbers are converted to per capita numbers, the trend is even more dramatic. We now have many fewer papers serving a much bigger population. (Kamarck and Gabriele 2015: 2)

In the case of television, experts in the journalism sector defended the value of this medium in the face of the disruptive forces set in motion by the internet and which threatened so many industries. Invoking that old belief that "a picture is worth a thousand words", it was assumed that this format would be able to stand firm in the wake of the arrival of the web, social networks and new technologies, which, rather than attacking it, would serve as a means to strengthen the television experience.

And so pay-TV increased its offer of channels, while open-TV optimized image quality thanks to new digital terrestrial television (DTTV) standards, including in both cases interactive resources and pay-per-view services.

Yet, the rise in connection speeds and the growth in online video consumption gave universal access to Smart TV, enabling users to choose between watching conventional television—whether open or pay—or viewing streaming apps: "in the world of Netflix and YouTube, who worries about getting home on time to watch the day's news broadcast?", asks Christian Leal, director of *Radio Bío-Bío's* digital platform, the online news site with the highest web traffic in Chile[1] (Leal 2017).

Figures published by Magna (IPG Mediabrands) confirm this trend. In 2017, for the first time ever, worldwide online advertising spending exceeded spending in television. More specifically, digital spending reached $209 billion while TV brought in $178 billion. It is forecast that by 2022 the gap will be even greater, that is, $347 billion vs. $183 billion (Kafka and Molla 2017).

It comes as little surprise, therefore, that a study conducted by the Pew Research Center should show that, between 2016 and 2017, the number of Americans obtaining their news from television and print newspapers fell from 57 to 50% and from 20 to 18%, respectively, while those getting their news online increased from 38 to 43%. The percentage share using the radio, meanwhile, remained stable (25% in both 2016 and 2017), because, it is argued, listening to a radio station is compatible with other daily activities such as working and driving (Gottfried and Shearer 2017).

These constant changes have forced the media to diversify their formats and to redesign their news outlets, so that today the news media have to be considered in terms of multi-screen spaces. All this brings with it the need for new strategies for disseminating news content and for maintaining journalistic visibility, in addition to the search for new finance models.

2.1 Social Networks and the Digital Duopoly

The scenario we have just described was, in many ways, foreseen by Ken Doctor, the expert media industry analyst,[2] in his *book Newsonomics:*

[1]According to Similar Web data, *Bío-Bío* Chile obtained an average traffic of 28 million monthly users between June and November 2017. Full details available at https://www.similarweb.com/website/biobiochile.cl.

[2]Ken Doctor continues to publish reports about the news media industry at his website http://newsonomics.com/ and to write opinion articles for Nieman Lab.

Twelve New Trends That Will Shape the News You Get. Published in 2010, the study identified the need for the news media to bridge various gaps. One of these was the financial gap, the result of the ending of the golden age in which the mainstream media had received billions of dollars of revenue from conventional advertising. Current figures may vary, but the numbers will never return to what they once were:

> The tens of billions of dollars that sustained news businesses, allowing them to pay tens of thousands of journalists won't be coming back. The new building blocks of the digital ad revolution will support heavier and heavier loads. They'll pay, slowly and over time, for more news to be reported and written by professionals. While they'll never pay the freight that the print business used to, by 2015, they'll pay for more than they do today. What about the rest of what's needed? (Doctor 2010: 220–221)

As a result, network and digital marketing has crossed paths with the news media, bringing about a major paradigm shift. It is no longer enough for the commercial department to spend its time looking for advertisers as a means of financing a paper. Today the media are "learning to sell themselves", as can be seen, for example, in the dissemination of their content via Google and Social Media ADS:

> Marketing has seen its own parallel revolution to what the news world has experienced. Much of it concerns viral marketing, parallel to the social networking revolution that we're in the midst of, and part of it is simply about old-fashioned, savvy promotion applied across media. Where once great mass markets, served by newspapers and broadcasters, were the easy, standard way to sell products and services, the viral Web is giving both marketers and media headaches and unexpected opportunities. (Doctor 2010: 194)

It is against this backdrop that social networks are acquiring an increasingly more important role in the dissemination of news. An online media outlet does not operate solely via its own website (Pedraza-Jiménez et al. 2016). Today, the communicative strategy of a news media firm, as with that of any other organization, requires the careful definition of its social media plans. That is, the implementation of editorial policies for the publication of its content on different social platforms.

The news media are no longer passive recipients of readers who visit the pages of their website. In addition to this, they implement active publication policies via their profiles on different social platforms, in which their (potential) readers are present (He and Pedraza-Jiménez 2015). In this way, the media take their content to where the readers are. This means that they are obliged to disseminate their news journalism via different social channels, most notably Facebook and Twitter. Although other platforms, including YouTube, Instagram, Snapchat and WhatsApp, are increasingly gaining in importance.

According to another Pew Research Center study, 67% of Americans—5% up on 2016 figures—report receiving some of their news via the social media. The three sites recording the greatest increase in information consumption are Twitter (up from 59 to 74%), YouTube (from 21 to 32%) and Snapchat (from 17 to 29%). Facebook remains stable with a slight increase (66–68%) (Shearer and Gottfried 2017).

However, the dependence on web traffic from such sites as Facebook is cause for constant criticism in the industry: First, owing to the site's Instant Article format that forced the online media to modify their mobile website codes to maintain the traffic originating from their fan pages, and, second, owing to an experiment launched in six countries shifting the focus in its News Feed from public news pages to friends' posts in the home page of each user profile. The outcome being that the traffic of the online media sites affected has fallen by 66% (Dojcinovic 2017).

At the beginning of 2018, Mark Zuckerberg explained in a post published on the same social network that users' content would be prioritized over that of fan pages in the feed of each profile:

> We're making a major change to how we build Facebook. I'm changing the goal I give our product teams from focusing on helping you find relevant content to helping you have more meaningful social interactions.
>
> We started making changes in this direction last year, but it will take months for this new focus to make its way through all our products. The first changes you'll see will be in News Feed, where you can expect to see more from your friends, family and groups.
>
> As we roll this out, you'll see less public content like posts from businesses, brands, and media. And the public content you see more will be held to the same standard—it should encourage meaningful interactions between people. (Zuckerberg 2018)

In light of the controversy caused, Facebook announced on its specialist blog, Journalism Project, that in future it will classify the news media according to how trustworthy they are considered to be by the users of its platform. However, for many digital media the only way to maintain their historical results now will be by investing in Social Media ADS. Meanwhile, though, Facebook has announced it will launch a new experiment in the United States to give more visibility to journalistic content according to the user's geolocation (Hardiman and Brown 2018).

The outcome is that various media firms are seriously proposing combatting the so-called "digital duopoly" formed by Facebook and Google. News Media Alliance, the main US newspaper industry trade group, seeks to obtain collective negotiating rights with both organizations so that the newspaper industry has a better system of revenue generation. Facebook has responded by saying that it is willing to seek joint solutions to help papers sell subscriptions on its site (Rutemberg 2017).

One firm announcing that it intends to go one step further in its attempt to counter this dependence on social networks is *BuzzFeed*, paradoxically a media company that we may never have heard of if it had not enjoyed explosive growth on Facebook in a brief ten-year period. In 2017 the firm achieved just 80% of its financial targets. This resulted in the laying-off of more than 100 employees and led to the firm drawing up an escape plan from the digital duopoly, which they accused of receiving massive advertising revenues while paying very little to content creators. An article in Nieman Lab put it like this:

> BuzzFeed plans to counter the dominance of Google and Facebook in two primary ways: One is by building a more diverse business model that's focused less on direct-sold advertising and more on commerce, programmatic advertising, studio development, and revenue from platforms. He [CEO Jonah Peretti] said that, by 2019, non-direct-sold revenue will account for over half of BuzzFeed's overall revenue, up from 25 percent this year. (Bilton 2017)

The most radical stance though was adopted by *Folha de Sao Paulo*, Brazil's leading newspaper (Bronosky and de Carvalho 2014: 32), which in February 2018 announced that it would no longer be updating its Facebook content after a 32% fall in traffic of the top 10 Brazilian papers during January, a figure that looks set to continue to fall after the changes announced by the Journalism Project (Folha 2018).

2.2 Models and Forecasts

Striking out on new paths, accepting new challenges and making new forecasts all require new business strategies. The paths that *BuzzFeed* and *Folha* are striking out on will be monitored very carefully by media firms having to face similar problems. Depending on how well they fare, one way or another, these media companies seem likely to influence the course of action adopted by their industry counterparts.

Yet, some companies do not find themselves subjected to such pressures by this situation, as they do not have large digital newsrooms dependent on constantly fluctuating analytics. These are the independent or niche media companies. Most of which were created in digital format, precisely because of the economic and logistical challenges of creating an analog format.

Different industry experts forecast that a series of factors will come together in 2018 that will help media firms of this type enjoy exponential growth. Among other reasons, they identify the relative ease of creating and maintaining a website or a profile in different social media:

> According to data from the Youth Economic Circle, an international non-profit association that promotes entrepreneurship among young people, 2018 will be the year for "niche" sites, portals set up as business ventures by those wanting to publicize their hobbies to the world. Their target audience is limited and they place greater value on aspects of the news story other than its immediacy.
>
> The goal of these sites is to go viral. The independence they enjoy from not having to adhere to editorial lines dictated by large conglomerates makes them very attractive to millennials, young professionals who consume news in a more fragmented and dispersed way than in the past. (ANP Chile 2017)

Above and beyond a media company's size, the international journalists' network, IJNet, has identified seven business models that could save the future of the news outlet (Chinula 2017). The list runs as follows:

- *Sponsored content*: original stories to promote a company. The content may be very similar to journalistic storytelling and just as attractive, but it needs to be tagged to distinguish it from pure editorial content.

- *Crowdfunding*: applicable equally to nonprofits dedicated to investigative journalism (*Ciper*, Chile) as to individual projects through such platforms as Kickstarter. The method has been incorporated by the *Guardian* in its membership scheme. It has also facilitated the creation of newspapers such as *De Correspondent* in the Netherlands and *FrontPage Africa* in Liberia.
- *Subscriptions*: there are newspapers, such as *The Information*, which is 100% based on this model, and *ElDiario.es* in Spain, which was born and managed according to this model (Sanabre Vives 2015). In general, it is a financial model that provides support rather than being a great business opportunity for large media companies, notable exceptions include *The New York Times*. Other exceptions include the *Financial Times* and *The Wall Street Journal*, which boast very successful subscriber bases, a model that we look at in more detail below.
- *Live journalism*: Social Media Live Streaming[3] allows the creation of projects for presenting news to a live audience. Leading US examples include The Boston Globe's *Globe Live*, and Gannett's *Arizona Storytellers Project*.
- *Donor funding*: its three best known forms are philanthropic backing, government funding and policies of corporate social responsibility (CSR). The first is best illustrated by South Africa's *Amabhungane*, funded by six donor organizations; the second by the support given by the French and Norwegian governments; and, the third, by Google News Lab and the Facebook Journalism Project.
- *Micropayments*: payment to access a single article. *Blendle*, a Dutch platform, employs this model charging an average of £0.50 per article, and so guarantees readers no ads and the possibility of getting their money back if they do not like what they read.
- *Quality journalism*: The *Washington Post* believes that 'fake news' and information overload lead users and companies to seek reliable content in reputable media, which in turn should lead to increased traffic and more advertising, or more subscriptions.

[3]The authors of this chapter have created an observatory of the uses of live video journalism on social platforms. It can be accessed at https://www.smls.info/.

In theory, all these new business models for news outlets should create new jobs. For example, the *Independent Journal Review*, with an average of 30 million unique visitors per month, recently hired an Audience Growth Director to consolidate its results (*Independent Journal Review*, n.d.).

3 Pay-for-News Models

When Greg Barton graduated from Leeds University with a degree in Business Studies in the late 80s, he eyed up his job options: business ventures with his friends, internships in France, etc. As none offered him sufficient income, he decided to try his luck in Chile in the early 90s, where he was quickly taken on by an English magazine to sell advertising to firms in the mining industry.

In 1994 he got a letter from his mother in which she enclosed an article about something new called the Internet. To find out more, he had to request authorization to access it on the computers at the University of Chile—the only place in the country with a connection at that time—and so he was able to scour the digital edition of *The Times*, thanks to which he realized that this new channel would allow him to create a newsroom, an online press office providing information about the different sectors making up Chilean industry. Later, in 1996, he founded *Business News Americas*—now known simply as *BNamericas*—one of the first digital media companies to operate a pay format and with content written in both English and Spanish.

Today *BNamericas*[4] employs more than 50 journalists—who receive a salary that doubles the income of traditional media writers—and has more than 1200 subscribers that include the leading firms in Chile, Brazil, Argentina and Mexico. Its business model is not only to deliver specialized news adapted to the needs of its subscribers, but also to prepare specific reports to help them make business decisions (Mente Emprendedora 2015).

Pay-for-news models existed long before the internet was created, although then the business focused on two types of agency offering two specific services:

[4] The English edition of *BNamericas* can be consulted at https://www.bnamericas.com/en/.

- *News agencies*: collect news from different locations and publish it in different formats for their clients (media firms that pay for specific news coverage). Some of the best known are *Reuters* (United Kingdom), *Associated Press* (USA), *EFE* (Spain), *DPA* (Germany), and *Xinhua* (China).
- *Communication agencies*: carry out analyses of the press and give their clients (usually companies) a report, known as a *Press Clipping*, in which they highlight the content of interest in different media sources. With the emergence of the digital media, this has become known on the web as "news aggregation" and allowed the birth of new media enterprises such as *The Huffington Post*.

3.1 Paywall and "The Chump Gap"

The current scenario—in which online advertising spending exceeds that in conventional channels, albeit concentrated in the digital duopoly—invites media firms to consider paywalls as a way to avoid their excessive dependence on advertising revenues.

Pay-for-news models are undergoing continuous change, as they face up to the dichotomy that *Newsonomics* calls "The Chump Gap", which can be summed up in one simple question: Why pay for a newspaper if I can read the news for free on the web?

> It's an absolutely fair question.
>
> Here's the problem. We'll all end up getting the quality of news and information that we pay for. We can't leave that quality—and quantity—to the vagaries of how the digital ad revolution plays out. First off, no one has any idea how much money the new ad businesses will throw off. Secondly, as we've seen throughout Newsonomics, the fortunes of the ad business have gotten disconnected from the news business.
>
> So, I think that leaves us saying, I'm not a chump, I'm a champion. Just as we pay for cable programming and broadband Internet and support all kinds of community and global organizations, we can support news and information. No, it doesn't have to mean throwing some dimes in a tin cup. It means stepping forward and proudly proclaiming your financial support, especially for community and investigative journalism. (Doctor 2010: 222)

Several recent studies, produced by highly reliable sources, have addressed how this gap has gradually been overcome, providing positive data for newspaper companies that want to go behind a paywall. They include the following:

- *In paywall age, free content remains king for newspaper sites*: an article published in the *Columbia Journalism Review* analyzed the 25 most read newspaper websites in the United States. Of these, 25% favor paywalls as one of their main sources of income, and only 10 of the 25 eschew any form of payment format for any of their content. The article highlights two payment models, the "leaky" website paywall with unlimited "side doors" (*The New York Times*, *The Wall Street Journal*, and *The Washington Post*) and the "hard" paywall (*Boston Globe* and *Boston.com*) (Stulberg 2017).
- *Digital News Report 2017*: the survey undertaken by Oxford University's Reuter Institute interviewed more than 70,000 people from 36 countries and found that the most cited reasons for paying were to get news access on their mobiles (30%), to be able to consume news from a range of sources (29%) and/or to take advantage of a good deal (23%) (Reuters Institute 2017: 34–37). The report also highlights the figures of subscribers in the Nordic countries: Norway (15%), Sweden (12%) and Denmark (10%) and their growth in the United States, where there was a leap in all payment formats from 9 to 16% between 2016 and 2017, attributable to findings that left-wing sympathizers under the age of 35 want to "help fund journalism" (Fletcher 2017).
- *Pay Models in European News*: another publication by the Reuters Institute, based on the study of 170 media outlets on the continent, concluded that 66% of newspapers and 71% of magazines include some type of subscriber pay model (Pellicer 2017). These percentages are highest in France (95%), Poland (90%) and Finland (87%). The United Kingdom is at the other end of the spectrum, with the lowest percentage of pay models (33%) but at the same time the highest monthly subscription charges (£18.87), largely attributable to the *Financial Times*, whose average price is £46.00 per month (Sehl et al. 2017).
- *Paywalls in Latin America*: a report drawn up by the Knight Center for Journalism at the University of Texas at Austin identifies the region's primary pay walls as those being operated by *Reforma* in Mexico, *Folha* in Brazil, and *Clarín* and *La Nación* in Argentina. Although all four have experienced a growth in readership in recent

months, their model has not been imitated by the region's other main newspapers (Nalvarte 2017b). The report highlights the unusual case of Chile which, despite leading internet penetration rates in Latin America, having achieved access rates to fixed and mobile connections (3G and 4G) of 97.5 for every 100 of its inhabitants (Subtel Chile 2017: 8), shows no great interest in adopting paywalls and the focus is still mainly oriented to print formats.

3.2 *Cause for Optimism*

In the light of the findings of the above reports, it can be inferred that US data have infected the entire industry with optimism, although everything points to the fact that the reasons underpinning this have more to do with politics than with the digital strategies of the news media. The Spanish newspaper *El Mundo* has the following to say:

> The air of optimism being breathed among part of the US press owes much to the widely acclaimed payment for content schemes. And what is particularly good is that this sudden boom in the number of readers prepared to pay for information – both in its printed and digital versions – has been a reaction to the attempts to manipulate public opinion perpetrated over the last few years, either via social networks, fake news or post-truth discourse. Some say that Trump has done more for the legacy of the media in this last year than the most reputable gurus have achieved in decades: The Times has almost doubled its digital subscriptions since the current US president came to power. In other words, readers want to be safe in the knowledge that their information has been corroborated and that it is critical of those in power, characteristics that have always distinguished it. And the good thing is that they have found this safety. (Lozano 2017)

The situation has stimulated other American media outlets to follow suit. This is the case of the magazine *Wired*, which since January has been working on introducing a paywall, its value proposition being that exclusive access will not exceed the value of a Spotify Premium subscription ($9.99 per month). If these objectives are met, its owner, Condé Nast, may replicate the model for all its publications before the end of 2018 (Mullin 2017).

Back in the UK, the current position of the *Financial Times* is no coincidence. For the first time in more than 130 years of history, the newspaper exceeded 900,000 paying readers, of these 700,000 are digital subscribers, corresponding, in the main, to corporate subscriptions (500,000). According to *Press Gazette* (Ponsford 2017), these figures may also have a political motivation, fueled in this case by Brexit. The paper's goal for 2018 is to exceed one million subscribers, providing a clear example of the fact that the price factor is not influential when it comes to investing in quality journalism.

For many in the news media, the "Chump Gap" is a forbidding bridge that has to be crossed over a dangerously swelling river in the middle of the jungle. Each firm must decide how to get across, should they opt for a *freemium*—a mix of free and premium content, for a *metered paywall*—payment for the news stories read, or, directly, for a *hard paywall*—all access requires payment or a free trial is available for a limited time period—. But as the leading media publishers with a pay model stress, once the decision is taken there is no going back: once you've decided to cross the river, stopping halfway across or going back to the start of the bridge could mean being dragged off by the current and thrown onto the rocks.

4 Sustainability and New Formats

Since the 1990s, and following a series of business scandals (Silverstein 2013), the generalized opinion was formed that every organization owes a duty of "responsibility". This means it must be answerable for the impacts it causes in its day-to-day running, impacts that are generated in three areas: the economic, the social and the environmental, an accounting framework known as the "triple bottom line". This is how the concept of CSR was born and, as a result, that of sustainability.

To verify the levels of CSR in each company and just how sustainable its management is, sustainability reports began to be produced. These, together with the firm's financial reports, analyze the evolution of the elements that make up the "triple bottom line" over the preceding year in terms of the firm's compliance with various standards and indicators. Thus, we saw the birth of the Global Reporting Initiative (GRI), an NGO responsible for promoting and validating sustainability reports. In addition, the regulations of the International Organization for Standardization for CSR (ISO 26000) were drawn up to provide reporting guidelines.

The latest version of the GRI, known as G4, was combined with ISO 26000 to create a unified format for verifying the level of social responsibility in companies. In this way, ISO 26000 establishes how sustainability can be defined in relation to a range of management indicators:

> Sustainable business for organizations means not only providing products and services that satisfy the customer, and doing so without jeopardizing the environment, but also operating in a socially responsible manner.
>
> Pressure to do so comes from customers, consumers, governments, associations and the public at large. At the same time, far-sighted organizational leaders recognize that lasting success must be built on credible business practices and the prevention of such activities as fraudulent accounting and labour exploitation. (ISO 2010: 5)

But how do these definitions, standards and indicators impact the news media? In other words: How does sustainability apply to the newspaper business? To answer the first question, we need to look at what the G4 and ISO 26000 reports have to say about the news media. Essentially, they define them as stakeholders; that is, as an interest group that can influence or be influenced by the activity of an organization, which means it is important that there is a process of engagement between the parties. The regulations emphasize the value of giving visibility to good actions and that the media report these good deeds.

In response to this, various companies have begun to organize "Sustainable Journalism Awards".[5] However, these are not awarded for business practices, but rather recognize the work of journalists that have written about environment friendly business initiatives, for example, reforestation programs, cutting water consumption in business operations, reducing the carbon footprint, etc.

The second question, in contrast, is somewhat more complex. A possible answer might be found in Latin America, where it is usual to speak of "sustainability factors for newspaper firms".

The Gabriel García Márquez Foundation for a New Ibero-American Journalism (FNPI) carried out a case study on the subject in Colombia, emphasizing these factors:

[5] Various Sustainable Journalism Prizes are awarded. Thompson Reuters Foundation and Barilla present the "Food Sustainability Media Award" for those who write about nutrition, the King of Spain Awards have a special section for "Environmental and Sustainable Development Journalism", and various Latin American countries give Awards for Sustainable Journalism (PESU).

> The sustainability of the media depends to a large extent on the new relationships that they forge with their audience when putting technology at their service. The challenge that journalism and the media face is thinking about how to use the information they obtain from their user web journeys to plan their narrative practices. (FNPI 2016: 9)

A definition frequently employed when explaining the concept of sustainability is that "the actions taken by a company today should not compromise its stability tomorrow". Applied to the media, this means a sustainable journalism is one that takes decisions today that allows it to confidently forecast future growth, and to achieve this it is very important that reader loyalty be cultivated.

Newsonomics argues that for this to happen a process of adaptation is first necessary, an idea that has obvious parallels with the survival of a particular species in a changing ecosystem: in line with Darwinian thinking, only the fittest news outlets will survive and retain our interest. However, as journalism is not a meritocracy, adaptability via increased quality do not necessarily go hand in hand:

> It's our new News Reality Show, in which the sharp-elbowed players—some we may like, some we may detest—use every means to win. With great frequency, someone gets kicked off the island. That's the new news world, which is no longer staid and steady. It seems no one is more than a few steps away from being pushed into the sea.
>
> Consider that we're at the beginning of this choice revolution. When we began reading news on the Internet in the mid-nineties, we were tethered to large, bulky desktop computers. We went to the only available digital reading source. Now we can take all manner of reading sources with us. First, the portable laptop joined the desktop. Now, though, we've got iPhones, Kindles, Sony Readers, and this year a slew of new more-paper-like screens will emerge. (Doctor 2010: 35)

There can be no place in this model for either the 'post truth' or 'fake news'. How can a digital newspaper be considered sustainable if it has been created by a user that only cuts and pastes stories from other sites—sometimes not even from trustworthy sources—without any verification of their veracity and with the sole objective of making money? Can a model survive such as the one created by young Americans who admit to writing news items in less than 10 minutes to "take people in and to get them to read the stories"? (CfA 2017). The answer seems to lie in the hands of the digital duopoly which, as we stressed earlier, is developing different strategies so that its algorithms do not allow the dissemination of content that have not gone through prior fact checking.

4.1 Indicators and Local Business Ventures

In the FNPI report mentioned above—entitled in Spanish *Ocho claves para entender las audiencias digitales en Colombia* (that is, eight ways to understand digital audiences)—a direct link is established between sustainability and engagement. To achieve this, the empowerment of audiences as producers of content presents itself as a solution to the continuing fall in advertising revenues that the newspaper industry faces.

Put succinctly, the digital news media in some countries, as illustrated in the report by the specific case of Colombia, are experiencing a true paradigm shift. Today, reader engagement is much more important than traditional performance indicators—ratings, circulation and number of visits—which have become increasingly fragmented (FNPI 2016: 24).

The Knight Center specifically organized the '10th Ibero American Colloquium for Digital Journalism', attended by the editors of Latin American and Spanish newspapers, to analyze cases of innovation and sustainability in journalism. One of the main conclusions to be drawn was that the best technology created for sustainable journalism are people, because if they are not the protagonists of change, all efforts will be in vain (Nalvarte 2017a).

Óscar Durán Ibatá, professor and researcher at the Jorge Tadeo Lozano University in Colombia, argues that sustainability in the media cannot hold out for a multi-million dollar investment, like Jeff Bezos's financial injection in the *Washington Post*, rather it requires the development of local initiatives. "The way things are, it would be a good idea to start creating our own media. Stop complaining about the good or bad that the media do, and propose something ... perhaps the answer lies in our own hands, in our own talent. It is about fully committing to the quality of information and content" (Durán Ibatá 2017).

However, local journalism is not synonymous with small-scale journalism. *Newsonomics* explains how the web has forced us to redefine and reinvent journalism of this kind because it is no longer limited simply to a single city or community. Technology allows us to expand our reach, yet at the same time it allows us to be as local as we want.

> Local's gotten all mixed up on the Web, though. We can see two big reasons for that.
>
> The first is that the Web lets us define "local" any way we want. It's like the city is one big Google map, with those plus and minus zooms. Care about your block, neighborhood, zip? You can zero in there, courtesy of technology brought to you by aggregators like Topix, Outside In, and even Google itself. Or maybe you do care about the city itself. Or the region. Follow your mouse and take in as much or as little of the city as you wish. News, entertainment listings, family events, parks, and more.
>
> The second is that the Internet has forced local media companies to redefine themselves. We no longer need those local editors to select stories and package news of the nonlocal world. (Doctor 2010: 40)

It seems, therefore, that the best way to identify indicators of sustainability in journalism is to study the key trends and measures being adopted by initiatives in local media outlets. Such ventures demonstrate greater flexibility and, above all, seem better able to adapt to the scenarios that are likely to emerge in the future, such as the recent modifications to the Facebook algorithm which should ensure them better results in 2018. Below we summarize three reports that make recommendations in this direction:

- *Small-market newspapers in the digital age*: this Tow Center report analyzes the way local newspapers are adapting to emerging trends. It highlights their audacity, ability to engage and to offer unique content of value for their communities. However, the report stresses that the sector needs to tell its own story better to its peers. Despite the unpredictability of its future, the authors argue that local journalism has recourse to many more tools of survival and sustainability than imagined (Ali and Radcliffe 2017).
- *8 Key Trends in Local Journalism*: Damian Radcliffe, professor at the University of Oregon and co-author of the previous report, explores how ten local news outlets in the US are responding to current challenges. Doubling down on local content, making a greater commitment to audiences, changing the business model, operating smaller and more visually oriented newsrooms, adopting multiple ways to increase income, promoting online and offline engagement, introducing greater diversity in staffing, and cultivating the local focus as a vanguard for the wider profession are the eight key ideas to emerge from his study (Radcliffe 2017).

- *5 keys to success for entrepreneurial journalists*: this report, prepared by SembraMedia for IJNet and based on a study of cases in Latin America and Spain, identifies five common keys to success: diversifying income sources, creating communities, diversifying media teams, ensuring journalists learn to tell their own stories so people contribute to their digital projects, and providing quality original content (Warner and Iastrebner 2017).

What would happen if we removed the labels "local" and "entrepreneurship" from the recommendations reported? We would probably find that each of the key trends is readily applicable to all types of news media, as we shall see in the case study dedicated to *The New York Times* in the following pages. Just as local journalism is not alone in having to win its readers' loyalty, innovative startups are not alone in having to create diverse media that can respond to the challenges of new technologies.

In short what we find is a series of paths towards sustainable management that are common for the entire newspaper industry, which means that the "triple bottom line" can be rewritten as follows:

1. *Finances*: the more diverse the income sources, the greater the possibilities of growth.
2. *Content*: focus on originality, quality and adaptability to each channel of dissemination, including new formats that create a sensation of exclusivity, such as interactive productions, visual journalism and immersive journalism.
3. *Audience*: broadening its reach is just the first step, the key lies in boosting 'engagement', increasing the loyalty of audiences and subscribers and promoting instances of co-creation.

4.2 *Examples: Latin America and Norway*

The good omens that allow us to talk about sustainability in Latin America include growth projections in mobile data traffic in the region of 600% for the period 2016–2021, which would be equivalent to a total of 728 million connected devices (Reuters 2017). Currently, 88% of social network users on the continent connect to them at least once a day (Tendencias Digitales 2016).

In parallel with this, Latin American news media appear to have achieved certain levels of maturity. According to the study 'Inflection

Point' conducted by SembraMedia, analyzing the sustainability of journalism in the region, four categories of digital news media can be identified according to their total revenues: 32% are classed as 'startups & stagnants' (between US$100 and $19,999), 23% as 'struggling & steady' (between US$20,000 and $99,999), 17% as 'steadfast and striving' (between US$100,000 and $499,999), and 12% as 'stars and standouts' (US$ 500,000 or more) (SembraMedia 2017).

These specific circumstances have allowed the development of various examples of innovation and new formats on the continent, as recorded in the report *Innovative Journalism in Latin America*:

- *Social Media Live Streaming*: reporting via Periscope and Facebook Live has allowed *Efecto Cocuyo* in Venezuela, *Cadena 3* in Argentina, and *El Financiero* in Mexico to grow their audiences.
- *Mixed reality*: immersive and virtual reality video productions as used by *Diario Financiero* in Chile, *Todo Noticias* in Argentina, and *TV Globo* in Brazil.
- *Infographics*: as used by *Pictoline* in Mexico to tell stories through illustrations.
- *Short videos*: strategies for attracting millennials, as practiced by *Upsocl* in Chile; *Sopitas* y *Click Necesario* in Mexico; *Remezcla* in the USA, and *Muy Liebre* in Argentina.
- *Data journalism*: as used by *La Nación* in Argentina, the region's powerhouse in this use of technology.
- *Fact checking*: as practiced by *Colombia Check, Chequeado* in Argentina, *ChecaDatosMx* and *El Sabueso* in México, and *Agência Lupa, Aos Fatos* and *Agência Pública* in Brazil in verifying public discourse and revealing false news (Knight Center 2017: 1–72).

As mentioned above under "Pay-for-news models", according to the *Digital News Report*, Norway leads the way in terms of boasting the highest percentage of subscribers to its newspapers: while 15% of readers of online news formats have an annual subscription, a further 11% acknowledge having used other payment methods to access journalistic information. The country's publishers recognize that the key to success lies in content for mobile devices.

Torry Pedersen was the CEO of *Verdens Gang*, the most widely read paper in the country. His success led to him being named 'editor-in-chief of the year' and to his accepting a greater challenge: appointment as Head of Publications at Schibsted Media, the parent company of one of the most profitable newspapers in Europe. For him, the key lies in the maxim 'mobile first': telling the stories (in the case below, of an escaped narcotics dealer enjoying some fine dining), organizing the newsroom in an integrated and attractive way via rapid navigation that includes videos in vertical format that are no more than a minute long:

> Different media are catering to different aspects of these elements with their output. At the time when the drug smuggler enjoyed his duck's breast there was no such thing as the digital motorway. No one carried a smartphone in their pocket and no one had been given the tools to bring the conversation into the public domain through social media. Digitalization has now made information limitless both geographically and in volume. Does this put new demands on how journalism is presented in order to keep its punch? I for one think that the answer is a resounding YES.
>
> But the increasingly frequent technological shifts mean we are facing huge challenges. In a media landscape where we have moved from a scarcity of information to being burdened by the glut of it, journalism can be sorted into three categories: continuous, context and depth. (Pedersen 2017)

In short, while those working in Latin America recognize that the sector's innovation experiences have not yet been sufficiently exploited, it is clear that the greater reach and visibility achieved from becoming more sustainable can generate new sources of income. In the case of Norway, the healthy outlook it shares with the other Nordic countries suggests it exploits the benefits of what might be considered a niche market. After all, in a country of just 5 million inhabitants, the monthly traffic of *Verdens Gang* reaches half that figure. This means, the results of the main newspapers in some countries are comparable to the figures obtained by local media outlets in others, if, that is, we take into consideration the number of inhabitants to which these media are directed. Once again, the need to 'redefine what is local' becomes more than apparent.

5 *The New York Times* Case: A Moving Audience

At the beginning of this decade, *Newsonomics* made the claim that the major new media companies had entered a phase of globalization, and that only the fittest would survive. And who were these companies? The list—made up primarily of US media—included such newspapers as *The New York Times*, *The Wall Street Journal*, *USA Today* and *The Washington Post*; various open TV channels, including *NBC*, *ABC* and *CBS*; a number of pay channels like *CNN* and *Fox News*; some new agencies, such as *The Associated Press*; radio stations, most notably *National Public Radio*; and, specialized media companies like *Bloomberg*.

The list also included a number of UK-based firms: *Financial Times*, *The Guardian* and *The Telegraph*; *BBC* Television; and agencies like *Reuters*. Together they formed the so-called "Digital Dozen". Sure, the list holds more than twelve names, but it was forecast that with mergers and collaborations the group would gradually be reduced to no more than a dozen. Only these companies were considered capable of competing in the new scenario faced by the media, centered on multiplatform (press, TV, radio, web) and cross promotion between the different media (Doctor 2010: 48–60).

Beyond these predictions, eight years on we can see that each of these media firms has maintained their dominance almost unaffected. Some have even expanded their borders: the local quickly became global. Christian Leal, of *Bío-Bío* radio, attributed, in part, the fall in visits that the Chilean digital news media industry suffered in 2017 to the 'foreign invasion' headed by the Spanish editions of *BBC Mundo* and *The New York Times*, as well as *The Huffington Post*, the Russian agency *RT*, and the Latin American edition of the Spanish newspaper *El País* (Leal 2017).

That *The New York Times*—a.k.a. the NYT—should top this list is no coincidence. The paper is typically held up as the model to follow not only by *Newsonomics*, but by the world's journalism industry in general. Ken Doctor interviewed Mark Thompson, NYT's CEO, who explained that one of the keys to its success is responding to the continuous movement that results in their digital reorganization every 18 months:

> We are constantly course-correcting, adjusting as we make progress. A new opportunity and a new shape becomes possible, and we move to the new one. This won't be the end of it: Everything is moving, our audience is moving, technology is moving, and we are working hard to make sure the organization is moving too. (Thompson 2017)

The NYT has been present on the web since 1996 and, according to its projections, in the most negative of scenarios, its print edition will survive for at least another ten years. One of the main changes it implemented was to transform the Newspaper Distribution Area into an avantgarde Digital Marketing Department under the umbrella of a unique strategy that combines audience, product, advertising and subscriptions.

These changes included a generational switch in the post of the newspaper's publisher: on January 1, 2018 Arthur Gregg Sulzberger replaced his father Arthur Ochs Sulzberger Jr., who had held the position since 1992, maintaining a family tradition dating back to 1896, when the Ochs Sulzberger bought the company.

But this has not been the only change at NYT. Mexican millionaire, Carlos Slim, the newspaper's leading individual shareholder, announced at the end of 2017 that he was selling more than half his stake in the company, valued at, US$250 million, but would retain an 8% holding.[6] The specialized press reported that the arrival of Slim in 2008 occurred at a time when the NYT found itself immersed in the subprime crisis, facing a fall in its advertising revenue, and a sharp decline in its print subscriptions. Although he increased his percentage holding in 2015, the entrepreneur never actually sat on the executive board and stayed out of all strategic decisions.

In short, in the light of the $64.6 million profit posted by the NYT between January and September 2017, it could be said that Slim's decision has more to do with taking advantage of the business's profitability than with any strategic considerations (Davis 2017).

5.1 *Reinventing Itself*

Can we, therefore, conclude that the constant adjustments made by *The New York Times* reflect a prior process of reinvention? This is the claim made by Ismael Nafría, digital news media consultant and author of the book 'The reinvention of The New York Times', and founder of the monthly newsletter "Boletin Tendencia@s," which analyzes the main changes in the newspaper's editorial line. His analysis identifies the ten lessons to be learned from NYT's digital reinvention:

- Unwavering commitment to quality journalism and to offering users a product they cannot do without
- A constantly changing business model: aware that users contribute more than advertisers

[6] On going to press, the percentage stake being put up for sale had not been confirmed.

- Placing main focus, on users, especially the paper's most loyal readers
- A very clearly defined vision, mission and value proposition
- Staff teams fully adapted to the digital and mobile era
- The future—and the present—lie with the mobile
- Journalism is becoming increasingly visual
- The road to digital transformation is long and full of challenges
- The print newspaper has to be constantly rethought
- All departments must work in close collaboration. (Nafría 2017a: 1)

Each of these lessons are drawn from more than 20 years of operating in digital environments as identified in the analysis of multiple internal documents produced in that period. The Catalan journalist explained in an interview how these experiences can serve as a point of reference for the world's media:

> *The New York Times* is a newspaper that believes in and is fully committed to quality journalism, it is a newspaper that understood that the business model had undergone a radical change, it is a newspaper with faith in what it does, it is a newspaper that knows what its mission is and most importantly of all: it is not afraid of change and of having to adapt.
>
> In one way or another, every newspaper has the potential to be the New York Times of its part of the world or of its subject specialization, for me this means being a point of reference…something which its readers cannot live without, a newspaper that commits itself heart and soul to quality. The case of the NYT shows us that the commitment to quality and being able to adapt without fear to the digital and mobile environment have their reward. The courage the newspaper has shown in facing up to the digital challenge, a path that is full of obstacles, is truly admirable. (Nafría 2017b)

A good example of this process are the latest set of guidelines for its newsroom on how to use social networks, published in October 2017. They stress the importance of their journalists not expressing partisan opinions on personal platforms that might undercut the paper's reputation, and of responding thoughtfully to criticisms of their work, bearing in mind that however private a social site may be everything posted there will be associated with the NYT. They also recommend that journalists be as transparent as possible if they have posted something in error and subsequently deleted it, and that they inform the privacy protection area immediately if they feel threatened by trolls (*The New York Times*, 2017).

The key to this reinvention can be summarized quite simply as 'understanding the language of each digital environment': Each update, each new function, each algorithm change and each new technology require rethinking the way content is distributed. This is the key to responding to constant change.

5.2 *Paths to Take*

Mark Thompson claims that the real challenge facing the NYT, and the newspaper industry in general, is "to find customers willing to pay for products that already exist". However, they would seem to be facing up to this challenge successfully after announcing that digital subscribers have reached around 2.5–2.1 million paying for digital access, 300,000 for its crossword site, and 30,000 for its cooking site—to which we can add the million readers of the print edition, which means that 60% of its income comes from its readers/subscribers/customers, an ideal balance for today's newspapers (Lozano 2017).

Chartbeat is a company analyzing the content of 50,000 leading media sites around the globe. Each year end, it identifies the stories that generated most engagement, based on total active reading time per user, and in that top 10, half the articles were published by the NYT. All of them highlight the themes that resonated with readers everywhere in 2017 (Chartbeat 2017):

- *Multiple Weapons Found in Las Vegas Gunman's Hotel Room (3rd place)*: an article summarizing events surrounding the Las Vegas shooting perpetrated by Stephen Paddock on October 1, 2017. The article includes videos, infographics, Google Maps satellite images and prominent social media publications.
- *Harvey Weinstein Paid Off Sexual Harassment Accusers for Decades (7th place)*: report condemning behavior of world-renowned US producer including testimonies of alleged victims of sexual harassment published on October 5, 2017. The article includes updates on reactions to the story, a link to Harvey Weinstein's statement in response to allegations, and a news podcast.
- *You May Want to Marry My Husband (8th place)*: letter published by the writer Amy Krouse Rosenthal, who upon learning that she

had only a few days to live wrote in praise of her husband's virtues, so that he might find someone to share his life with after she had gone. The 'dating profile' was published on March 4, 2017, with versions in Chinese and Spanish. The author died just nine days later.

- *Pictures From Women's Marches on Every Continent (9th place)*: on January 21 and 22, the 2017 Women's March was celebrated. Although the main demonstration was organized in Washington to denounce Donald Trump's sexist discourse, a total of 673 marches were held in 55 countries. The next day, a special graphic was made showing the highlights of each event, 360° videos and an interactive map.
- *The Lost Children of Tuam (10th place)*: report on the disappearance of almost 800 children from an orphanage in Ireland. It was published on October 28, 2017 and included several current images and videos, but all specially treated to be seen in black and white.

The FNPI has also carried out an analysis of the keys to the success of the Spanish version of the NYT. The report highlights the special emphasis given to health journalism, something that is reflected in the newsletter published for the paper's subscribers. Each issue of this newsletter includes the week's five most engaging news items and at least two of these tend to be related to health. Yet, paradoxically, unlike the English version, the Spanish edition does not have a specific health section.

Why has the 'Gray Lady' of journalism undertaken to provide this content for its Spanish-speaking readers? Here, we identify five common characteristics that make these articles dealing with health of such interest to these readers:

- *Local themes of global interest*: pets, food and obesity are the topics typically addressed. Although the focus might be on local problems, comparative graphics for the rest of the world are included to offer a broader context.
- *A minimum of three sources*: with the exception of opinion articles, it is usual that each article contains the views of experts, a variety of testimonies and official sources.
- *Room for the reporter to show their human side*: journalists are given room to write opinion pieces in which they can communicate their own ideas using their own personal style.

- *Do not accept everything unquestioningly*: articles question everything from popular beliefs, the paper's own previous articles, and, especially, scientific studies.
- *Busting myths*: investigating questions we have all asked from time to time and responding to them in a highly readable way. For example, does air conditioning cause nasal congestion? Can you be fat and healthy? Or how much sugar is there in a glass of wine? (FNPI, n.d.)

One of the main lessons to be learnt from the NYT's multimedia news agenda is that it never loses the ability to amaze—engaging with its readers is just one more path that journalism can take to achieve this much sought after sustainable management.

6 Conclusions and Future Challenges

We have examined a series of cases, as illustrated and described in a variety of reports and studies, that seek to relate new business models with emerging news formats, including different interactive platforms and immersive journalism. Here, with the exception of a few media companies—like *The New York Times* with its almost uniquely successful experience in obtaining subscriptions for its digital version—the majority are experimenting with a wide range of exploratory situations and models. Some of the main options involve exploring the use of the new formats that we have described and which are dealt with in other chapters of this book. This is the case of interactive video streaming, new forms of virtual reality and augmented reality, developed to increase audiences and to attract young audiences, and with them better advertising revenues, and new subscription methods, implemented to strengthen reader loyalty.

In short, news media companies (including publicly owned enterprises) should be concerned that investment in these new formats is sustainable, either because it increases their audiences and advertising revenue, or because it provides readers with exclusive content, thus boosting subscription numbers and reducing the subscriber abandonment rate. These new formats have been responsible for what are truly spectacular projects. A good case in point is provided by the multimedia documentaries being produced by various companies, for example, *The New York Times*' 'Snow Fall' report (Freixa et al. 2014).

Finally, it seems clear that adopting innovative and exploratory initiatives like those being taken by the best and most creative news media companies—as we have shown throughout this chapter—is the only way forward to preserve the social communication industry. Indeed, only in this way can we hope to safeguard the independence of the media and the vital function they fulfill in our democratic societies.

References

Ali, C., and D. Radcliffe. 2017. *Small-Market Newspapers in the Digital Age*. New York: Tow Center for Digital Journalism. Retrieved from https://www.cjr.org/tow_center_reports/local-small-market-newspapers-study.php.

ANP Chile. 2017, December 20. *2018, el año de los medios digitales independientes*. Retrieved from Asociación Nacional de la Prensa: http://anp.cl/noticias/nota-1/.

BBC News. 2017, November 2. *What is 2017's Word of the Year?* Retrieved from http://www.bbc.com/news/uk-41838386.

Bilton, R. 2017, December 13. *"The Media is in Crisis": Jonah Peretti Lays Out His Vision for a More Diversified BuzzFeed*. Retrieved from Nieman Lab: http://www.niemanlab.org/2017/12/the-media-is-in-crisis-jonah-peretti-lays-out-his-vision-for-a-more-diversified-buzzfeed/.

CfA. 2017. *How Google Makes Millions Off of Fake News*. Washington, DC: Campaign for Accountability.

Chartbeat. 2017. *2017 Top Stories*. Retrieved December 31, 2017, from http://2017.chartbeat.com/stories.

Chinula, M. 2017, June 19. *7 Business Models That Could Save the Future of Journalism*. Retrieved from IJNet: https://ijnet.org/en/blog/7-business-models-could-save-future-journalism.

Davis, M. 2017, December 19. *Carlos Slim Plans to Slash New York Times Holdings*. Retrieved from https://www.bloomberg.com/news/articles/2017-12-19/biggest-new-york-times-investor-slim-hatches-deal-to-slash-stake.

Doctor, K. 2010. *Newsonomics: Twelve New Trends That Will Shape the News You Get*. New York: St. Martin Press.

Dojcinovic, S. 2017, November 15. *Hey, Mark Zuckerberg: My Democracy Isn't Your Laboratory*. Retrieved from *The New York Times*: https://www.nytimes.com/2017/11/15/opinion/serbia-facebook-explore-feed.html.

Durán Ibatá, Ó. 2017, July 31. *Dejemos de quejarnos, armemos nuestros propios medios*. Retrieved from *Puroperiodismo*: http://www.puroperiodismo.cl/?p=28314.

Engel Bronosky, M., and J. Maurício de Carvalho (eds.). 2014. *Jornalismo e convergência*. São Paulo: Cultura Acadêmica.

Fletcher, R. 2017. *Paying for News*. Retrieved December 31, 2017, from Digital News Report: http://www.digitalnewsreport.org/survey/2017/paying-for-news-2017/.

FNPI. 2016. *Ocho claves para entender las audiencias digitales en Colombia*. Bogotá: Fundación Gabriel García Márquez para el Nuevo Periodismo Iberoamericano.

FNPI. n.d. *Periodismo de salud, contenido clave en el NY Times en español*. Retrieved December 30, 2017, from Fundación Gabriel García Márquez para el Nuevo Periodismo Iberoamericano: http://www.fnpi.org/es/blog/periodismosalud/periodismo-de-salud-contenido-clave-en-el-ny-times-en-espanol.

Folha. 2018, February 9. *Facebook Says It Wants 'High Quality' News*. Retrieved from http://www1.folha.uol.com.br/internacional/en/brazil/2018/02/1956092-facebook-says-it-wants-high-quality-news.shtml.

Freixa, P., J. Soler-Adillon, C. Sora, and J. Ribas. 2014. Snow Fall and A Short History of the Highrise: Two Approaches to Interactive Communication Design by *The New York Times*. *Textual & Visual Media* 7: 63–84.

Gottfried, J., and E. Shearer. 2017, September 7. *Americans' Online News Use is Closing in on TV News Use*. Retrieved from Pew Research Center: http://www.pewresearch.org/fact-tank/2017/09/07/americans-online-news-use-vs-tv-news-use/.

Hansen, E., and E. Goligoski. 2018. *Guide to Audience Revenue and Engagement*. New York: Tow Center for Digital Journalism.

Hardiman, A., and C. Brown. 2018, January 28. *News Feed FYI: More Local News on Facebook*. Retrieved from Facebook Newsroom: https://newsroom.fb.com/news/2018/01/news-feed-fyi-local-news/.

He, X., and R. Pedraza-Jiménez. 2015. Chinese Social Media Strategies: Communication Key Features from a Business Perspective. *El Profesional de la Información* 24 (2): 200–209.

Independent Journal Review. n.d. *Audience Growth Director*. Retrieved May 30, 2017, from Media Group of America: http://ijr.applytojob.com/apply/nQho2HRY6h/Audience-Growth-Director.

ISO. 2010. *ISO 26000 project overview*. Geneva: International Organization for Standardization.

Kafka, P., and R. Molla. 2017, December 4. *2017 Was the Year Digital Ad Spending Finally Beat TV*. Retrieved from *Recode*: https://www.recode.net/2017/12/4/16733460/2017-digital-ad-spend-advertising-beat-tv.

Kamarck, E., and A. Gabriele. 2015. The News Today: 7 Trends in Old and New. *Center of Effective Public Management of Brookings*, 11.

Kleis Nielsen, R. 2016. The Business of News. In *The SAGE Handbook of Digital Journalism*, ed. T. Witschge, C.W. Anderson, D. Domingo, and A. Hemida, 51–67. London: Sage.

Knight Center. 2017. *Innovative Journalism in Latin America*. Texas: Open Society Foundations. Retrieved from https://knightcenter.utexas.edu/books/IJENGLISH1.pdf.

Leal, C. 2017, December 29. *Medios digitales 2017 en Chile: ¿el año en que tocamos techo?* Retrieved from *Puroperiodismo*: http://www.puroperiodismo.cl/?p=28718.

Lozano, V. 2017, November 7. *3,5 millones de lectores del 'Times'*. Retrieved from *El Mundo*: http://www.elmundo.es/opinion/2017/11/07/5a00aca822601dd0228b4596.html.

Mente Emprendedora. 2015, January 26. *ME56: Greg Barton – BNAméricas: Líder en Información de Negocios en America Latina*. Retrieved from http://menteemprendedora.com/greg-barton.

Mullin, B. 2017, November 29. *Paywall Will Be Wired's 'Hedge Against the Future'*. Retrieved from *The Wall Street Journal*: https://www.wsj.com/articles/paywall-will-be-wireds-hedge-against-the-future-1511956800.

Nafría, I. 2017a. *La reinvención de The New York Times*. Createspace Independent Publishing Platform.

Nafría, I. 2017b, November 6. Ismael Nafría: "Cada medio puede ser, en cierta medida, el New York Times". *Distintas Latitudes* (F. Luján, Interviewer). Retrieved from Distintas Latitudes: https://distintaslatitudes.net/ismael-nafria-cada-medio-puede-ser-el-new-york-times.

Nalvarte, P. 2017a, April 27. *Latin American and Spanish News Sites Experiment to Reach Audience and Finance Quality Journalism*. Retrieved from Knight Center for Journalism in the Americas: https://knightcenter.utexas.edu/blog/00-18319-latin-american-and-spanish-news-sites-experiment-reach-audience-and-finance-quality-jo.

Nalvarte, P. 2017b, November 15. *Paywalls in Latin America: A Special Report from the Knight Center on Digital Subscriptions in the Region's Newspapers*. Retrieved from Knight Center for Journalism in the Americas: https://knightcenter.utexas.edu/blog/00-19010-paywalls-latin-america-special-report-knight-center-digital-subscriptions-regions-news.

Newman, N. 2018. *Digital News Project 2018*. University of Oxford. London: Reuters Institute. Retrieved from https://reutersinstitute.politics.ox.ac.uk/sites/default/files/2018-01/Journalism%2C%20Media%20and%20Technology%20Trends%20and%20Predictions%202018%20Newman.pdf.

Nieman Journalism Lab. 2017, June 9. *Newsonomics: CEO Mark Thompson Thinks The New York Times Can "Aspire to a Different Order of Magnitude"*. Retrieved from http://www.niemanlab.org/2017/06/newsonomics-ceo-mark-thompson-thinks-the-new-york-times-can-aspire-to-a-different-order-of-magnitude/?relatedstory.

Pedersen, T. 2017, December 13. *Fill It with Facts*. Retrieved from *WAN-IFRA*: https://blog.wan-ifra.org/2017/12/13/fill-it-with-facts.

Pedraza-Jiménez, R., L. Codina, and J. Guallar (eds.). 2016. *Calidad en sitios web. Método de análisis general, e-commerce, imágenes, hemerotecas y turismo*. Barcelona: Colección EPI Scholar. Editorial UOC.

Pellicer, M. 2017, May 18. *Modelos de pago en los medios europeos*. Retrieved from https://miquelpellicer.com/2017/05/modelos-pago-los-medios-europeos/.

Ponsford, D. 2017, November 21. *Financial Times Surpasses 700,000 Digital Subscribers and Boasts Highest Readership in 130-Year History*. Retrieved from *Press Gazette*: http://www.pressgazette.co.uk/financial-times-surpasses-700000-digital-subscribers-and-boasts-highest-readership-in-130-year-history/.

Radcliffe, D. 2017, October 18. *8 Key Trends in Local Journalism*. Retrieved from MediaShift: http://mediashift.org/2017/10/8-key-trends-local-journalism/.

Reuters. 2017, June 14. *Tráfico datos móviles A.Latina se disparará al 2021 por mayor uso smartphones y video: Cisco*. Retrieved from https://lta.reuters.com/article/internetNews/idLTAKBN1952QM-OUSLI.

Reuters Institute. 2017. *Digital News Report 2017*. London: University of Oxford.

Rutemberg, J. 2017, July 9. *News Outlets to Seek Bargaining Rights Against Google and Facebook*. Retrieved from *The New York Times*: https://www.nytimes.com/2017/07/09/business/media/google-facebook-news-media-alliance.html?ref=nyt-es&mcid=nyt-es&subid=article.

Sanabre Vives, C. 2015. A Model for Website Analysis and Conception: The Website Canvas Model Applied to Eldiario.es. *Hipertext.net* 13: 1–19.

Sehl, A., A. Cornia, R. Kleis Nielsen, and F. Simon. 2017. *Pay Models in European News*. Oxford: Reuters Institute. Retrieved from http://www.digitalnewsreport.org/publications/2017/pay-models-european-news/?utm_source=API+Need+to+Know+newsletter&utm_campaign=77ea87d438-EMAIL_CAMPAIGN_2017_05_18&utm_medium=email&utm_term=0_e3bf78af04-77ea87d438-45825977#the-sample.

SembraMedia. 2017. *Inflection Point*. California: Omidyar Network.

Shearer, E., and Gottfried, J. 2017. *News Use Across Social Media Platforms*. Washington, DC: Pew Research Center.

Silverstein, K. 2013, May 14. *Enron, Ethics And Today's Corporate Values*. Retrieved from *Forbes*: https://www.forbes.com/sites/kensilverstein/2013/05/14/enron-ethics-and-todays-corporate-values.

Stulberg, A. 2017, September 22. *In Paywall Age, Free Content Remains King for Newspaper Sites*. Retrieved from *Columbia Journalism Review*: https://www.cjr.org/business_of_news/newspaper-paywalls.php.

Subtel Chile. 2017, July 31. *Sector Telecomunicaciones Tercer Trimestre*. Santiago de Chile: Ministerio de Transportes y Telecomunicaciones. Retrieved from http://www.subtel.gob.cl/wp-content/uploads/2018/01/PPT_Series_SEPTIEMBRE_2017_V1.pdf.

Tendencias Digitales. 2016. *Usos de Internet en Latinoamérica*. Caracas: Tendencias Digitales & Mercantil.

The New York Times. 2017, October 13. *The Times Issues Social Media Guidelines for the Newsroom*. Retrieved from https://www.nytimes.com/2017/10/13/reader-center/social-media-guidelines.html.

Thompson, M. 2017, June 9. Newsonomics: CEO Mark Thompson Thinks *The New York Times* Can "Aspire to a Different Order of Magnitude". *Nieman Lab* (K. Doctor, Interviewer). Retrieved from http://www.niemanlab.org/2017/06/newsonomics-ceo-mark-thompson-thinks-the-new-york-times-can-aspire-to-a-different-order-of-magnitude/.

Warner, J., and M. Iastrebner. 2017, January 12. *5 Keys to Success for Entrepreneurial Journalists*. Retrieved from IJNet: https://ijnet.org/en/blog/5-keys-success-entrepreneurial-journalists.

Zuckerberg, M. 2018, January 12. *One of Our Big Focus Areas for 2018 is Making…* Retrieved from Facebook: https://www.facebook.com/zuck/posts/10104413015393571.

CHAPTER 7

Authors' Rights and the Media

Javier Díaz-Noci

1 Introduction

New journalistic narratives, characterized by a clear trend towards the use of multimedia and transmedia strategies, are posing a number of additional problems to the legal field of intellectual property and copyright, which is already subject to many different pressures. Clearly, the greatest challenge faced by intellectual property is the equitable regulation of users' rights, both as regards access to culture and in terms of the impact on their status as authors of intellectual works or transformers of derivative works. Active users, who no longer limit themselves to being mere passive consumers or, at most, disseminators of intellectual works, have seen their creative possibilities multiply, and today demand that their place in the world of creation and intellectual property be recognized. And here one particular term has acquired great significance: innovation.

User interaction and the creation of derivative works, some of unprecedented levels of innovation, need to be legally regulated. In parallel with this, intellectual property needs to protect another aspect of user interests; indeed, since the birth of copyright law the spirit of the law has

J. Díaz-Noci (✉)
Department of Communication, Pompeu Fabra University, Barcelona, Spain
e-mail: javier.diaz@upf.edu

M. Pérez-Montoro (ed.), *Interaction in Digital News Media*,
https://doi.org/10.1007/978-3-319-96253-5_7

allegedly been both to protect authors and to ensure a general and fair access to knowledge.

Storytelling has evolved immeasurably throughout history, but it has taken a qualitative leap in recent decades with the popularization of digital tools, which allow much greater flexibility in the creation of copyright works. All parties involved in the creation and distribution of complex intellectual works, especially those characterized by interactivity and described in detail in the preceding chapters, are engaged in a struggle to defend their interests. Another problem posed by the tension between the necessary legal harmonization of copyright laws and the legal fragmentation imposed by national sovereignty is the way in which the European Union faces the pressure exerted by each agent involved in intellectual creation, and more specifically by the media industry. This gives rise to the need to reconcile the legitimate interests of authors (generally workers, both salaried and freelancers), media owners (especially, in the declining press industry) and active users. For instance in March 2018, the Committee of Ministers approved recommendations in which they recognize that "Intermediary services may also be offered by traditional media, for instance, when space for user-generated content is offered on their platforms".[1]

Naturally, this period of legal change is equally a response to the way in which the News Media have begun to renew their business models, as we have seen in Chapter 6. This overhaul of the economics of the media cannot be understood without an exhaustive examination of related legal aspects.

The collective work, comprising individual contributions gathered together under the initiative and coordination of a corporate entity, is probably the most significant of these and it remains one of the cornerstones of media protection. We analyze this particular legal category as well, both when we address calls from the media (or more specifically, the newspaper) industry for the European Union to enact a so-called *press publishers' right*; and, when we consider the intellectual property rights on user-generated content (specifically those published by the media).

[1] *Recommendation CM/Rec(2018)2 of the Committee of Ministers to member States Adopted by the Committee of Ministers on 7 March 2018 at the 1309 meeting of the Ministers' Deputies on the roles and responsibilities of internet intermediaries.* See also *Recommendation CM/Rec(2018)1[1] of the Committee of Ministers to member States on media pluralism and transparency of media ownership*, adopted at the same meeting.

2 A Legal Branch in Tension

The ever-changing realities of media contents throughout the history of communication—dating back over some four centuries—have obliged copyright and intellectual property laws to adapt constantly to rapid technical, economic and social changes. Our times are no different in this respect: together with the adoption of the World Wide Web in a mobile environment (Díaz Noci 2017), we live in an era of information abundance, in which the legislative powers are forced to respond to these necessities and to address the interests of authors, right holders and (even) active users. Copyright seeks to strike the right balance between many different forces. Although in the Civil Law tradition the term *property* is preferred, in practice, it has little to do with *real property*, that is, ownership of material assets. The rights for intellectual creations are not of this type.

Various new legal figures are involved. The joint work is probably the legal category that best applies to the works studied in the previous chapters, especially works of multimedia that exploit information visualization and interaction. Yet, the derivative work needs to be more carefully regulated insofar as interactive tools mean earlier works can be readily transformed. In spite of legal doctrine in favor of the general implementation of 'fair use' or 'fair dealing', the solution of a limited set of exceptions to intellectual rights is to be imposed in Continental Europe. This will create a landscape in which the different actors involved in the process of producing and disseminating news have to reorient their strategies. These include media companies, whose lobbying activity seeks to enact new intellectual property rights to help them face the challenges of the digital world; journalists, whose role as authors is endangered by the global crisis journalism currently finds itself in; and active audiences, whose claims for the recognition of their authors' rights seem about to achieve some limited success, as it happened in Canada, the first country to enact such a right. User-generated content, when it is not fully authored by that user, must be of non-commercial use, otherwise the law usually blocks the legality of the derivative work, unless permission is sought and granted by the copyright holder or 'fair use' has been observed.

The concept of collective work, which served its purpose in the analogue world (especially that of the printing press) is under threat in the digital world, undermined by many factors and agents that have emerged with the rise of the World Wide Web and the triumph of globalization.

The tension that exists when seeking to balance the right of access to culture, the right to earn a living creating intellectual works and the right of individuals and corporations to obtain a return on their investment in expensive, complex production structures has underpinned copyright law. This is arguably one of the most sensitive issues when dealing with the copyright on news reporting: how to share the rights and benefits between the producer of the collective work (a corporate or legal entity) and the individual author of each work published in it. This is the question that we address throughout this chapter, i.e. whether copyright law needs to be reformed and, if so, which direction these reforms need to take, with specific reference to news reporting, a social activity in perpetual movement and immersed in a crisis of values and professionalization.

Here we are dealing with a new doctrinal category of rights, in line with Lionel Bently's definition of this phenomenon as the shift *from property rights to the rights to remuneration* (Bently 1994: 982). Remuneration is the key concept if we accept that convergence is unavoidable in news production and dissemination these days. The aggregation and syndication of content, the possibilities of which are multiplied by digital technology, is another reason that might account for this movement from media companies lobbying to facilitate the management of all intellectual works created under their orders. Bently has accurately defined this, since "entrepreneurial works are now of greater economic importance than traditional authorial works", to the extent that, as we shall see in the next section, media companies, especially the European newspaper industry, are enjoying a degree of success in their lobbying activity. All this could explain the interest shown by the industry to present a change in the profile of journalists as a reality, given the new tasks imposed on them by digital technology—including, multimedia, search engine organization,[2] curation of contents, and the management of social networks.

Assignees do not *possess* intellectually created works as they have to be returned to the public domain once the rights on these goods expire,

[2]Nordermann (2018), on discussing the Decision of the German Bundesgerichtshof of September 11, 2017, file number I ZR 11716: "For search engines, more generous duties apply than for ordinary linkers. This is due to recognition of the role of search engines for the fundamental rights of internet users. Search engines need to be aware of a right infringement before they have a duty to act".

some years after the author's death. It is generally accepted that this time limitation is 70 years *post mortem auctoris*, in order to protect the authors' and their heirs' right to enjoy the fruits of these works. Such a period of years might be deemed excessive for certain kinds of perishable, or even ephemeral, intellectual goods, including news, and would appear to need revision. Companies, however, could be trying to avoid this limitation by digitizing their archives and offering them to the public, even on a fee-paying basis. Thus, there is the possibility of creating anthologies by using search engines of intellectual works—for instance, news, drawings, and photographs created more than 70 years after the author's death—whose exploitation rights have expired and in the hope of being able to monetize them in a near future. As websites are, ultimately, database systems managed through an interface, *sui generis* rights on databases also need to be carefully considered. Once again, the tensions generated by increasing levels of technical complexity make it more difficult to enact a series of different rights using just one act, or even one branch of the law (that is, intellectual property law plus, at least, competition law), so that a greater legal coordination is needed to address these emerging problems. It is perhaps best summed up by Swindler: "… the protection of news property has been worked out gradually and tentatively and for the most part in terms of the degree of original creative effort on the part of the individual writer or artist which can be discerned in the published material" (1959: 318).

Just before the advent of the World Wide Web, the major changes to intellectual property rights were foreseen and clearly defined by Georges Koumantos at the Madrid Convention on Intellectual Property held in 1979. Koumantos identified three trends that represented turning points in the development of intellectual property (Koumantos 1981: 14) and which seemed likely to be further strengthened by the development of the World Wide Web.

First, the agents protected by the international conventions are more often the organizations who disseminate the work, and under whose orders the collective work is produced, than individual authors. This means, plainly and simply, that intellectual property law tends to protect economic interests more than it does cultural interests.

Second, authors' rights surrender to illegal facts in the same measure that technology augments its strength, not only because it makes it easier and more accurate to reproduce perfect copies of any intellectual work, but also because it makes it easier to conceal any illegal behavior.

Internationalization of communication systems, whose paradigm is the internet, poses problems that from a legal point of view are not new—basically, determining which substantive and procedural rules and courts are competent when parties of different national origin are involved—but whose proliferation is exponential to the development of the use of the web. As a result, this means lawsuits can be afforded by nobody other than a rich corporation. The efforts taken by the European Union to put some order into copyright litigation in what is otherwise a fragmented national landscape is a clear example of this.

Third and most importantly, the authors' rights system has been exposed to major modifications in structure. Until the end of the twentieth century and the appearance of the globalized communication network, intellectual property protection was an *erga omnes* right which prevented anyone not authorized by the author (or copyright holders) to use the work without permission. This situation is undergoing a change, the clearest example being the claims for such an exclusive right made by corporate entities. Georges Koumantos affirmed in 1979 that this opposition right is becoming a simple compensation right.

The main reason for such a major transformation is explained by George Koumantos. More than ideological, the main reason is economic, reflecting the fact that the mass media has grown with the emergence of large, transnational, complex corporations operating under national laws in a globalized online journalism, in which new actors, such as aggregators or social networks, like Google and Facebook, have imposed a new set of rules. Parallel to this, users, somewhat shyly it must be said, have begun to demand a more active role, propelled by the internet and the World Wide Web and thanks to increased capabilities of editing, publishing, modifying and disseminating contents using digital tools in a network of global hypertext, which has greatly enhanced the active participation of the public (see Ihlebaek and Krumsvik 2015), to the point that they wish to be granted recognition as authors or, at least, as co-authors.

The circle is closing in this millennium. In 2004, the International Labour Office held a meeting on the future of work and quality in the information society, a sector "marked by innovation, communication and creativity". The report confirmed the fact that "the workforce in the creative industries has grown faster than in other sectors", but at the same time "the emergence of ICTs has fostered an environment where violation of intellectual property may flourish", thus "employers and creative workers share a strong interest in the role of copyright and neighboring rights" (International Labour Office 2005: 24–25). In 2014, a report, signed by Andrew Bibby, observed a "shift to atypical and freelance working" due to a "decline in traditional jobs" and recommended solutions based on, for instance, collective bargaining and competition law.

The prevalence of multiplatforms in the editorial field, most obviously as this impinges on the economics of the media, and the creation of multimedia groups has not helped matters, since workers are not always sure whether they are supplying intellectual goods for one company or for the whole group. The increasing complexity of contracts makes it difficult for workers to determine whether they are signing away their right to negotiate with third parties, but based on the legal notices of these media organizations, the latter automatically consider that these rights as being assigned to the company and the group or trust, including all contents sent by users.

3 How to Regulate User-Generated Contents

The main issue we consider is the copyright on user-generated content. In a somewhat limited way, such a right was adopted in 2012 in Canada, while the European Union, at that moment, was reluctant to follow suit (see *Copyright in the Knowledge Economy* report, 2008) deeming it "too early" (see Díaz Noci 2016a: 49 ff.). The Canadian *Copyright (Modernization) Act*, passed in June 2012, included this new right, but actually it referred solely to derivative works by users as long as they were not for commercial use or as long as the pre-existing work developed by the user to produce a new, transformative work was reserved by copyright holders. This is the case of most contents published by media worldwide, insofar as they typically reserve the exclusive rights of any economic exploitation for the companies, and force users who want to produce a derivative work to actually acquire the rights on the pre-existing work, while the resulting work must be for non-commercial uses, which places a barrier on such supposedly innovative products.

Somewhat surprisingly, the European Union has re-introduced user-generated content into its *Proposal for a Directive on Copyright in the Digital Single Market*, via Article 13 which refers to information society providers ("information society providers that store and provide to the public access to large amounts of works or other subject-matter uploaded by users"). Thus, at some point it was proposed that user's rights be taken into consideration. This occurred in February 2017, when *rapporteur* Marc Joulaud recognized users as "active contributors" in his draft opinion addressed to the European Parliament's Committee on Culture and Education and to Committee on Legal Affairs, insisting that he does not focus on technical aspects but rather on the "principal purpose" (Joulaud 2017: 5). There is interest in certain sectors of the European legislature in developing the notion of user-generated content as one of the motors of innovation and creativity, a notion that has always underpinned intellectual property laws. Joulaud appears to be in favor of creating "a new pillar to protect consumers' legitimate practices", and he calls for a more precise definition of what might be considered user-generated content ("an image, a set of moving images with or without sound, a phonogram, data, or a combination of the above, which is uploaded or displayed on a digital content platform by one or more users", pp. 36–37) and for its interpretation on the primary basis of exceptions, something not covered to date by the strict, mandatory list provided by the European institutions. Fair use (or fair dealing) seems to be an appropriate way to cover users' stimulating practices and cross-border uses, mentioned also by the *Directive Proposal.* Marc Joulaud proposed defining user-generated content, accepting that it "may comprise extracts or quotations of protected works or other subject-matter, which may be altered, combined or transformed for different purposes by users" (Joulaud 2017: 15). He also includes "content automatically generated by an act of hyperlinking related to a press publication", a practice which many press groups find unacceptable. The *rapporteur* calls for a system of obliging platforms which provide direct access to user-generated content "to conclude licensing agreements with rightholders".

Both Marc Joulaud and other MEPs, including Catherine Stihler, have defined what the exceptions to user-generated content should be and the conditions they must fulfill: quotations or extracts from pre-existing works must be related to works previously made available to the public legally; with express mention of the source, author's name (respecting, in this way, the moral right of paternity), unless it is impossible, e.g. when the pre-existing work is an orphan work; when the use of the derivative work is "solely for non-commercial uses" (according to Stihler's proposal) or "used in accordance with fair practice". Finally, it is important that the new, derivative work has, as Stihler proposes, "a certain level of creativity […] which substantially differentiates it from the original work". As such, these proposals do not contradict many of the copyright provisions already in force in many national laws.

However, events seem to have taken a worrying turn. Many voices have expressed misgivings about the way the proposals on the rights of press publishers and user-generated content are presented in the *Directive Proposal*. The RCUK Centre for Copyright and New Business Models in the Creative Economy, along with the University of Glasgow, the University of Cambridge and Tilburg University addressed an open letter to the European Parliament and Council condemning press publishers' rights, which in their opinion "will deter communication of news, obstruct online licensing, and negatively affect authors", recalling that media companies are already able to acquire exclusive rights on these contents by means of employment contracts. As we have seen, national laws, such as the French, have enforced exactly this, so there is a way to achieve these goals without any need to change the nature of copyright law at the European level (see Coche 2018: "The most adequate solution to address this issue would be adopting enforcement rules by inserting a legal presumption in favor of press publishers"; furthermore, she insists in removing proposals for a new press publishers' right).

The letter also stresses that "the author's share will become smaller" and that this "will hinder European innovation compared to the rest of the world". The letter takes an even firmer stance against the rights on user-generated contents introduced by the European institutions when trying to oblige internet providers and platforms to scrutinize and filter all possible illegal contents, most of them produced by users, simply because they are against copyright holders or because they are fake news, libelous or commit any other legal (criminal) offence. This obligation, if eventually enacted, could go against the general obligation of no monitoring contents established by the Court of Justice of the European Union in two cases, *Scarlet Extended* (C 70/10) and *Netlog/Daban* (C 360/10).

According to another open letter addressed to the European institutions by the Max Planck Institute for Innovation and Competition, on September 8, 2017, criticizing Article 13 of the *Directive Proposal* because, in their opinion, it "creates legal uncertainty [...], can enable abusive behavior, thereby threatening freedom of expression and information". The Institute proposes an alternative, which includes the aforementioned "implementation of a mandatory exception for private, non-commercial exploitation of works in social networks not affecting the rightholder's normal exploitation of works", a "mandatory remuneration [...] payable by platform providers" and a "simplification of trans-European licensing mechanisms".

4 Sharing the Benefits

The movement toward the clarification of the legal complexity surrounding intellectual property is not only of a conceptual or philosophical order, but also one motivated by purely economic reasons. By calling for an effective publisher's exclusive right to clear copyright, legal entities are, we believe, initiating what amounts to a subtle substitution of entrenched legal concepts. Legal reforms, such as the one made in France, and the ancillary rights enacted in Germany and Spain, which have enjoyed limited practical success (albeit sufficient to promote legal reform in the European Union through an intense lobbying campaign), are representative of a clear movement toward achieving this objective. Indeed the progress made would seem to confirm Eric Easton's claim that the newspapers' quest for copyright protection was a step "toward a property-based, rather than service-based, ethos" (Easton 2004: 522).

The position defended by Europe's leading scholars is, however, categorical:

> Copyright law is linked to the freedom of the authors to create and should remunerate the creative authors in first instance. Therefore copyright law should not grant rights ab initio to persons other than the individual creators. This principle (the *author principle*) applies to the exclusive rights within the copyright bundle [...]. We believe copyright is not the correct instrument by which to confer rights on legal entities to protect their investments. (European Copyright Society 2015: 2)

It is interesting to examine how the media industry has moved to protect its interests by promoting legal reform, the outcome of which, at the time of writing this chapter, is uncertain in the European Union. The tensions between authors and companies—not to mention users—is well exemplified by the debate surrounding the *Public consultation on the role of publishers in the copyright value chain and on the "panorama exception"* launched by the European Commission in March 2016. The opinions submitted by different organizations highlight the distance in the positions of the actors involved in the news reporting business.

On the one hand, press publishers call for full control of the contents they offer, as they currently do but in a contractual manner, using their terms of use to clearly state that all that is produced as a result of their investment and under their supervision is owned by the company, and that the company has full permission to publish, communicate, remove or modify everything submitted by users with no compensation, in principle, in exchange for permitting users a non-exclusive use of their works, so they could exploit them separately. Companies strictly forbid any derivative use of their contents, but reserve for themselves any derivative use of the user-generated content.

Whilst author and user organizations advocate "a strong public domain to benefit users, creators, educators, researchers, and cultural heritage institutions" (Tarkowski 2016: 6, on behalf of Communia, an association with a mission to foster the public domain), press publishers lobby in favor of their own interests, at a time when European associations are split down the middle—since the beginning of 2016, the publishers in eleven countries decided to (supposedly amicably) leave the European Newspaper Publishers' Association (ENPA) and create News Media Europe (NME). Led by *Grupo Vocento* in Spain (the media group that headed lobbying in favor of reforming Art. 32.2 of the Spanish *Intellectual Property Act* in 2014), the main European press publishers are moving toward a concentration of the printed newspaper sector to better defend their interests. And even if we accept that they are, as Communia's document says "a relatively small number of traditional publishers who by no means represent the wide variety of active publishers" (ibidem), they are powerful.

Tension is also building between public and private interests. Access to knowledge and information is a basic right, but its application is difficult and controversial when there is no clear alternative to copyright, as a monopoly given to authors or publishers. If "copyright is inherently unjust", because it has been "privatized", as Marieke van Schijndel and Joost Smiers suggest in their essay *Imagining a World without Copyright* (2005), and because copyright law (especially the authorial branch of it) pays little attention to who they call "the average artist", and to journalists and even users, as intellectual workers acting to satisfy the market rather than following the impulse of personal creation and artistic inspiration, then we have to implement alternatives to that ownership system. Van Schijndel and Smiers propose *collective ownership* and, theoretically at least, it is easy to link this concept to the public domain *latu senso*: this can include orphan works, for instance, or public works that are made rapidly available and whose validity is rapidly outdated, like hot news. In a sense, a misappropriation tort based on this doctrine could work for news, as Eric Easton (2004) suggests, but this needs to be compensated with a term of duration much shorter than the currently existing one of the lifetime of the author plus 70 years.

Finally, various territorial problems have emerged, for which there appear to be no easy solutions (for a discussion of some of these, see Díaz Noci 2017: 210 ff.). It is not always readily determinable, in a globalized world of virtual dissemination of contents (via the internet), in which national law or jurisdictional territory copyright infringement should be pursued. In Europe, legal doctrine is based on several criteria, including the country of the defendant's residence, or the country in which the infringement was produced (though this is not always easy to determine either). The Court of Justice of the European Union holds that damages should be claimed in each country in which they are produced, which could be virtually any country in the digital world. Thus, it obliges the plaintiff to roam from country to country and from court to court, and to spend vast sums of money to make his claim, according to the so-called *Shevill case*, 1995 (*Fiona Shevill, Ixora Trading Inc., Chequepoint SARL and Chequepoint International Ltd v Presse Alliance SA*, C-68/93), which determined the meaning of Article 5 of the Brussels Convention ("Place where the harmful event occurred"). This has been subsequently modified in later cases, to the point that when the rights of the person are involved it is accepted that there is only one place in which damages can be claimed (see *eDate/ Martinez*C-509/09, C-161/09). Yet, such legal initiatives, and the reforms made to certain national laws, are of limited impact (Aguilar-Paredes et al. 2016).

5 The Reaction of Media Industries

There is, however, one question that needs careful consideration: resistance to change, sometimes defined as *resilience*, among news organizations. First, the assumption that journalists, and more recently active users, are real authors is weak in some countries. Authors' rights (another term used, especially in Civil Law countries of French influence) are not equally enacted. For instance, moral rights, which were only recently assumed by Common Law countries in the 1990s, and which are unknown in the legal traditions of the United States and the

United Kingdom, where a more entrepreneurial conception of copyright is considered more natural, are not equally recognized for all kinds of authors. Journalists, unlike some other authors, have no 'paternity' right (the right to be mentioned as the creator of his or her work) under the British *Copyright Act*, for instance—even when most companies prefer to credit them as authors, despite being under no obligation to do so. On the other hand, moral rights, including the paternity right and integrity right (works cannot be modified without their authors' permission) are undeniable and unwaivable in many Civil Law acts. Yet, in Spain 23% of journalists, according to a survey carried out in 2007, believed they had no rights over the works they produce, and 58% confessed that they received no remuneration for the reproduction of the contents they produce for a media group. As a result, 48% of Spanish journalists consider the recognition of their authors' rights as being far from sufficient.

The question is, as Richard Danbury has posed, whether the crisis in commercial news is "sufficient to merit intervention".[3] At a seminar on this very subject, held at the University Pompeu Fabra in November 2014, one of the conclusions reached by participants was precisely that legislation can have costly, unforeseen results and that it would be preferable for the legislator to structure the law in such a way as to remove all barriers to reaching private agreements and to minimize transaction costs. Tolerating, if not exactly encouraging, the production of derivative works, can also act as an incentive for the economy. Eric Easton explains that certain transformative uses of the journalism work product "i.e., new products in the same market, or the same product in different markets, should be encouraged", so in practice "the duration of any protection available should be severely limited" (Easton 2004: 523). Yet, in the European Union at least, newspaper publishers are moving in exactly the opposite direction. Easton puts his faith in the efforts of "individual reporters and editors" to preserve quality journalism, which requires enforcing individual, personal rights of all types; meanwhile, publishers put their faith in weakening these individual (author and user) rights and gaining an exclusive *quasi*-property on all the work they can lay their hands on.

A reflection of this point of view is the struggle being maintained by media groups against the press clipping activities of firms whose

[3] http://www.cipil.law.cam.ac.uk/aboutresearchappraising-potential-legal-responses-threats-production-news-digital-environment-ahrc.

business is reproducing the contents of others without adding their own intellectual contribution (the "extra element doctrine"). For example, this served as the catalyst for the Spanish Intellectual Property Law (TRLPI 1/1996) reformed first in 2006 and later in 2015, in this case to enact an unsuccessful, unwaivable right in favor of press publishers against aggregators. Indeed, Google News abandoned the Spanish market before the legal reform was enforced. In November 2012, newspaper publishers in Brazil decided to ban the search engine aggregator from using their content. The German press publishers lobbied the Government and the Parliament in the same way, trying to ensure payment for the inclusion of hyperlinks to news items published by their online newspapers. In Belgium, the Court held in *Copiepresse* v. *Google* that "the mere grouping of fragments of published articles, due to the lack of any commentary by Google, does not amount to reporting current events", a fact recognized even in the *Report to the Council, the European Parliament and the Economic and Social Committee on the application of Directive 2001/29/EC on the harmonization of certain aspects of copyright and related rights in the information society.*

Yet, the situation is not entirely new and has obvious parallels with the *industrial media*. In 1925/26, the International Labour Office commissioned a report on the work conditions of journalists that would reflect "...the conditions of journalism [...] against a background of an emerging media culture with the rise of broadcasting, the success of picture magazines, and the triumph of the movies" (Hardt 2005: 6). The report described the rapid process of capitalistic concentration, so that "the journalist of our days is dependent on a vast organization of a more or less industrial type", but, nevertheless, "sets store by his intellectual status".

The situation gained a degree of clarification following the ruling in the *Infopaq* case (*Infopaq International A/S* v. *Dankse Dagblades Forening*, Case C-508 [2009] E.C.D.R. 16.). The European Court of Justice, at the behest of the Supreme Court of Denmark, held that originality could be found even in short excerpts, concluding that "it is only through the choice, sequence and combination of those words that the author may express his creativity in an original manner and achieve a result which is an intellectual creation". The European Court of Justice left the national legislators and courts to decide where such excerpts might constitute an original creation, but, as Hasan A. Deveci says, "cases around the world suggests it can" (Deveci 2011: 473).

The question is whether the law should protect the interests of authors or the interests of the media, and here different solutions have been adopted in both Common Law and in Civil Law countries. Common Law countries are reluctant to recognize authors' moral rights and even more reluctant to recognize journalists' (and users') moral rights, so all protection of news stories is considered as 'work made for hire' (for instance, "Copyright in works created by journalists in the course of their employment by publishers of newspapers, magazines and similar periodicals", Australia. Copyright Law Review Committee, 1994: 1). In other countries, including Brazil, the question has been neglected: "*A LDA* [the old Intellectual Property Law of Brazil, *Lei n° 5.988/73*, not amended in the current act, *Lei 9.610/98*] *mantém pecaminoso silêncio em torno dos direitos autorais decorrentes das obras de autor assalariado*" (Viera Manso 1989: 20).

Civil Law countries have also taken steps in this direction, giving more primary exploitation rights to the corporate entities, although they are reputed to be authorial systems. The whole thing began in France. The so-called *Loi Hadopi* (a reform of the *Code de la Propriété Intellectuelle* in 2009, carried out under Nicolas Sarkozy's right wing government) provided for the exploitation rights of journalist-produced works under its Sect. 6 ("*Droit d'exploitation des oeuvres des journalistes*"), specifically attributing ab initio these rights to the media companies or *titres de presse*, defined as "*l'organe de presse à l'élaboration duquel le journaliste professionnel a contribué*", in a permanent or occasional manner, since an exclusive assignment to the employer is established by the law (see, in general terms, Lucas-Schloetter 2005, on the regime of salaried authors).

This position seems to run contrary to the general rule emanating from the intellectual property acts of France and of the countries that followed its model, including Spain—and the Spanish-speaking countries of Latin America—and Italy: that is, the special recognition of collective works made under the initiative and scrutiny of a person, other than those that effectively produce the individual works, of the condition of this juridical persons as the author of the collective work. This, at least, means the recognition of corporate entities as authors of the individual works composed by newspapers and which already belong to the natural persons that produce them. The definition of a newspaper, and subsequently, a website, as a collective work is guaranteed by many media companies using a contractual clause attached to a labor or freelance contract or to collective agreements. However, the situation has changed since then: first of all, contracts have been modified. In the print world, they used to be limited in geographical scope, but now they cover the transnational uses of the work.

Certain limitations, beyond those usually recognized by any copyright act, were accepted by doctrine. Lucien Solal explains that the collective work was not to be protected, as their parts (drawings, news items, literary and scientific articles, photographs) are, but that the news itself was not copyrightable, meaning the "*simple reproduction d'un fait, sans aucune mise en forme*" (Solal 1959: 107). The *Loi Hadopi* has dramatically reversed the tendency of French law, which since the act of 1957 established that "*pour tous les oeuvres publiées dans un journal ou récueil périodique, l'auteur conserve, le droit de les fair reproduire et de les exploiter*".

6 Automated News

Another concern for the law is the growing importance of what has been called "automated journalism" (or "robot journalism"), defined as

> the process of using software or algorithms to automatically generate news stories without human intervention – after first programming the algorithm, of course. Thus, once the algorithm has been developed, it allows each step of the news production process to be automated, from the collection and analysis of data, to the actual creation and publication of news. (Graefe 2016: 9)

It is a product of *database journalism* (Weeks 2014: 5), susceptible to being classified as protectable, under copyright laws, as databases or as *sui generis* rights. The process was developed around 2014, when Ken Schwencke, then a journalist hired by the *Los Angeles Times* daily newspaper (and its online edition), designed an algorithm to produce some news items about a low intensity earthquake on March 17, 2014. He signed the piece as the author. One year later, in March 2015, *Le Monde* used another algorithm, designed by Data2Content and Syllabs, to prepare and display a range of news items on the electoral results.

Another form of automated journalism are chatbots (a neologism formed using *chat* and *robots*). These are instant messenger services combined with a personalization tool, so it can be argued that they create nothing that did not exist previously. The question, from a legal point of view, is which legal category should be used to protect the resulting piece of work, and who should be considered its author. On occasions, when a journalist is the author of the algorithm and, so, manages the whole news item production process, although leaving the big data mining in the "hands" of the software to ensure their correct output, he or she can properly claim to be the author of the literary piece. This is the case of Ken Schwencke, who operates as both programmer and journalist. In the case of the information items published by *LeMonde.fr*, they were not signed by any journalist, and since they are part of a collective work, it is supposed that the exploitation rights, according to the contractual terms, are assigned to the company. Yet, what would happen if one of these automatically produced pieces were to be deemed libelous or defamatory, which party would be considered liable (Weeks 2014: 75).

From the point of view of copyright, probably the main issue involved is the question of originality, which lies not in the literary part of the piece but in the design of the software—even more so than in the design of the database, as the software searches, mines and exploits. Lin Weeks is right to assert that "at the highest level of abstraction, automated journalism stories consist of an algorithm, of input (known in the industry as clean data), and of prose output" (Weeks 2014: 85). In line with Weeks, the protection of the algorithm itself, considered, we should add, as a form of software, is uncontroversial; more problematic is how to protect the output itself. Another issue is how the media treat certain kinds of information—in principle, not mere data—in order to display it automatically, a question that has been examined by Jop Esneijer: "Note that automated scanning of tweets and blogs for relevant content and copy or even publishing them [...] would in principle also require the authorization of the original author as these are acts of copying or making available to the public, unless they are excepted, for example because they fall under the quotation right" (Esneijer et al. 2012: 43).

7 Legal Reforms in Europe

The solutions to the problems outlined in the preceding sections are multiple and complex. However, it is perhaps, interesting, to focus on two aspects that have come under close scrutiny recently, and which have stirred up considerable controversy. These are the so-called press publishers' right and rights on user-generated content.

Newspaper publishers insist that the landscape is changing so rapidly that laws that were perfectly applicable when the printing press were the main source of income for news companies are in need of an overhaul. "In the non-digital past, a publisher's right was not considered necessary", states one report (EPC et al. 2016: 3). The industry highlights the fact that "quality journalistic content – whether breaking news or in-depth investigative reports, sports coverage or feature writing – is not just popular to read and share across social media, but expensive to produce, so media companies need to make profits to stay in business, pay their journalists and contributors, and equipped to carry the risks and liabilities of production, and publishing". They complain that "unlike other content producers, [they] do not possess any rights of their own at European level", so that they have "to rely on the assignment of rights by their authors" (ibidem). What the European news industries claim for themselves is explicitly the "same rights as *producers* from other creative industries" (ibidem), namely the want a status for their contents equal to that commanded by the products of audiovisual work on the Continent, and they even implicitly imagine a future similar to the situation enjoyed by their counterparts in the United States:

> A press publisher does not merely publish content created by journalists and photographers. The publisher is responsible for overseeing the entire operation involved from the initial concept to the financing, production and management of a newspaper or magazine, in print or online, and takes legal responsibility together with the editor for the making available to the public of the final published edition(s) and any updates thereafter. Crucially, the publisher creates an editorial brand. (EPC et al. 2016: 4)

The movements lobbying for this "exclusive right for publishers" (Kala 2015 [on behalf of the ENPA]: 3) are in a sense waging a war against open licenses—and in favor of a broad interpretation of extended collective licenses in the case of massive digitization, where the numbers of authors and copyright holders to negotiate with is so huge that it is effectively impossible to grant an individual license to any one of them. The main journalists' association, the International Federation of Journalists, continues to campaign in favor of their members' rights, and, for instance, in a contract model launched to avoid abusive contractual terms, freelancers are encouraged to negotiate the following clause:

> All author's rights in the work shall remain with *author* who will retain their exclusive rights. The licence granted to publish or broadcast will be

limited to the first publication/broadcast only. Unless there is express written agreement to the contrary, the licence shall expire 3 months after the delivery date referred to in clause 2 and once the licence has expired ***publisher/broadcasting company*** shall destroy all copies of the work. Any modification of the work shall be subject to prior authorization by ***author***. (point 8a of the *IFJ/EFJ Contract's Check List for Freelance Journalists*, 2009)

Various platforms have been created to fight for authors' rights.[4] Art. 3.3 of the recommendation of the European Commission on May 24, 2011 [*A Single Market for Intellectual Property Rights. Boosting Creativity and Innovation to Provide Economic Growth, High Quality Jobs and First Class Products and Services in Europe*][5] recognized that authors should expect a fair return for their work and a far return also when their work is modified or reused. This is highlighted by the European Commission to Parliament, in the aforementioned document: "Fair compensation of authors and performers [is a] mechanism [which] includes the regulation of certain contractual practices, unwaivable remuneration rights, collective bargaining and collective management of rights" [COM (2015) 626 Final]. "Journalists are authors", Art, 3.3.5. of that document unequivocally states. In this regard, we would endorse the words that Mike Holderness, head of the copyright group of the International Federation of Journalists, pronounced at a seminar organized at the Pompeu Fabra University in November 2014: "Sustainable journalism requires it to be possible for independent journalists to make a living from journalism, rather than from sponsorship or patronage, for example – to be *professionals*".

8 Do Media Companies Need an Ancillary Right? Press Publishers' Right

Many voices in Europe have raised serious concerns about the convenience and viability of ancillary rights for press publishers (see Tarkowski 2016: 8; European Copyright Society 2016). A study conducted by

[4]See *Plataforma por los Derechos de Autor de los Periodistas*. Madrid: Federación de Asociaciones de Periodistas (FAPE), July 2014.

[5]Retrieved from http://ec.europa.eu/internal_market/copyright/docs/ipr_strategy/COM_2011_287_en.pdf.

Martin Kretschmer, Séverine Dusollier, Christophe Geiger and P. Bernt Hugenholtz in 2016 highlights the fact that the European Commission is not explaining "what kind of right is envisaged" (European Copyright Society 2016: 3). The study mentions, along with the German and Spanish reforms, Sect. 8 of the British *Copyright, Patents and Designs Act* "on the typographical arrangement of a published edition", lasting 25 years, and the European *Database Directive 96/9/EC* providing a *sui generis* right for publishers, lasting 15 years, "and none appears to have had the intended consequences" (ibidem: 4). On the other hand, defense against free riders, which were not a major problem in a purely analogue world, justifies legal intervention, according to the European newspaper publishers (EPC et al. 2016: 6).

In seeking ancillary rights, newspaper publishers are adding a "highly problematic extra layer of rights", as some leading European scholars on intellectual property have pointed out (European Copyright Society 2016: 6). In their opinion, such measures would be difficult to apply effectively since it would result in an increase in transaction costs and create more confusion for users. As Mireille M. M. van Eecheoud claims, "neither the Impact Assessment nor the Commission Communication explains in what way the introduction of an additional layer of rights would facilitate the clearing of rights for online uses and reduce transaction costs". Resorting to the language of economics, Jeff Borland and Philip L. Williams explain "the problem is that technological developments have raised the transactions costs of license agreements between journalists and the users of newspaper articles—where transaction costs include the cost of discovering the parties to the negotiation, the cost of conducting the negotiations, and the costs of enforcing the contract" (Borland and Williams 1993: 352). As they rightly point out in their 1993 article, two models exist: one to assign copyright to the publisher, so the journalist receives a fixed monetary payment, a salary (and sometimes some general compensation for further reproductions of the work); the other to assign copyright to journalists, so their incomes consist of a combination of a fixed wage plus variable royalties. The authors, in accordance with a risk-sharing approach, are in favor of assigning copyright to the publisher to ensure copyright protection of works on the market. This, needless to say, is the most widespread model and, most probably, the one that will be favored by European institutions.

Users find themselves in no-man's land, a view which is shared by the European Copyright Society (2016: 16). Companies, on their side, are tirelessly fighting for an ancillary right for themselves, at least in Europe and in Brazil. The *resilience* of these industries is a major problem in constructing the future of copyright law. While Pamela Samuelson seems right to affirm that "in numerous respects, copyright law today serves well the interests of authors, those to whom authors assign or license their rights, and the public, but in some important respects, this law is askew" (Litman and Samuelson 2010: 1245), but at the same time it is difficult not to think that this is also the case faced by news reporting. However, a number of business models, albeit shyly, are beginning to appear on the horizon of the news industry: non-profit and, in the Common Law tradition, charitable trusts, and it is true that a huge amount of innovation in news presentations originates from one of these trusts, the Scott Trust,[6] owner of one of the fiercest defenders of the *digital first* strategy, *The Guardian*, although the paper is losing huge amounts of money, to the point that former editor-in-chief, Alan Rusbridger, failed to be elected as its president. As is made evident in the preamble to the reform of the German Law on Intellectual Property 2014, any legal reform that is made "should not be understood as a legislative form of protection of old and outdated business models".

The position is extremely controversial. Whilst the great press publishers (the smaller ones are not in favor of this movement, see NERA 2015) and many scholars, at the request of the European institutions and the MEPs, have insisted in the inconvenience of enacting such a particular right. OpenForum Europe has published a couple of reports on this very question (see Díaz Noci 2016b; Van Eecheoud 2017), and Lionel Bently, Martin Kretschmer and others published *Strengthening the Position of Press Publishers and Authors and Performers in the Copyright Directive* at the request of the European Parliament's Policy Department for Citizens' Rights and Constitutional Affairs of the JURI committee. All were skeptical, if not reluctant to accept the necessity of enacting such a right for press publishers, as was the final report of a research project led by professors Lionel Bently and Ian Hargreaves (*Evaluating potential legal responses to threats to the production of news in a digital era*, Danbury 2016). Many of these arguments were adopted by two of the *rapporteurs* of the European Union, the official one by MEP Theresa Comadini Cachia and the complementary one by MEP Catherine Stihler,

[6]https://www.theguardian.com/the-scott-trust.

and published on February 2, 2017 (see *Draft Report on the proposal for a directive of the European Parliament and of the Council on copyright in the Digital Single Market (COM(2016)0593 – C8-0383/2016 – 2016/0280(COD))*, supported by smaller media organizations such as Open Media, whose digital rights specialist, Ruth Coustick-Deal, said in March 2017 that "this is an issue of fundamental rights, and once again we see the need for the European Parliament to step in and undo the damage being inflicted by the European Commission. Cachia's proposed updates to copyright legislation are a strong step in the right direction, but more needs to be done to ensure the ability of all Europeans to access information online and express themselves freely."[7] Theresa Comadini Cachia was subsequently replaced by conservative MEP Axel Voss, whose position is closer to that of the leading newspaper publishers of Europe, summed up in their need for a right to "compete effectively and profitably on all platforms" under the umbrella of "freedom of the press and democracy" (available at www.publishersright.eu, a website devoted to promoting this initiative). This, however, as MEP Julia Reda insists, could go against the EU's link doctrine as determined in the so-called *Svensson* case (European Court of Justice, C-466/12). The European Court of Justice observed that "it must be observed that making available the works concerned by means of a clickable link, such as that in the main proceedings, does not lead to the works in question being communicated to a new public". The Court observed that, actually, the clickable links do not create a new public, so the authorization of the copyright holders is not needed. Finally, the Court stated that "article 3(1) of Directive 2001/29 must be interpreted as precluding a Member State from giving wider protection to copyright holders by laying down that the concept of communication to the public includes a wider range of activities than those referred to in that provision." Moreover, on March 26, 2015, the CJEU held in *C More Entertainment AB v Linus Sandberg*, C-279/13 that 'making available' was not a public communication act and that a link which provided the chance to watch a sports event is not copyright infringement. In that decision, the court made an interpretation of Article 3(2) of *Directive 2001/29/EC*, since the defendant provided in its website links to "gain access to the live broadcast [...] of ice hockey games without having to pay the sum asked

[7] http://infojustice.org/archives/37935.

by the operator of the other site", whereas the website to which the hyperlinks lead is of public access. Finally, a third case should be mentioned, namely *GS Media BV* v. *Sanoma Media Netherlands BV, Playboy Enterprises International Inc., Britt Geertruida Dekke* (Case C-160/15), in which once again the CJEU was asked "if anyone other than the copyright holder refers by means of a hyperlink on a website controlled by him to a website which is managed by a third party and is accessible to the general internet public, on which the work has been made available without the consent of the rightholder" and if this is to be considered a communication to the public according to Article 3(1) of the aforementioned *Directive 2001/29*. Thus, in general, it is legal to post a link to free contents on the Web, and not legal to post a link to unpermitted contents (in the CJUE's own words, "the posting of a hyperlink on a website to works protected by copyright and published without the author's consent on another website does not constitute a 'communication to the public' when the person who posts that link does not seek financial gain and acts without knowledge that those works have been published illegally"). Since most of the contents posted by the media are free, such linking activity is not easily forbidden.

While in the Common Law arena, the question is examined in the light of fair use or fair dealing, in the Civil Law arena, it has to be examined according to a closed list of exceptions. Media companies though have insisted (the case, for instance, of *Grupo Vocento* in Spain) in tackling linking practices exhaustively.

9 Conclusions and Future Directions

As we have seen, innovation is a commonly invoked theme when addressing current developments and reforms of intellectual property law. Just how the innovative practices of enterprises, authors and engaged users can be enhanced is a subject for some debate, concerning as it does issues on which scholars tend to hold a fairly fixed opinion but on which legislative politicians are split. The active lobbying of various influential groups—notably the leading European news organizations—which face a structural crisis in their business model, seeks a radical change in the European copyright rules, as they strive to broaden the conception of copyright on the Old Continent as well as in other economies, especially in that of America. Various aspects require careful consideration, including, the need to support a major industry (media companies), to protect their investment (news stories are expensive and digital technologies favor dissemination but not, necessarily, creation), and to ensure fair competition is licitly upheld by the media. At the same time, however, authors need to be protected by means of fair contracts, which is a clear invocation of contract law and freedom of speech. In this respect, both a press publisher's right and a restrictive consideration of user-generated contents, imposing on Internet providers the obligation of monitoring contents, can run counter to freedom of speech and innovation. It is presumably for this reason that the press publishers' right that has been announced has acquired the nickname of "link tax" or "snippet tax". At the same time, it is questionable whether this press publishers' right is sufficient to solve the newspaper industry's economic problems and whether it is the best instrument to address the crisis faced by newspapers (though not necessarily by journalism). Resistance to change and an aversion to having to face new economic risks by experimenting with new business models could explain this position, a position, however, that is not shared by the so-called *minor players*, that is, the smaller, digital-born media.

Scholars call for the implementation of fair use in the Civil Law tradition, instead of opting for a closed, mandatory list of exceptions. However, if this system of exceptions and limitations is to be kept—as seems likely—then the legislature needs to consider enacting a new list in relation to user-generated contents, as proposed by Catherine Stihler and Marc Joulaud.

Only time will tell which direction Europe's institutions will eventually take, how the countries of Europe will go about adopting these provisions, and what decisions the media will adopt in response to the paradigm shift in their business models. We are clearly living in critical times for the future of intellectual property law—a branch that is subject to many competing tensions—as well as other legal fields, including competition, contract and media law, not to mention the basic tent of freedom of speech. As the *Proposal for the Directive on Copyright* states, legal reforms in the field of intellectual property must encourage innovation while protecting the fundamental rights of all agents involved in the communication process. Just how our institutions manage to achieve these goals, and the extent to which it favors us all, remains to be seen.

References

Aguilar-Paredes, Carlos, Mario Pérez-Montoro, and Lydia Sánchez-Gómez. 2016. The Ecosystem for Accessing TV Series and Films in Spain: An Outline of the Situation Following the *Intellectual Property Act 2015. El profesional de la información* 25 (6): 870–881.

Bently, L. 1994. Copyright and the Death of the Author in Literature and Law. Book Review. *Modern Law Review* 57 (6): 973–986.

Bibby, A. 2014. *Employment Relationships in the Media Industry.* Geneva: International Labour Office.

Borland, J., and P.L. Williams. 1993. An Economic Analysis of the Division of Copyright Between Newspaper Publishers and Journalists. *The University of New South Wales Law Journal* 16 (2): 351–362.

Coche, Eugénie. 2018. *Copyright Reform: A New Right for Press Publishers—To Have or Not to Have*? Amsterdam: Kluwer Copyright Blog. Retrieved from http://copyrightblog.kluweriplaw.com/2018/03/13/copyright-reform-new-right-press-publishers-not/.

Danbury, Richard. 2016. *Is an EU Publishers' Right a Good Idea?* Final Report on the AHRC Project: Evaluating Potential Legal Responses to Threats to the Production of News in a Digital Era. Cambridge: Centre for Intellectual Property and Information Law, Faculty of Law, University of Cambridge.

Deveci, H.A. 2011. Hyperlinks Citations, Reproducing Original Works. *Computer Law & Security Review* 27: 465–478.

Díaz Noci, Javier. 2016a. Authors' Rights: Journalists, Audiences and News Organizations. In *Shaping the Future of News Media*, ed. Carles Singla, Irene Da Rocha, and Xavier Ramon. Barcelona: Integrated Journalism in Europe and European Commission. Retrieved from http://integratedjournalism.upf.edu/wp-content/uploads/2016/04/Proceedings-book.pdf.

Díaz Noci, Javier. 2016b. *Press Publishers and Copyright. A Meeting Organized by OpenForum Europe and Held at the European Parliament, Brussels, October 17, 2016.* Brussels: Open Forum Europe. Retrieved from http://www.openforumeurope.org/wp-content/uploads/2016/10/PRESS-PUBLISHERS_RIGHT_OPENFORUMEUROPE.pdf.

Díaz-Noci, Javier. 2017. Copyright and User-Generated Contents for Mobile Devices: News, Entertainment, and Multimedia. In *Between the Public and Private in Mobile Communication*, ed. Ana Serrano, 199–217. London: Routledge.

Easton, E.B. 2004. Who Owns 'The First Rough Draft of History'?: Reconsidering Copyright in News. *Columbia Journal of Law and Arts* 27: 521–595.

Esneijer, J., O. Nieuwenhuis, C. Mijs, C. Versloot, N. Helberger, B. van der Sloot, and T. McGonagle. 2012. *Making User Created News Work.* TNO 2012 R11277. Amsterdam: IViR.

European Copyright Society. 2015. *Opinion on the Reference to the CJEU in Case C-572/13* Hewlett-Packard Belgium SPRL v. Reprobel SCR. Retrieved from https://europeancopyrightsociety.org/opinion-on-reprobel/.

European Copyright Society. 2016. *Answer to the EC Consultation on the Role of Publishers in the Copyright Value Chain*. Retrieved from https://europeancopyrightsocietydotorg.files.wordpress.com/2016/06/ecs-answer-to-ec-consultation-publishers-role-june16.pdf.

European Publishers Council (EPC), European Newspaper Publishers' Association (ENPA), European Magazine Media Association (EMMA), and News Media Europe (NME). 2016. *Publishers in the Digital Age. Adequate Legal Protection Is Needed to Ensure the Diversity of the Press and the Future of Quality Journalism in Europe*. Retrieved from www.publishersright.eu.

Graefe, A. 2016. *Guide to Automated Journalism*. New York: Tow Center for Digital Journalism, Columbia University.

Hardt, H. 2005. International Labour Office: Conditions of Work and Life of Journalists. *Javnost—The Public* 12 (1): 5–14.

Ihlebaek, K.A., and A.H. Krumsvik. 2015. Editorial Power and Public Participation in Online Newspapers. *Journalism* 6 (4): 470–487.

International Labour Office. 2005. *Note on the Proceedings. Tripartite Meeting on the Future of Work and Quality in the Information Society: The Media, Culture, Graphical Sector, Geneva, 18–22 October 2004*. Geneva: International Labour Office.

Joulaud, Marc. 2017. *Draft Opinion of the Committee on Culture and Education for the Committee on Legal Affairs on the Proposal for a Directive of the European Parliament and of the Council on Copyright in the Digital Single Market*. Brussels: European Parliament.

Kala, M. 2015. *Copyright in the EU Digital Single Market. 10 Recommendations of the Newspaper and News Media Sector*. Brussels: European Newspaper Publishers' Association (ENPA).

Koumantos, G. 1981. Défis et promesses du mass média pour le droit d'auteur. *Droit d'Auteur*, Janvier.

Litman, J., and P. Samuelson. 2010. The Copyright Principles Project: Directions for Reform. *Berkeley Technology Law Journal* 25 (3): 1175–1245.

Lucas-Schloetter, A. 2005. La création salariée et le droit contractuel d'auteur. Étude de droit comparé. *Pe.i. Revista de Propiedad Intelectual* 21: 15–79.

NERA. 2015. *Impact of the New Article 32.2 of the Spanish Intellectual Property Act*. Report for the Spanish Association of Publishers of Periodical Publications (AEEPP). Madrid: NERA.

Nordermann, Jan Bernd. 2018. *The German Bundesgerichtshof Applies the Latest CJEU Case Law on Liability for Linking to Search Engines*. Amsterdam: Kluwer Copyright Blog. Retrieved from http://copyrightblog.kluwer.com/2018/03/06/german-bundesgerichtshof-applies-latest-cjeu-case-law-liability-linking-search-engines/.

Recommendation CM/Rec(2018)2 of the Committee of Ministers to Member States Adopted by the Committee of Ministers on 7 March 2018 at the 1309 Meeting of the Ministers' Deputies on the Roles and Responsibilities of Internet Intermediaries. Brussels: Council of Europe.

Solal, L. 1959. *Dictionnaire du droit de la presse.* Paris: Syndicat National de la Presse Quotidienne Régionale.

Swindler, W.F. 1959. News: Public Right v. Property Right. *Faculty Publications. College of William & Mary Law School,* Paper 1614.

Tarkowski, A. 2016. *Response to the Public Consultation on the Role of Publishers in the Copyright Value Chain and on the 'Panorama Exception'.* Brussels: Communia International Association on the Public Domain. Retrieved from http://www.communia-association.org/.

Van Eecheoud, M.M. Mireille. 2017. *A Publisher's Intellectual Property Right: Implications for Freedom of Expression, Authors and Open Content Policies.* Brussels: OpenForum Europe.

Viera Manso, E. 1989. *Contratos de direito autoral.* São Paulo: Editora Revista dos Tribunais.

Weeks, L. 2014. Media Law and Copyright Implications of Automated Journalism. *Journal of Intellectual Property and Entertainment Law* 4 (1): 67–94.

CHAPTER 8

Scientific Production on Interaction in Digital News Media

Ernest Abadal and Javier Guallar

1 Introduction

Interaction in the news is an emerging subject that has already accumulated a considerable number of academic studies. Studies in the field include those that analyse the use of a system of interacting with the news or with news information on digital media, either to encourage public participation or to create spaces for discussion and interaction between media outlets and citizens. Traditionally, printed newspapers communicated mainly in one direction. They transmitted messages to their audience, who received them without being able to interact except through specific sections such as 'Letters to the Editor'. However, the opportunities provided by digital dissemination, the development of techniques, and mechanisms for participation (comments, surveys, forums, votes, etc.) and the technological advance of software and devices (particularly smartphones) have changed the situation

E. Abadal (✉) · J. Guallar
Department of Information Science and Media Studies,
University of Barcelona, Barcelona, Spain
e-mail: abadal@ub.edu

J. Guallar
e-mail: jguallar@ub.edu

M. Pérez-Montoro (ed.), *Interaction in Digital News Media*,
https://doi.org/10.1007/978-3-319-96253-5_8

considerably, and various levels of immediate interaction with audiences have been attained.

Perhaps, Kiousis (2002) was one of the first to define in greater depth the concept of interactivity in relation to the news, in a paper that has become a classic in the field and, as we will see below, has been cited many times. In this text, numerous definitions of the concept of interactivity are analysed in the context of communication and an operational definition is proposed:

> Interactivity can be defined as the degree to which a communication technology can create a mediated environment in which participants can communicate (one-to-one, one-to-many, and many-to-many) both synchronously and asynchronously and participate in reciprocal message exchanges (third-order dependency). (Kiousis 2002: 379)

A practical approach to this topic is described by Suau and Masip (2013), who distinguish between selective interactivity, participatory interactivity and productive interactivity. The first type represents the lowest level of interactivity and refers to services that enable a minimum amount of interaction between the audience and the system: RSS, email alerts, the opportunity to contact journalists or the media outlet, etc. The second, participatory interactivity, permits contact between users and the media within parameters that are previously established by the media outlet, such as comments, voting and 'likes', among many other features. The third, productive interactivity, involves the creation of user generated content (UGC). Finally, some literature reviews on this subject are useful, as they help to put it into context (Masip et al. 2010; Suau and Masip 2013; Baños et al. 2017).

Bibliometric studies are increasingly used to demonstrate the state of science in a certain discipline or specialisation. Hundreds of examples can be found, from odontology (De-la-Flor et al. 2017), women in science (Dehdarirad et al. 2015) and open educational resources (Zancanaro et al. 2015) to social media (Kapoor 2017), open access (Miguel et al. 2016; Rodrigues et al. 2016) and the dissemination of innovation (Zhai et al. 2018).

Bibliometric studies are clearly useful. They identify the main authors in the field, the journals that are most frequently used, collaborations between authors, and the main subject areas that are focused on, among other aspects. Bibliometric studies do not analyse the content in depth as a literature review would, but they do give a general overview of the output in a discipline or specific subject area.

In this chapter, we aim to follow the approach of bibliometric studies, and analyse scientific output on interactivity in digital news to determine its evolution over time, authorship (including collaborations between authors and their affiliations), the most notable journals, and the subject areas that are addressed.

2 Methodology

Our bibliometric analysis used Scopus (Elsevier) as a reference. This is a multidisciplinary database that has indexed around 18,000 academic journals since 2001 and in which the social sciences are well-represented. Scopus has notable search features that enable searches to be limited to papers' keywords, for example.

Even though the Web of Science currently indexes around 20,000 journals,[1] we did not use it in this study as searches cannot be limited to keywords. GoogleScholar includes an even greater number of sources (not only journal titles, but also books). However, it was not used because its search features are very basic, and the downloads of records includes less information that the other two databases mentioned above.

The main terms used in the search were 'interactivity' and 'news', with some variations or synonyms for each term, as we will see below. We also considered the concept 'participatory journalism' as its presence is notable in the area under study.

Generally, subject searches are carried out on the title, abstract and keywords fields, and may produce a number of documents that bear little relation to the subject of the search. To eliminate any imprecise references, the search was limited to the keyword field (including author keywords and indexed keywords), except in the case of 'participatory journalism', which is already considered a very specific term. Therefore, the resulting search equation (which can be copied by anybody interested in the Scopus advanced search page) was as follows:

[1] Since 2015, it has also included the journals in the Emerging Sources Citation Index, which number over 7000.

KEY (interactivity AND media) OR KEY (interactiv* AND news) OR KEY (interactiv* AND journalism) OR KEY (interactiv* AND newspaper) OR TITLE-ABS-KEY ('participatory journalism')[2]

A total of 858 records were found. A considerable number of these were papers and conference papers from the area of information technology, which address the subject from a strictly technological perspective that does not accurately reflect the focus of the study, defined at the start of this text. Therefore, we decided to limit the search to exclude publications from the fields of information technology and engineering.

After the application of this filter, the total number of records selected was 440 (on the date 26 February 2018). These records were used in the bibliometric study.

The same search in the WoS generated a total of 2765 records (4441 before the exclusion of information technology), many of which were not closely related to the subject of interest, as the terms could not be limited to the 'keywords' field. In the case of GoogleScholar, a total of 4828 documents were found when the search was limited to terms that appear in the title. In this case, the limitations were due to the lack of standardisation of records, the impossibility of eliminating references from the information technology field, and the difficulties in downloading records.

No time limit was used. Therefore, the final selection of publications for analysis contains items from any year, specifically from 1989 to the current time.

The following indicators were analysed: evolution over time, authorship, affiliation, type of document, language, journal, most cited papers and subject areas.

To exploit the results, we used spreadsheets with the bibliographic references and thus generated the tables for each of the indicators. We also used the programme VOSviewer (van Eck 2010), developed at Leiden University, which can help create networks of bibliographic data (coauthorship networks, index terms, etc.) presented in a very visual, easy-to-understand way.

[2] KEY is an operator for limiting the search to subject fields that, in the case of Scopus, are Author Keywords and Controlled Keywords. The sign * can be used to include singular and plural forms.

3 Results and Discussion

Below, we discuss the results for each of the indicators. The tables were compiled directly from the data downloaded from Scopus and the networks were mapped using VOSviewer. The total number of units analysed is specified for each table (whether 440 publications, 770 authors, etc.).

3.1 Evolution Over Time

The earliest document is dated 1989. From this date up to 2004, the average annual number of publications was very low, at fewer than 10 references. Between 2005 and 2014, the number of records increased in a sustained, constant manner from 12 to 50, a figure that has not been surpassed. It remains to be seen whether this figure is maintained in the coming years. The graph does not include the nine documents from 2018, as they would distort the overall linear pattern.

Therefore, we can state that the study of interactivity entered a period of greater implementation in digital media from the start of the second decade of digital journalism, in around 2005. This division into periods coincides with the stages that several authors have identified in the evolution of digital media (for example Abadal and Guallar 2010: 39): in 2005, the middle phase of 'digital social multimedia' began, in which online media outlets made major advances in the expansion of some of their defining characteristics, such as interactivity and multimediality (Fig. 1).

3.2 Authorship

Numerous researchers have published on the subject under study: a total of 770 authors were found. A considerable number of these authors (690) have published just one paper on the topic. A total of 80 researchers published at least two papers, and within this group, 20 authors could be considered the most prominent in the field, with three or four papers in Scopus (Table 1). No authors published over four papers on this subject. The authors who published four papers are David Domingo, Avery E. Holton, Edgar Huang, Anders Olof Larsson, Steve Paulussen and Oliver Quiring.

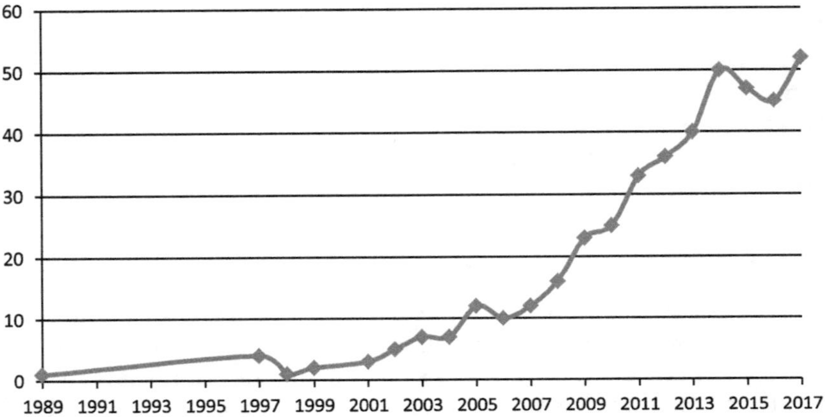

Fig. 1 Evolution in number of publications by year

Table 1 Authors with the highest number of publications on the subject

Authors	*Affiliation*	*Hits*
Domingo, David	Université Libre de Bruxelles, Belgium / Universitat Rovira i Virgili, Spain	4
Holton, Avery E.	Texas Communication, USA	4
Huang, Edgar	Indiana University-Purdue, University Indianapolis, USA	4
Larsson, Anders Olof	Westerdals Oslo School of Arts, Communication and Technology, Norway	4
Quiring, Oliver	Johannes Gutenberg University of Mainz, Germany	4
Paulussen, Steve	University of Antwerp, Belgium	4
Barnes, Renee	University of the Sunshine Coast, Australia	3
Borger, Merel	University of Amsterdam, Netherlands	3
Coddington, Mark	Washington and Lee University, USA	3
Hermida, Alfred	University of British Columbia, USA	3
Ksiazek, Thomas B.	Villanova University (Philadelphia), USA	3
Lewis, Seth C.	University of Minnesota, USA	3
Masip, Pere	Universitat Ramon Llull, Barcelona, Spain	3
Palomo, Bella	Universidad de Málaga, Spain	3
Scacco J.M.	Purdue University, USA	3
Quandt, Thorsten	University of Münster, Germany	3
Sanders, José	Radboud University, Nijmegen, Netherlands	3
Singer, Jane B.	City University, London, UK	3
Stroud, Natalie Jomini	University of Texas, Austin, USA	3
Thurman, Neil	City University, London, UK	3

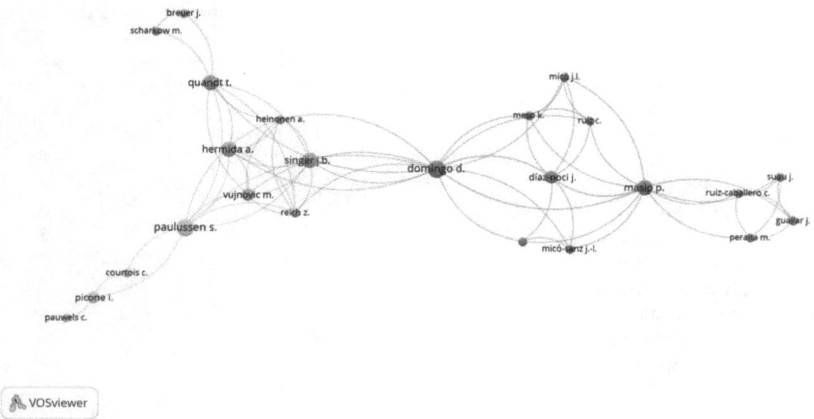

Fig. 2 Network of coauthorship

Therefore, rather than a few authors with considerable output on this subject, we found a varied group of 20 authors with significant output. The list of the 20 most prominent authors revealed a high number of researchers who work in the USA (8), a wide range of European countries (Germany, Netherlands, Spain and the UK with two authors; Belgium and Norway with one) and one researcher from Australia.

The analysis of coauthorship (Fig. 2, generated by VOSviewer) illustrates the relationships between researchers. The results show that the Spaniard David Domingo, from the Université Libre de Bruxelles, Belgium (and previously from the Universitat Rovira i Virgili, Spain) is the researcher with the most coauthorship relations involving colleagues from other European countries and from the United States. Therefore, he occupies the central node of academic output on interactive media. Other prominent collaborators are Jane Singer (British), Alfred Hermida (American), Steve Paulussen (Belgian), Thorsten Quandt (German) and Javier Díaz-Noci and Pere Masip (both Spanish), who form nodes in other coauthorship relations.

3.3 Affiliation

The authors are affiliated with a wide range of institutions in America and Europe. Notably, the list of affiliations only includes universities, with no independent research centres or centres outside of universities.

Table 2 Institutions with the highest numbers of publications ($n = 770$)

University	*Country*	*Documents*
University of Texas at Austin	USA	11
University of Zurich	Switzerland	7
University of Florida	USA	6
Universitat Pompeu Fabra	Spain	6
Universiteit Gent	Belgium	6
Pennsylvania State University	USA	5
Universidad de Málaga	Spain	5
Vrije Universiteit Amsterdam	Netherlands	5
Universitat Rovira i Virgili	Spain	5
University of Ljubljana	Slovenia	5
Tampereen Yliopisto	Finland	4
Radboud University Nijmegen	Netherlands	4
University of Toronto	Canada	4
San Diego State University	USA	4
University of Maryland	USA	4
Universidade da Coruña	Spain	4
University of Iowa	USA	4
Indiana University-Purdue University	USA	4
University of Utah	USA	4
Universitat Ramon Llull	Spain	4
Temple University	USA	4
Johannes Gutenberg Universitat Mainz	Germany	4
University of the Sunshine Coast	USA	4
Universidad de Sevilla	Spain	4

An assessment by country reveals that the USA is in first place, with ten universities on the list. Europe has 13 universities on the list, including a strong presence of Spanish universities: Pompeu Fabra (6), Málaga (5), Rovira i Virgili (5), Coruña (4), Ramon Llull (4), and Sevilla (4).

The University of Texas at Austin, USA, is clearly the leading institution in interactive media research, with 11 papers indexed in Scopus. This is followed by the University of Zurich, Switzerland, with seven, and a varied group of European and US universities with between five and six papers indexed in Scopus (Table 2).

3.4 *Type of Document*

Journal papers were the most common type of document found, accounting for almost three quarters of the total number of publications

Table 3 Document type ($n = 440$)

Document type	*Hits*	%
Article	322	73.4
Conference Paper	54	12.3
Book Chapter	23	5.2
Book	3	0.7
Other	38	8.6

(73%). The percentage of conference papers was considerably lower (12%). The distribution by type of document would have varied greatly if information and technology publications had been included, as conferences are one of the most common forms of disseminating results in this field. Consequently, we can confirm that publication in academic journals plays a central role in the discipline of Communication, and in the subject under study (Table 3).

3.5 *Language*

English is the main language used in the documents (almost 90%). The only other language with a notable presence is Spanish, although in a much lower percentage of papers (close to 10%) and with an area of influence that is centred on Spain and Hispanic America. It is surprising that only six other languages were found, and in negligible percentages of papers (Table 4).

Table 4 Output by language ($n = 440$)

Language	*Hits*	%
English	390	89
Spanish	38	9
English; Spanish	4	0.9
French	2	0.4
Slovenian	2	0.4
Afrikaans	1	0.2
English; Portuguese	1	0.2
German	1	0.2
Italian	1	0.2

Table 5 Journals with the most published papers (6 texts or more)

Journals	*Number*	*Year first included in Scopus*	*Country*
Digital Journalism	20	2010	UK
New Media and Society	20	1999	USA
Journalism Studies	19	2010	UK
Journalism Practice	17	2015	UK
Estudios Sobre el Mensaje Periodístico	11	2010	Spain
Journalism	11	2000	USA
Computers in Human Behavior	8	1985	UK
Comunicar	8	2008	Spain
Newspaper Techniques	8	1999	Germany
Convergence	7	1996	USA
Revista Latina de Comunicación Social	7	2011	Spain
Observatorio	6	2011	Portugal
El Profesional de la Información	6	2006	Spain

3.6 *Journals*

The total number of journals that have published a paper on this subject is 167. There is wide dispersion, as 120 journals (71%) have only published one paper on this subject.

Table 5 lists the 13 journals that have published six or more papers on this subject. Journals that are particularly notable for their high output in this area are *Digital Journalism*, *New Media and Society*, *Journalism Studies*, *Journalism Practice*, *Estudios sobre el Mensaje Periodístico* and *Journalism*. (Note that *Journalism Practice* was only included in Scopus in 2015, which makes its prominent position commendable.)

These journals were mainly published in three countries: the UK and Spain, each with four journals, and the USA with three, while Germany and Portugal also had a published journal on the list. Overall, European journals predominated over US journals (ten journals compared to three).

3.7 *Most Cited Papers*

The twenty most cited papers are shown in Table 6. All of them correspond to papers in scientific journals. The relationship between the most relevant and influential papers to date in the scientific output on the topic, and the journals, authors and corresponding subject areas reveals some data of interest.

Table 6 Most cited papers (the first twenty) ($n = 440$)

Authors	*Title*	*Year*	*Source title*	*Cited by*
Kiousis S.	Interactivity: A concept explication	2002	New Media and Society	244
Sundar S.S., Kalyanaraman S., Brown J.	Explicating web site interactivity: Impression formation effects in political campaign sites	2003	Communication Research	218
Thurman N.	Forums for citizen journalists? Adoption of user generated content initiatives by online news media	2008	New Media and Society	194
Lewis S.C.	The tension between professional control and open participation: Journalism and its boundaries	2012	Information Communication and Society	187
McMillan S.J.	A four-part model of cyber-interactivity: Some cyber-places are more interactive than others	2002	New Media and Society	144
Nip J.Y.M.	Exploring the second phase of public journalism	2006	Journalism Studies	119
Bucy E.P.	Interactivity in society: Locating an elusive concept	2004	Information Society	101
Chung D.S.	Profits and perils: Online news producers' perceptions of interactivity and uses of interactive features	2007	Convergence	96
Ou C.X., Pavlou P.A., Davison R.M.	Swift guanxi in online marketplaces: The role of computer-mediated communication technologies	2014	MIS Quarterly: Management Information Systems	92
Bødker S.	A human activity approach to user interfaces	1989	Human-Computer Interaction	88
Lowry P., Romano N., Jenkins J., Guthrie R.	The CMC interactivity model: How interactivity enhances communication quality and process satisfaction in lean-media groups	2009	Journal of Management Information Systems	86
Burton S., Soboleva A.	Interactive or reactive? Marketing with Twitter	2011	Journal of Consumer Marketing	85
Sundar S.S.	Theorizing interactivity's effects	2004	Information Society	83
Ruiz C., Domingo D., Micó J.L., Díaz-Noci J., Meso K., Masip P.	Public sphere 2.0? The democratic qualities of citizen debates in online newspapers	2011	International Journal of Press/Politics	77

(continued)

Table 6 (continued)

Authors	*Title*	*Year*	*Source title*	*Cited by*
Wu G.	Conceptualizing and measuring the perceived interactivity of websites	2006	Journal of Current Issues and Research in Advertising	74
Lawson-Borders G., Kirk R.	Blogs in campaign communication	2005	American Behavioral Scientist	73
Labrecque L.I.	Fostering consumer-brand relationships in social media environments: The role of parasocial interaction	2014	Journal of Interactive Marketing	69
Cover R.	Audience inter/active: Interactive media, narrative control and reconceiving audience history	2006	New Media and Society	67
Steensen S.	Online journalism and the promises of new technology: A critical review and look ahead	2011	Journalism Studies	67
Karlsson M.	The immediacy of online news, the visibility of journalistic processes and a restructuring of journalistic authority	2011	Journalism	59
MacGregor P.	Tracking the online audience: Metric data start a subtle revolution	2007	Journalism Studies	54

A wide range of authors was found, although only one had two papers in this ranking (S. Shiam Sundar). In a comparison of the list of most cited authors with that of the authors with the most publications (Table 1), only four authors coincide: David Domingo, Seth C. Lewis, Pere Masip and Neil Thurman.

Three of the journals had more than one paper among the top twenty. Notably, *New Media & Society* had four papers in this ranking, three of which were among the top five (positions 1, 3 and 5). This was followed by *Journalism Studies*, with three papers (both these journals were highlighted in Table 5, which confirms their highly relevant role in the subject area), and *Information Society*, with two. The remaining journals (up to 11) had only one paper on this list. We also found some journals from disciplines other than Communication, for example, *MIS Quarterly* (Library and Information Science) and *Human Computer information* (Applied Psychology).

In a comparison of the list of journals with the most cited papers and the list of journals with the highest number of papers published on the subject (Table 5), three journals coincide (*New Media & Society, Journalism* and *Journalism Studies*). None of the journals that coincide on both lists are published in Spain. This could be because the Spanish language has a smaller scope and diffusion than English.

Some papers had a broader focus than the subject of interactivity in journalism, and addressed topics such as interactivity as a concept, its application to websites, by citizens or in political communication, as well as user perceptions and technological aspects. Other papers centred on the use of interactivity in digital journalism and included specific aspects such as citizen journalism, participation in the media, readers' comments, the relation with social media such as Twitter or audience measurement.

3.8 Subject Areas

Using the VOSviewer tool, we mapped the network of relations between the 74 terms that appeared at least five times in the keywords field (either Author Keywords or Indexed keywords)[3] (Fig. 3).

[3] Some of them are shown in Table 7.

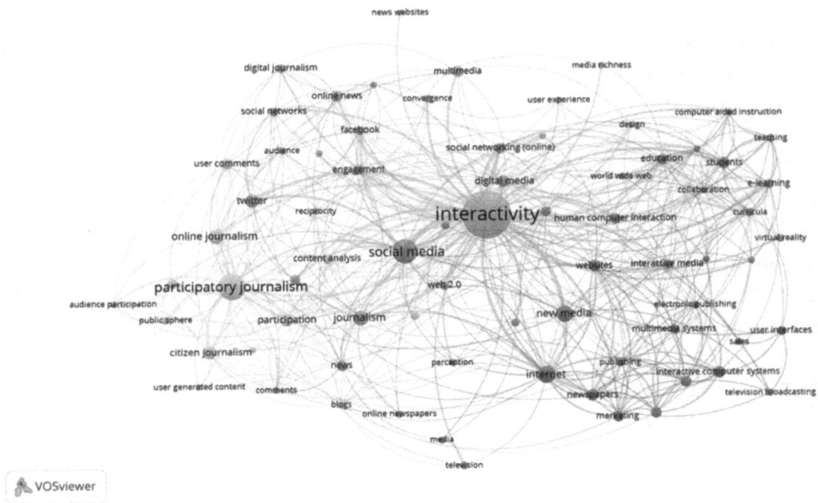

Fig. 3 Network of subject areas

According to the search of the Scopus database, the main keyword is the term interactivity, as expected. Hence, it is the central concept in the subject area under study and is present predominately in the research.

Further, two terms were found to be highly relevant: participatory journalism and social media. The first of these terms illustrates the clear consolidation of interactivity, as it refers to a specific type of interactivity in the media, that of audience participation. The second term, social media, highlights the expanding role of social networks in relations between media outlets and users, and shows that much of the interactivity between media and audiences is channelled through social media platforms.

Among the other keywords, we can find, (a) very general concepts such as internet, new media, online journalism, digital media or newspapers; (b) concepts that identify specific elements of interactivity in the media such as participation, citizen journalism, user comments or multimedia; and (c) some very specific terms such as Twitter.

Table 7 complements the network of interrelations as it contains a list of keywords along with the absolute values of how many times they appeared in the selected records.

Table 7 Most commonly used keywords

Keyword	*Hits*
Interactivity	264
Participatory journalism	81
Social media	69
Internet	34
New media	31
Journalism	26
Online journalism	25
Participation	22
Citizen journalism	21
Twitter	20
Digital media	16
Newspapers	15
User comments	15
Online news	15
Multimedia	15
Websites	14
Students	14
Interactive computer systems	14
Social networking	13
Human computer interaction	13
Marketing	12
Online systems	12
Newsprint	12
Education	12
Content analysis	12
News	12

4 Conclusions

Bibliometric studies applied to a specific subject, in this case, interactivity in digital news, provide an overview of various aspects of publications. These include distribution over time, authorship and affiliation, the most dynamic journals, and the most common languages or subject areas.

In terms of evolution over time, we found a considerable increase in publications on this subject from 2005, after digital journalism had become totally consolidated and social networks had appeared.

Regarding the most prolific authors, a relatively large group of 20 researchers emerged who work at US and European universities and are distributed almost equally between these geographic regions. The institution with the highest number of publications is the University of Texas at Austin, USA, followed at a distance by many European and US universities.

An analysis of coauthorship relations revealed various clusters, in which David Domingo plays a notable role as a bridge between several groups of European and US authors.

The predominant language in the publications was English (almost 90%), followed at a distance by Spanish (almost 10%). The other six languages identified did not reach 1% of the total.

The journals *New Media & Society*, *Digital Journalism*, *Journalism Studies* and *Journalism Practice* have published the most papers on this subject. The first of these journals is from the USA; the other three from the UK. It is highly commendable that the list of journals that have published most papers on interactivity contains four journals published in Spain and one in Portugal. The romance languages spoken in these two countries are less commonly used in scientific communication.

In terms of subject areas, the main keyword was the term interactivity. This was followed by the terms participatory journalism and social media, around which various clusters of interrelations formed.

As a final comment, we should mention the absence of Asia in the results. It is surprising that no Asian authors, universities or journals were found.

References

Abadal, Ernest, and Javier Guallar. 2010. *Prensa digital y bibliotecas*, Gijón: Trea, 170, ISBN 9788497044462.

Baños-Moreno, María-José, Juan-Antonio Pastor-Sánchez, and Rodrigo Martínez-Béjar. 2017. Interactividad en periódicos en línea: del modelo facsímil al multimedia. *Anales de Documentación* 20 (2). http://dx.doi.org/10.6018/analesdoc.20.2.282401.

Dehdarirad, Tahereh, Anna Villarroya, and Maite Barrios. 2015. Research on Women in Science and Higher Education: A Bibliometric Analysis. *Scientometrics* 103: 795. https://doi.org/10.1007/s11192-015-1574-x.

De la Flor-Martínez M., et al. 2017. Evaluation of Scientific Output in Dentistry in Spanish Universities. *Med Oral Patol Oral Cir Bucal* 22 (4): e491–e499, July 1, 2017. http://www.medicinaoral.com/medoralfree01/v22i4/medoralv22i4p491.pd.

Kapoor, Kawaljeet Kaur, et al. 2017. Advances in Social Media Research: Past, Present and Future. *Information Systems Frontiers*. https://doi.org/10.1007/s10796-017-9810-y.

Kiousis, S. 2002. Interactivity: A Concept Explication. *New Media & Society* 4 (3): 355–383. http://doi.org/10.1177/146144480200400303.

Masip, Pere, Javier Díaz-Noci, David Domingo, Josep-Lluís Micó-Sanz, and Ramón Salaverría. 2010. Investigación internacional sobre ciberperiodismo: hipertexto, interactividad, multimedia y convergencia. *El profesional de la información* 19 (6) (November–December): 568–576. https://doi.org/10.3145/epi.2010.nov.02.

Miguel, Sandra, Ely Francina Tannuri de Oliveira, and Maria Cláudia Cabrini Grácio. 2016. Scientific Production on Open Access: A Worldwide Bibliometric Analysis in the Academic and Scientific Context. *Publications* 4 (1): 1. https://doi.org/10.3390/publications4010001.

Rodrigues, R.S., V. Taga, and M.F. Passos. 2016. Research Articles About Open Access Indexed by Scopus: A Content Analysis. *Publications* 4 (4): 31. https://doi.org/10.3390/publications4040031.

Suau, Jaume, and Pere Masip. 2013. Exploring Participatory Journalism in Mediterranean Countries. *Journalism Practice*. http://dx.doi.org/10.1080/17512786.2013.865964.

van Eck, N.J., and L. Waltman. 2010. Software Survey: Vosviewer, a Computer Program for Bibliometric Mapping. *Scientometrics* 84: 523. https://doi.org/10.1007/s11192-009-0146-3.

Zancanaro, Airton, José Leomar Todesco, Fernando Ramos. 2015. A Bibliometric Mapping of Open Educational Resources. *The International Review of Research in Open and Distributed Learning* 16 (1): 1–23. http://dx.doi.org/10.19173/irrodl.v16i1.1960.

Zhai, Yujia et al. 2018. Measuring the Diffusion of an Innovation: A Citation Analysis. *Journal of the Association for Information Science and Technology* 69 (3): 368–379. https://doi.org/10.1002/asi.23898.

CHAPTER 9

Interaction in Digital News Media: Trends, Challenges, and Lessons Learned

Mario Pérez-Montoro and Pere Freixa

1 Introduction

The emergence and growth of the digital news media have been facilitated by advances in the technologies and resources that make that media possible and, above all, by the gradual introduction of new ways of articulating the information ecosystem that these digitally-based resources now permit. At the epicenter of all this sits interaction, understood in a very broad, multidimensional, sense, as a differentiating factor that characterizes not only the texts produced in this context but also very much the medium itself (Nash 2014). Recognizing the value of interactivity in the digital media means situating dialogue at the very heart of the communication event that takes place between the different actors involved in the process: emitters, receivers, texts, and the system itself, which, in

M. Pérez-Montoro (✉)
Department of Information Science and Media Studies,
University of Barcelona, Barcelona, Spain
e-mail: perez-montoro@ub.edu

P. Freixa
Department of Communication, Pompeu Fabra University, Barcelona, Spain
e-mail: pere.freixa@upf.edu

M. Pérez-Montoro (ed.), *Interaction in Digital News Media*,
https://doi.org/10.1007/978-3-319-96253-5_9

the digital universe, is dynamic and plays an active role. A number of foundational definitions, such as those provided by Rafaeli (1988) and Jensen (1998), allow us to understand interactivity as the complete system of communication exchanges that take place on an interactive continuum. Hypertextuality, linking the elements of multimedia, the active exploration of links and the dialogues that result from these dynamics allow us to define a media with its own characteristics, as will have been made evident throughout the preceding chapters.

Our intrinsic perspective on the interactive text has revealed, as we shall see in the next subsection, that the creation of interactive stories, as well as their emission and exploration by the audience, are not exempt from difficulties. Indeed, it is essential to consider the role of the user in the text design process. Here, UX design, one of the specialist areas of interaction design, has developed as a discipline capable of developing powerful methodological tools to facilitate the design process as well as of assessing the reception of finished interactive products (Soler-Adillon et al. 2016). The multimedia potential of interactive texts is apparent in interactive visualizations and documentaries, in those based on the visual image and text as well as in 360° film and VR immersive projects which the media is setting great store by. In each of these works, authors have to select the resources they want to use to promote the interaction that can generate interest and engagement with users.

Interactivity does not refer exclusively to interactive texts. As we shall see in Sect. 3—Scenarios of Interaction—the different focuses of interest dealt with have enabled us to consider a broad panorama in which interaction allows us to pose questions about aspects such as business models, the legal dimensions concerning the authorship of interactive texts and academic studies of the digital news media.

2 Interactive Products

This book has taken the concept of interactivity as its guiding thread for conducting its assessment of the various dimensions of, and the challenges posed by, the digital news media, our main source of information in the digital sphere. Moreover, the concept of interaction has allowed us to highlight those characteristics of the information systems developed on the web and for the web that enable us to differentiate and identify the very features that define them. We have seen how the term interactivity accepts a number of different meanings depending on whether we place it in its technological, discursive, or procedural dimension. The ubiquity of interactivity in all phases and areas of the digital news media merely serves to confirm its centrality as a differentiating element in its own right.

Access to information, difficulties in resolving the uncertainties that arise between the narrative and the exploratory experience, and the configuration of complex information systems have all been examined in Chapter 2. From the examples analyzed, we have seen that, for most authors, interactivity defines strategies for understanding the communication act, whether it be in documentaries or in the news. Likewise, we have also seen the impossibility of disassociating user interactivity; indeed, in each project, the authors conceive the audience in a different way: as co-authors, as users, as participants, as public, or as collaborators. We see how different proposals are developed for each of these profiles and how each of these proposals presupposes resolving its own communication situations. In *Proyecto Quipu* and *Out My Window*, for example, from the very outset, the authors incorporate within the project the group of participants that are its actual object of focus. They are part of the design of the whole system; they collaborate in its definition and provide the contents that feed it. In other examples, like *Documenting Hate*, the definition of user roles and the design of the information system are completed a priori by the authors, who take responsibility for the overall interaction design. In fact, all three examples illustrate one of the biggest challenges that these projects face: the dependence on the audience to contribute content.

Audience participation emerges as an essential element of the digital news media and, with varying degrees of intensity, the activation of that participation is essential for interactive dialogue to take place. Participation, often in the form of exploration, as in *Pregoneros de Medellín* and *Out My Window*, allows us to see how meaning emerges from the interactive text with each individual's reading experience. Via the actions they take, users activate the complete information system on which the interactive documentary and structured journalism are based.

Moreover, as we have seen throughout this book, the intensive use of information visualization in journalistic content is another characteristic feature of the digital news media. Here, again, a number of interesting conclusions have been drawn.

First, we should emphasize the increase in the narrative weight given to information visualization in journalistic pieces. A shift has taken place from the classic context in which visualizations served as a mere support to textual argumentations, to the point that they are now at the center of the interaction between the medium and the consumer. Today, resources of this type have, in many cases, become the main contribution of the piece—more important than the text—allowing the user to navigate in an interactive mode through the story told and designed by the author.

Second, we have learned that the classic conceptual schema is no longer useful for analyzing new visualization proposals. The rigid, classic distinction between infographics and visualization has been destroyed by products that naturally articulate infographics (figurative resources) and data visualizations (abstract resources) to tell stories in a more appropriate fashion. We need more complex, faceted conceptual taxonomies that facilitate this analysis and that include aspects such as the narrative genre, visual narrative, narrative structure, interaction driver, and the visualization–story ratio.

Finally, based on a detailed analysis, we have been able to identify a general trend in recent proposals in which a linear order and limited interactivity dominate the narrative. This responds mainly to a strategy of ensuring products function independently of the screen size used by the audience to consume them. However, aside from this general tendency, we have identified a series of different types of pattern that appear to characterize the visualization products being developed today, and which run on a hypothetical scale of interactivity from the simplest to the most complex. We have labeled these as "Intro and chart," "multiple views," "guided dashboards," "quick overview, stacked details," "quick overview, annotated chart," "complex overview, quick details," and the "martini glass structure."

Likewise, we have been able to examine new narratives based on technology advances, such as the emergence, in 2015, of virtual reality in the digital news media. Certainly, the advances associated with mobile devices have made it possible to open up to wider audiences the chance of exploring immersive experiences associated with the telling of news stories. We have seen how 360° filming is allowing interactive documentary and film reports to be rethought by raising many interesting questions about such aspects as point of view, framing, camera location, and movement. The perception of space as a whole means using the camera as just one more element of the choreography that the user will later explore through his or her virtual recreation. Verisimilitude and realism strengthen the hyper-realistic sensation of virtual reality, despite the narrative doubts that are raised by the difficulty of combining interaction with narrative, as we saw in Chapter 2, and which works like *Aamir* remind us of.

We have seen that the choice of VR and immersive, interactive environments as media for informing reality is justified on the grounds that such immersive experiences provide a high degree of emotional intensity for the users that experience them. Most authors and media organizations that are taking this road claim that immersion favors user identification with the situations experienced by the characters in their stories, as is the case in *Clouds Over Sidra*, and that this identification facilitates greater social empathy, although many question marks still hang over this capacity of the media and its effectiveness. Some theoreticians and academics argue that there is a possibility that the effects are the opposite to those sought and that they produce negative stereotypes or counterproductive behaviors.

Another interesting question that we have been able to identify is the dilution and redefinition of the concepts of virtuality and reality in such works as *Hunger in Los Angeles* by Nonny de la Peña, in which recorded images, audio files, and virtual recreations are presented together to form a hyper-realistic scenario that the spectator can freely explore. In these works, as we have seen, the aim is for the user to have firsthand experiences with a high emotional content, although they do not dispel doubts about the difficulties found when seeking to combine story development with the potential of the interaction as a generator of narrative meaning.

Finally, we are seeing how advances in virtual reality as applied to the digital news media are occurring simultaneous in two scenarios, which we might label as scenarios of high and low technology. The latter, based on mobile devices and smartphones—logically of wider implementation for reasons of cost—is conditioned by the coexistence of numerous platforms and technologies that are being developed simultaneously. This so-called "cardboard phase" is favoring the emergence of novel forms of interaction in which users can experience a sense of place as well as visually explore complete scenarios, interacting using gaze direction and head movements.

We want to conclude this section with the conclusions and lessons learned from our discussion of the design of interactive products. Neither new narrative proposal, nor any proposal based on information visualization, virtual reality, or any other technology advance, will work properly if it is not designed in accordance with certain methodological standards.

First, the design must be user-centered. The success of these products depends on our acquiring an exhaustive understanding of the target audiences, of their context of use and of user expectations. The audience, the end user of these products, must be right at the heart of all the design decisions taken.

Second, as designers we must deploy a carefully structured methodological strategy that guarantees the communicative efficiency of our interactive products. This strategy requires the implementation of two types of research method: those that facilitate generative research and those that enable evaluative research.

The former, generative research, allows us to analyze the entire universe of users: the users' product requirements, and the users' needs and objectives that can be met with these products. It is a research stage that has to be conducted prior to product design. To meet these objectives, it is necessary to undertake a series of methodological proposals in a coordinated and structured fashion that include inquiry (with the organization of interviews, focus groups, and surveys), field studies (employing observation methods and contextual inquiry), and participatory research (including card sorting, collages, and interactive modeling).

To make sense of the findings obtained from these methodological procedures, all the information collected has to be analyzed and interpreted. After submitting the information to methods of data reduction, analysis, and conclusion drawing techniques, the results can then be communicated as structured findings.

Once we have a design proposal for an interactive product based on the analytical results provided by these techniques, evaluative research allows us to verify the communicative effectiveness and efficiency of the product and the level of user satisfaction. To do so requires deploying, in an articulated and iterative manner, a series of methodologies that allow us to re-evaluate and redesign the interactive proposals using the results that continue to emerge. The main methodologies here include those of inquiry (such as interviews, focus groups, and standardized surveys), user testing (such as task-based and A/B testing), and those based on physical-psychological measures (such as eye tracking, facial expression, and heart rate).

3 Scenarios of Interaction

Having considered the various trends and challenges associated with those characteristics that form an intrinsic part of interactive products, and having summarized the lessons that have been learned with regard to them, in this section, we examine the role played by these products in the other scenarios addressed in this book.

We start with that of emerging business models. The economic crisis, the fake news phenomenon, and the battering that the sector's reputation took as a result, combined with the pressing need to develop new methods to market and disseminate digital contents via social networks have ushered in significant changes in the strategies of economic sustainability employed by the digital news media. We have been able to analyze the main business models being deployed by the news media in an environment in which the classic formulas, centered on advertising, have proved insufficient to guarantee their economic viability. Attempts have been made to introduce models based, primarily, on sponsored content, crowd funding, subscriptions, donor funding, and micropayments. However, with the exception of some well-established media organizations, such as *The New York Times* and just a few others in each country, these efforts are proving insufficient to ensure the economic sustainability pursued by the industry.

In this new economic scenario, interactive content seems set to play a crucial role. Investment in this content aims at satisfying a series of key objectives: first and foremost, increasing the potential audience of the digital news media, by exploiting interest in this interactive content, among a public who, initially, for cultural or social reasons, was somewhat estranged from it—something essential, even for those companies that are enjoying some success with their subscription models; second, increasing audience engagement and loyalty by promoting these media products, where the publication of quality products of this type clearly favors these factors; and, third, increasing the traffic and the influence of news media websites by offering interactive products. These three factors (audience growth, engagement and loyalty, and traffic) are all clearly aimed at achieving two fundamental strategies that can guarantee the economic viability of the media: a revaluation of the price of advertising and an increase in the number of subscriptions.

Parallel to the economic issues concerning interactive content stand closely associated questions of a legal nature; indeed, it is difficult to design new business models that ensure the viability of the news media without rethinking the question of the intellectual property of those contents. Promoting innovation in the media, and creating new narrative strategies, requires the rethinking of intellectual property law, along with other legal branches such as competition law, to support these new proposals.

Clearly, what is needed is the reform—an effective harmonization—of intellectual property laws that can protect the two main agents on the journalistic stage: the media and the authors of their content. But also, and in particular, to protect and promote the innovation that may result from the derivative works permitted by the law, that is, from user-generated contents. In the case of the media, this means legislation that protects their investments (in personnel and technology) and which ensures fair competition in the newspaper industry. In the case of the authors, it means legislation that guarantees fair contracts and freedom of expression. In the case of active users, it means a law that protects and which does not cut back on the contents that are being legally produced, and all this while legislating to ensure that internet providers facilitate the fair diffusion of these media.

The book concludes by examining a critical dimension for the advancement and development of new interactive proposals: scientific and academic output focused on content of this type in journalistic environments. Bibliometric studies of this kind are clearly useful and allow a number of interesting conclusions to be drawn.

An examination of the different subjects and areas addressed in the academic literature shows that output on interactives while covering a wide range of conceptual, technological, and pragmatic questions, focuses above all on themes related to interactivity, that is, participatory journalism and the social media. Interestingly, the literature on interactives is not dominated by a single author or small group of authors; rather, there are some twenty academics, mainly European and American, who have gained some prominence in the field. Similarly, the weight of this output is not concentrated in just a few journals, but rather it is distributed among the journals of communication studies, although New Media & Society, Digital Journalism and Journalism Studies stand out slightly above the rest. Yet, as in many other academic fields, the dominant language of articles in this discipline is English.

In this regard, the leading research centers are located primarily in the USA, with an important role being played by the University of Texas at Austin, although there are a number of research centers working in this field throughout Europe. Surprising, perhaps, is the virtual absence in this field of study of Asian universities, journals, and authors.

References

Jensen, Jens. 1998. "Interactivity": Tracking a New Concept in Media and Communication Studies. *Nordicom Review* 19: 185–202.

Nash, Kate. 2014. Clicking on the World: Documentary Representation and Interactivity. In *New Documentary Ecologies*, ed. K. Nash, C. Hight, and C. Summerhayes, 50–66. Basingstoke: Palgrave Macmillan.

Rafaeli, Sheizf. 1988. From New Media to Communication. *Sage Annual Review of Communication Research: Advancing Communication Science* 16: 110–134.

Soler-Adillon, Joan, Carles Sora, Pere Freixa, and Joan-Ignasi Ribas. 2016. A Profile of the Interactive Communication Professional: Foundations, Current Trends and Perspectives. *El profesional de la información* 25 (2): 196–208.

Index

M. Pérez-Montoro (ed.), *Interaction in Digital News Media*,
https://doi.org/10.1007/978-3-319-96253-5